A Rogue By Compulsion
An Affair Of The Secret Service

By

Victor Bridges

Double 9
BOOKS

A Rogue By Compulsion
An Affair Of The Secret Service
by Victor Bridges

ISBN: 978-93-59957-30-2
Published by

DOUBLE 9 BOOKS

2/13-B, Ansari Road
Daryaganj, New Delhi – 110002
info@double9books.com
www.double9books.com
Tel. 011-40042856

ABOUT THE AUTHOR

Hugh Stowell Scott was an English author who wrote under the name Henry Seton Merriman. He was born on May 9, 1862, and died on November 19, 1903. The Sowers, his best-known book, was published thirty times in the UK. He was born in Newcastle upon Tyne and worked as an underwriter at Lloyd's of London. After that, he started traveling and writing books, many of which became great hits. Scott went to India as a tourist in 1877 and 1878, and the setting for his 1896 book Flotsam was India. He really loved traveling, and he did a lot of it with his friend and fellow author Stanley J. Weyman. On June 19, 1889, Scott married Ethel Frances Hall, who was born in 1865 and died in 1943. They didn't have any kids. Scott was surprisingly humble and quiet for his personality. He died at Melton, Suffolk, in 1903 of appendicitis. He was 41 years old. In his will, Scott gave £5,000 to Evelyn Beatrice Hall, who was his sister-in-law and a fellow writer. Hall is best known for writing The Friends of Voltaire, a biography. Scott described the legacy as a "token of my gratitude for her continued assistance and literary advice, without which I should never have been able to have made a living by my pen."

CONTENTS

CHAPTER I
A BOLT FOR FREEDOM

Most of the really important things in life—such as love and death—happen unexpectedly. I know that my escape from Dartmoor did.

We had just left the quarries—eighteen of us, all dressed in that depressing costume which King George provides for his less elusive subjects—and we were shambling sullenly back along the gloomy road which leads through the plantation to the prison. The time was about four o'clock on a dull March afternoon.

In the roadway, on either side of us, tramped an armed warder, his carbine in his hand, his eyes travelling with dull suspicion up and down the gang. Fifteen yards away, parallel with our route, the sombre figure of one of the civil guards kept pace with us through the trees. We were a cheery party!

Suddenly, without any warning, one of the warders turned faint. He dropped his carbine, and putting his hand to his head, stumbled heavily against the low wall that separated us from the wood. The clatter of his weapon, falling in the road, naturally brought all eyes round in that direction, and seeing what had happened the whole eighteen of us instinctively halted.

The gruff voice of the other warder broke out at once, above the shuffling of feet:

"What are you stopping for? Get on there in front."

From the corner of my eye I caught sight of the civil guard hurrying towards the prostrate figure by the wall; and then, just as the whole gang lurched forward again, the thing happened with beautiful abruptness.

A broad, squat figure shot out suddenly from the head of the column, and, literally hurling itself over the wall, landed with a crash amongst the thick undergrowth. There was a second shout from the warder, followed almost instantly by a hoarse command to halt, as the civil guard jerked his carbine to his shoulder.

The fugitive paid about as much attention to the order as a tiger would to a dog whistle. He was off again in an instant, bent almost double, and bursting through the tangled bushes with amazing swiftness.

Bang!

The charge of buckshot whistled after him, spattering viciously through the twigs, and several of the bolder spirits in the gang at once raised a half-hearted cry of "Murder!"

"Stop that!" bawled the warder angrily, and to enforce his words he quickened his steps so as to bring him in touch with the offenders.

As he did so, I suddenly perceived with extraordinary clearness that I should never again get quite such a good chance to escape. The other men were momentarily between me and the warder, while the civil guard, his carbine empty, was plunging through the trees in pursuit of his wounded quarry.

It was no time for hesitation, and in any case hesitation is not one of my besetting sins. I recollect taking one long, deep breath: then the next thing I remember is catching my toe on the top of the wall and coming the most unholy purler in the very centre of an exceptionally well armoured blackberry bush.

This blunder probably saved my life: it certainly accounted for my escape. The warder who evidently had more nerve than I gave him credit for, must have fired at me from where he was, right between the heads of the other convicts. It was only my abrupt disappearance from the top of the wall that saved me from being filled up with lead. As it was, the charge whistled over me just as I fell, and a devilish unpleasant noise it made too.

I didn't wait for him to reload. I was out of that bush and off up the hill in rather less time than it takes to read these words. Where I was going I scarcely thought; my one idea was to put as big a distance as possible between myself and the carbine before its owner could ram home a second cartridge.

As I ran, twisting in and out between the trees, and keeping my head as low as possible, I could hear behind me a hoarse uproar from my fellow-convicts, who by this time were evidently getting out of hand. No sound could have pleased me better. The more boisterous the good fellows became the less chance would the remaining warder have of worrying about me. As for the civil guard—well, it seemed probable that his time was already pretty fully engaged.

My chief danger lay in the chance that there might be other warders in the immediate neighbourhood. If so, they would doubtless have heard the firing and have come running up at the first alarm. I looked back over my shoulder as I reached the top of the plantation, which was about a hundred yards from the road, but so far as I could see there was no one as yet on my track.

My one chance lay in reaching the main wood that borders the Tavistock road before the mounted guard could come up. Between this and the plantation stretched a long bare slope of hillside, perhaps two hundred yards across, with scarcely enough cover on it to hide a rabbit. It was not exactly an inviting prospect, but still the place had to be crossed, and there was nothing to be gained by looking at it. So setting my teeth I jumped out from under the shelter of the trees, and started off as fast as I could pelt for the opposite side.

I had got about half-way over when there came a sudden shout away to the right. Turning my head as I ran, I saw through the thin mist a figure in knickerbockers and a Norfolk jacket vaulting over the low gate that separated the moor from the road.

I suppose he was a tourist, for he had a small knapsack fastened to his back and he was carrying a stick in his hand.

"Tally-ho!" he yelled, brandishing the latter, and then without hesitation he came charging across the open with the obvious intention of cutting me off from the wood.

For the first time in three years I laughed. It was not a pretty laugh, and if my new friend had heard it, his ardour in the chase might perhaps have been a trifle cooled. As it was he came on with undiminished zest, apparently quite confident in his ability to tackle me single-handed.

We met about ten yards this side of the nearest trees.

He rushed in on me with another "whoop," and I saw then that he was a big, powerful, red-faced fellow of a rather coarse sporting type—the kind of brute I've always had a peculiar dislike for.

"Down you go!" he shouted, and suiting the action to the word, he swung back his stick and lashed out savagely at my head.

I didn't go down. Instead of that I·stepped swiftly in, and striking up his arm with my left hand, I let him have my right bang on the point of the chin. Worlds of concentrated bitterness were behind it, and he went over backwards as if he had been struck by a coal-hammer.

It did me a lot of good, that punch. It seemed to restore my self-respect in a way that nothing else could have done. You must have been a convict yourself, shouted at and ordered about like a dog for three weary years, to appreciate the full pleasure of being able once more to punch a man in the jaw.

At the moment, however, I had no time to analyze my feelings. Almost before the red-faced gentleman's shoulders had struck the ground I had reached the railing which bounded the wood, and putting one hand on the top bar had vaulted over into its inviting gloom.

Then, just for an instant, I stopped, and, like Lot's wife, cast one hasty glance behind me. Except for the motionless form of my late adversary, who appeared to be studying the sky, the stretch of moor that I had just crossed was still comfortingly empty. So far no pursuing warder had even emerged from the plantation. With a sigh of relief I turned round again and plunged forward into the thickest part of the tangled brake ahead.

It would have been difficult to find a better temporary hiding-place than the one I had reached. Thick with trees and undergrowth, which sprouted up from between enormous fissures and piles of granite rock, it stretched away for the best part of a mile and a half parallel with the main road. I knew that even in daylight the warders would find it no easy matter to track me down: at this time in the afternoon, with dusk coming rapidly on, the task would be an almost impossible one.

Besides, it was starting to rain. All the afternoon a thick cloud had been hanging over North Hessary, and now, as scratched and panting I forced my way on into the ever-increasing gloom, a fine drizzle began to descend through the trees. I knew what that meant. In half an hour everything would probably be blotted out in a wet grey mist, and, except for posting guards all round the wood, my pursuers would be compelled to abandon the search until next morning. It was the first time that I had ever felt an affection for the Dartmoor climate.

Guessing rather than judging my way, I stumbled steadily forward until I reached what I imagined must be about the centre of the wood. By this time I was wet through to the skin. The thin parti-coloured "slop" that I was wearing was quite useless for keeping out the rain, a remark that applied with almost equal force to my prison-made breeches and gaiters. Apart from the discomfort, however, I was not much disturbed. I have never been an easy victim to chills, and three years in Princetown had done nothing to soften a naturally tough constitution.

Still there was no sense in getting more soaked than was necessary, so I began to hunt around for some sort of temporary shelter. I found it at last in the shape of a huge block of granite, half hidden by the brambles and stunted trees which had grown up round it. Parting the undergrowth and crawling carefully in, I discovered at the base a kind of hollow crevice just long enough to lie down in at full length.

I can't say it was exactly comfortable, but penal servitude has at least the merit of saving one from being over-luxurious. Besides, I was much too interested in watching the steady thickening of the mist outside to worry myself about trifles. With a swiftness which would have been incredible to any one who didn't know the Moor, the damp clammy vapour was settling down, blotting out everything in its grey haze. Except for the dripping brambles immediately outside I could soon see absolutely nothing; beyond that it was like staring into a blanket.

I lay there quite motionless, listening very intently for any sound of my pursuers. Only the persistent drip, drip of the rain, however, and the occasional rustle of a bird, broke the silence. If there were any warders about they were evidently still some way from my hiding-place, but the odds were that they had postponed searching the wood until the fog lifted.

For the first time since my leap from the wall I found myself with sufficient leisure to review the situation. It struck me that only a very hardened optimist could describe it as hopeful. I had made my bolt almost instinctively, without stopping to think what chances I had of getting away. That these were meagre in the extreme was now becoming painfully clear to me. Even if I managed to slip out of my present hiding-place into the still larger woods of the Walkham Valley, the odds were all in favour of my ultimate capture. No escaped prisoner had ever yet succeeded in retaining his liberty for more than a few days, and where so many gentlemen of experience had tried and failed it seemed distressingly unlikely that I should be more fortunate.

I began to wonder what had happened to Cairns, the man whose dash from the ranks had been responsible for my own effort. I knew him to be one of the most resourceful blackguards in the prison, and, provided the civil guard's first shot had failed to stop him, it was quite likely that he too had evaded capture. I hoped so with all my heart: it would distract quite a lot of attention from my own humble affairs.

If he was still at liberty, I couldn't help feeling enviously how much better his chances of escape were than mine. In order to get away from the Moor it was plainly necessary to possess oneself of both food and clothes, and I could think of no other way of doing so except stealing them from some lonely farm. At anything of this sort I was likely to prove a sorry bungler compared with such an artist as Cairns. He was one of the most accomplished cracksmen in England, and feats which seemed impossible to me would probably be the merest child's play to him.

Still it was no good worrying over what couldn't be helped. My first job was to get safely into the Walkham woods; after that it would be quite time enough to think about turning burglar.

I sat up and looked out into the mist. Things were as bad as ever, and quite suddenly it struck me with considerable force that by lying low in this fashion I was making a most unholy idiot of myself. Here I was growing cold and stiff, and wasting what was probably the best chance I should ever have of reaching Walkhampton. In fact I was playing right into the hands of the warders.

With an impatient exclamation I jumped to my feet. The only question was, could I find my way out of the wood, and if I did, how on earth was I to strike the right line over North Hessary? It was quite on the cards I might wander back into Princetown under the happy impression that I was going in exactly the opposite direction.

For a moment I hesitated; then I made up my mind to risk it. After all the fog was as bad for the warders as it was for me, and even if I failed to reach the Walkham Valley I should probably find some other equally good shelter before it lifted. In either case I should have the big advantage of having changed my hiding-place.

Buttoning up my slop, I advanced carefully through the dripping brambles. One could see rather less than nothing, but so far as I could remember the main Tavistock road was on my right-hand side. This would leave North Hessary away to the left; so turning in that direction I set my teeth and took my first step forward into the darkness.

I don't suppose you have ever tried walking through a wood in a fog, but you can take my word for it that a less enjoyable form of exercise doesn't exist. I have often wondered since how on earth I managed to escape a sprained ankle or a broken neck, for carefully as I groped my way forward it was quite impossible to avoid all the numerous crevices and overhanging boughs which beset my path.

I must have blundered into about fourteen holes and knocked my head against at least an equal number of branches, before the trees at last began to thin and the darkness lighten sufficiently to let me see where I was placing my feet. I knew that by this time I must be getting precious near the boundary of the wood, outside which the warders were now doubtless posted at frequent intervals. So I stopped where I was and sat down quietly on a rock for a few minutes to recover my breath, for I had been pretty badly shaken and winded by my numerous tumbles.

As soon as I felt better I got up again, and taking very particular care where I was treading, advanced on tiptoe with a delicacy that Agag might have envied. I had taken about a dozen steps when all of a sudden the railings loomed up in front of me through the mist.

I put my hand on the top bar, and then paused for a moment listening breathlessly for any sound of danger. Except for the faint patter of the rain, however, everything was as silent as the dead. Very carefully I raised myself on the bottom rail, lifted my legs over, one after the other, and then dropped lightly down on to the grass beyond.

As I did so a man rose up suddenly from the ground like a black shadow, and hurling himself on me before I could move, clutched me round the waist.

"Got yer!" he roared. Then at the top of his voice—"Here he is! Help! Help!"

CHAPTER II
A BICYCLE AND SOME OVERALLS

I was taken so utterly by surprise that nothing except sheer strength saved me from going over. As it was I staggered back a couple of paces, fetching up against the railings with a bang that nearly knocked the breath out of me. By a stroke of luck I must have crushed my opponent's hand against one of the bars, for with a cry of pain he momentarily slackened his grip.

That was all I wanted. Wrenching my left arm free, I brought up my elbow under his chin with a wicked jolt; and then, before he could recover, I smashed home a short right-arm punch that must have landed somewhere in the neighbourhood of his third waistcoat button. Anyhow it did the business all right. With a quaint noise, like the gurgle of a half-empty bath, he promptly released me from his embrace, and sank down on to the grass almost as swiftly and silently as he had arisen.

I doubt if a more perfectly timed blow has ever been delivered, but unfortunately I had no chance of studying its effects. Through the fog I could hear the sound of footsteps—quick heavy footsteps hurrying towards me from either direction. For one second I thought of scrambling back over the railings and taking to the wood again. Then suddenly a kind of mischievous exhilaration at the danger gripped hold of me, and jumping over the prostrate figure on the ground I bolted forwards into the mist. The warders, who must have been quite close, evidently heard me, for from both sides came hoarse shouts of "There he goes!" "Look out there!" and other well-meant pieces of advice.

It was a funny sort of sensation dodging through the fog, feeling that at any moment one might blunder up against the muzzle of a loaded carbine. The only guide I had as to my direction was the slope of the ground. I knew that as long as I kept on going uphill I was more or less on the right track, for the big granite-strewn bulk of North Hessary lay right in front of me, and I had to cross it to get to the Walkham Valley.

On I went, the ground rising higher and higher, until at last the wet slippery grass began to give way to a broken waste of rocks and heather.

I had reached the top, and although I could see nothing on account of the mist, I knew that right below me lay the woods, with only about a mile of steeply sloping hillside separating me from their agreeable privacy.

Despite the cold and the wet and the fact that I was getting devilish hungry, my spirits somehow began to rise. Good luck always acts on me as a sort of tonic, and so far I had certainly been amazingly lucky. I felt that if only the rain would clear up now and give me a chance of getting dry, Fate would have treated me as handsomely as an escaped murderer had any right to expect.

Making my way carefully across the plateau, for the ground was stiff with small holes and gullies and I had no wish to sprain my ankle, I began the descent of the opposite side. The mist here was a good deal thinner, but night was coming on so rapidly that as far as seeing where I was going was concerned I was very little better off than I had been on the top of the hill.

Below me, away to the right, a blurred glimmer of light just made itself visible. This I took to be Merivale village, on the Tavistock road; and not being anxious to trespass upon its simple hospitality, I sheered off slightly in the opposite direction. At last, after about twenty minutes' scrambling, I began to hear a faint trickle of running water, and a few more steps brought me to the bank of the Walkham.

I stood there for a little while in the darkness, feeling a kind of tired elation at my achievement. My chances of escape might still be pretty thin, but I had at least reached a temporary shelter. For five miles away to my left stretched the pleasantly fertile valley, and until I chose to come out of it all the warders on Dartmoor might hunt themselves black in the face without finding me.

I can't say exactly how much farther I tramped that evening. When one is stumbling along at night through an exceedingly ill-kept wood in a state of hunger, dampness, and exhaustion, one's judgment of distance is apt to lose some of its finer accuracy. I imagine, however, that I must have covered at least three more miles before my desire to lie down and sleep became too poignant to be any longer resisted.

I hunted about in the darkness until I discovered a small patch of fairly dry grass which had been more or less protected from the rain by an overhanging rock. I might perhaps have done better, but I was too tired to bother. I just dropped peacefully down where I stood, and in spite of my bruises and my soaked clothes I don't think I had been two minutes on the ground before I was fast asleep.

* * * * *

Tommy Morrison always used to say that only unintelligent people woke up feeling really well. If he was right I must have been in a singularly brilliant mood when I again opened my eyes.

It was still fairly dark, with the raw, sour darkness of an early March morning, and all round me the invisible drip of the trees was as persistent as ever. Very slowly and shakily I scrambled to my feet. My head ached savagely, I was chilled to the core, and every part of my body felt as if it had been trampled on by a powerful and rather ill-tempered mule.

I was hungry too—Lord, how hungry I was! Breakfast in the prison is not exactly an appetizing meal, but at that moment the memory of its thin gruel and greasy cocoa and bread seemed to me beautiful beyond words.

I looked round rather forlornly. As an unpromising field for foraging in, a Dartmoor wood on a dark March morning takes a lot of beating. It is true that there was plenty of water—the whole ground and air reeked with it—but water, even in unlimited quantities, is a poor basis for prolonged exertion.

There was nothing else to be got, however, so I had to make the best of it. I lay down full length beside a small spring which gurgled along the ground at my feet, and with the aid of my hands lapped up about a pint and a half. When I had finished, apart from the ache in my limbs I felt distinctly better.

The question was what to do next. Hungry or not, it would be madness to leave the shelter of the woods until evening, for not only would the warders be all over the place, but by this time everyone who lived in the neighbourhood would have been warned of my escape. My best chance seemed to lie in stopping where I was as long as daylight lasted, and then staking everything on a successful burglary.

It was not a cheerful prospect, and before the morning was much older it seemed less cheerful still. If you can imagine what it feels like to spend hour after hour crouching in the heart of a wood in a pitiless drizzle of rain, you will be able to get some idea of what I went through. If I had only had a pipe and some baccy, things would have been more tolerable; as it was there was nothing to do but to sit and shiver and grind my teeth and think about George.

I thought quite a lot about George. I seemed to see his face as he read the news of my escape, and I could picture the feverish way in which he would turn to each edition of the paper to find out whether I had been recaptured. Then I began to imagine our meeting, and George's expression when he realized who it was. The idea was so pleasing that it almost made me forget my present misery.

It must have been about midday when I decided on a move. In a way I suppose it was a rash thing to do, but I had got so cursedly cramped and cold again that I felt if I didn't take some exercise I should never last out the day. Even as it was, my legs had lost practically all feeling, and for the first few steps I took I was staggering about like a drunkard.

Keeping to the thickest part of the wood, I made my way slowly forward; my idea being to reach the top of the valley and then lie low again until nightfall. My progress was not exactly rapid, for after creeping a yard or two at a time I would crouch down and listen carefully for any sounds of danger. I had covered perhaps a mile in this spasmodic fashion when a gradual improvement in the light ahead told me that I was approaching open ground. A few steps farther, and through a gap in the trees a red roof suddenly came into view, with a couple of chimney-pots smoking away cheerfully in the rain.

It gave me a bit of a start, for I had not expected to run into civilization quite so soon as this. I stopped where I was and did a little bit of rapid thinking. Where there's a house there must necessarily be some way of getting at it, and the only way I could think of in this case was a private drive up the hill into the main Devonport road. If there was such a drive the house was no doubt a private residence and a fairly large one at that.

With infinite precaution I began to creep forward again. Between the trunks of the trees I could catch glimpses of a stout wood paling about six feet high which apparently ran the whole length of the grounds, separating them from the wood. On the other side of this fence I could hear, as I drew nearer, a kind of splashing noise, and every now and then the sound of somebody moving about and whistling.

The last few yards consisted of a strip of open grass marked by deep cart-ruts. Across this I crawled on my hands and knees, and getting right up against the fence began very carefully to search around for a peep-hole. At last I found a tiny gap between two of the boards. It was the merest chink, but by gluing my eye to it I was just able to see through.

I was looking into a square gravel-covered yard, in the centre of which a man in blue overalls was cleaning the mud off a small motor car. He was evidently the owner, for he was a prosperous, genial-looking person of the retired Major type, and he was lightening his somewhat damp task by puffing away steadily at a pipe. I watched him with a kind of bitter jealousy. I had no idea who he was, but for the moment I hated him fiercely. Why should he be able to potter around in that comfortable self-satisfied fashion, while I, Neil Lyndon, starved, soaked, and hunted like a wild beast, was crouching desperately outside his palings?

It was a natural enough emotion, but I was in too critical a position to waste time in asking myself questions. I realized that if burglary had to be done, here was the right spot. By going farther I should only be running myself into unnecessary risk, and probably without finding a house any more suitable to my purpose.

I squinted sideways through the hole, trying to master the geography of the place. On the left was a high bank of laurels, and just at the corner I could see the curve of the drive, turning away up the hill. On the other side of the yard was a small garage, built against the wall, while directly facing me was the back of the house.

I was just digesting these details, when a sudden sigh from the gentleman in the yard attracted my attention. He had apparently had enough of cleaning the car, for laying down the cloth he had been using, he stepped back and began to contemplate his handiwork.

It was not much to boast about, but it seemed to be good enough for him. At all events he came forward again, and taking off the brake, proceeded very slowly to push the car back towards the garage. At the entrance he stopped for a moment, and going inside brought out a bicycle which he leaned against the wall. Then he laboriously shoved the car into its appointed place, put back the bicycle, and standing in the doorway started to take off his overalls.

I need hardly say I watched him with absorbed interest. The sight of the bicycle had sent a little thrill of excitement tingling down my back, for it opened up possibilities in the way of escape that five minutes before had seemed wildly out of reach. If I could only steal the machine and the overalls as well, I should at least stand a good chance of getting clear away from the Moor before I was starved or captured. In addition to that I should be richer by a costume which would completely cover up the tasteful but rather pronounced pattern of my clothes.

My heart beat faster with excitement as with my eye pressed tight to the peep-hole I followed every movement of my unconscious quarry. Whistling cheerfully to himself, he stripped off the dark blue cotton trousers and oil-stained jacket that he was wearing and hung them on a nail just inside the door. Then he gave a last look round, presumably to satisfy himself that everything was in order, and shutting the door with a bang, turned the key in the lock.

I naturally thought he was going to stuff that desirable object into his pocket, but as it happened he did nothing of the kind. With a throb of half-incredulous delight I saw that he was standing on tiptoe, inserting it into some small hiding-place just under the edge of the iron roof.

I didn't wait for further information. At any moment someone might have come blundering round the corner of the paling, and I felt that I had tempted Fate quite enough already. So, abandoning my peep-hole, I turned round, and with infinite care crawled back across the grass into the shelter of the trees.

Once there, however, I rolled over on the ground and metaphorically hugged myself. The situation may not appear to have warranted such excessive rapture, but when a man is practically hopeless even the wildest of possible chances comes to him like music and sunshine. Forgetting my hunger and my wet clothes in my excitement, I lay there thinking out my plan of action. I could do nothing, of course, until it was dark: in fact it would be really better to wait till the household had gone to bed, for several of the back windows looked right out on the garage. Then, provided I could climb the paling and get out the bicycle without being spotted, I had only to push it up the drive to find myself on the Devonport road.

With this comforting reflection I settled myself down to wait. It was at least four hours from darkness, with another four to be added to that before I dared make a move. Looking back now, I sometimes wonder how I managed to stick it out. Long before dusk my legs and arms had begun to ache again with a dull throbbing sort of pain that got steadily worse, while the chill of my wet clothes seemed to eat into my bones. Once or twice I got up and crawled a few yards backwards and forwards, but the little additional warmth this performance gave me did not last long. I dared not indulge in any more violent exercise for fear that there might be warders about in the wood.

What really saved me, I think, was the rain stopping. It came to an end quite suddenly, in the usual Dartmoor fashion, and within half an hour most of the mist had cleared off too. I knew enough of the local weather signs to be pretty certain that we were in for a fine night; and sure enough, half an hour after the sun had set a large moon was shining down from a practically cloudless sky.

From where I was lying I could, by raising my head, just see the two top windows of the house. About ten, as near as I could judge, somebody lit a candle in one of these rooms, and then coming to the window drew down the blind. I waited patiently till I saw this dull glimmer of light disappear, then, with a not unpleasant throb of excitement, I crawled out from my hiding-place and recrossed the grass to my former point of observation. Very gingerly I lifted myself up and peered over the top of the paling. The yard was in shadow, and so far as I could see the back door and all the various outbuildings were locked up for the night.

Under ordinary circumstances I could have cleared that blessed paling in about thirty seconds, but in my present state of exhaustion it proved to be no easy matter. However, with a mighty effort I at last succeeded in getting my right elbow on the top, and from that point I managed to scramble up and hoist myself over. Then, keeping a watchful eye on the windows, I advanced towards the garage.

I found the key first shot. It was resting on a little ledge under the roof, and a thrill of joy went through me as my fingers closed over it. I pushed it into the keyhole, and very carefully I turned the lock.

It was quite dark inside, but I could just see the outline of the overalls hanging on the nail. I unhooked them, and placing the coat on the ground I drew on the oily trousers over my convict breeches and stockings. I could tell by the feel that they covered me up completely.

As I picked up the coat something rattled in one of the side pockets. I put my hand in and pulled out a box of wax matches, which despite the dampness of the garment still seemed dry enough to strike. For a moment I hesitated, wondering whether I dared to light one. It was dangerous, especially if there happened to be a window looking out towards the house, but on the other hand I badly wanted a little illumination to see what I was doing.

I decided to risk it, and closing the door, struck one against the wall. It flared up, and shading it with my hand I cast a hasty glance round the garage. The bicycle was leaning against a shelf just beyond me, and on a nail above it I saw an old disreputable-looking cap. I pounced on it joyfully, for it was the one thing I needed to complete my disguise. Then, wheeling the bicycle past the car, I blew out the match and reopened the door.

Stepping as noiselessly as possible on the gravel, I pushed the bike across the yard. There was a large patch of moonlight between me and the end of the drive, and I went through it with a horrible feeling in the small of my back that at any moment someone might fling up a window and bawl out, "Stop thief!" Nothing of the kind occurred, however, and with a vast sense of thankfulness I gained the shelter of the laurels.

The only thing that worried me was the thought that there might be a lodge at the top. If so I was by no means out of the wood. Even the most guileless of lodge-keepers would be bound to think it rather curious that I should be creeping out at this time of night accompanied by his master's bicycle.

Keeping one hand against the bushes to guide me, and pushing the machine with the other, I groped my way slowly up the winding path. As I came cautiously round the last corner I saw with a sigh of relief that my fears were groundless. A few yards ahead of me in the moonlight was a plain white gate, and beyond that the road.

I opened the gate with deliberate care, and closed it in similar fashion behind me. Then for a moment I stopped. I was badly out of breath, partly from weakness and partly from excitement, so laying the machine against the bank I leaned back beside it.

Everything was quite still. On each side of me the broad, white, moonlit roadway stretched away into the night, flanked by a row of telegraph poles which stood out like gaunt sentries. It was curious to think that they had probably put in a busy day's work, carrying messages about me.

There was a lamp on the front bracket, and as soon as I felt a little better I took out my matches and proceeded to light it. Then, wheeling my bike out into the roadway, I turned in the direction of Devonport and mounted. I felt a bit shaky at first, for, apart from the fact that I was worn out and pretty near starving, I had not been on a machine for over three years. However, after wobbling wildly from side to side, I managed to get the thing going, and pedalled off down the centre of the road as steadily as my half-numbed senses would allow.

For perhaps a quarter of a mile the ground kept fairly level, then, breasting a slight rise, I found myself at the top of a hill. I shoved on the brake and went slowly round the first corner, where I got an unexpected surprise. From this point the road ran straight away down through a small village, across a bridge over the river, and up a short steep slope on the farther side.

I took in the situation at a glance, and, releasing my brake, I let the old bike have her head. It certainly wouldn't suit me to have to dismount in the village and walk up the opposite slope, and I was much too exhausted to do anything else unless I could take it in a rush.

Down I went, the machine flying noiselessly along and gathering pace every yard. I had nearly reached the bottom and was just getting ready to pedal, when all of a sudden, I caught sight of something that almost paralyzed me. Right ahead, in the centre of the village square, stood a prison warder. His back was towards me and I could see the moonlight gleaming on the barrel of his carbine.

CHAPTER III
A DUBIOUS REFUGE

I was going so fast that everything seemed to happen simultaneously. I had one blurred vision of him spinning round and yelling to me to stop: then the next moment I had flashed past him and was racing across the bridge.

Whether he recognized me for certain I can't say. I think not, or he would probably have fired sooner than he did: as it was, my rush had carried me three quarters of the way up the opposite hill before he could make up his mind to risk a shot.

Bang went his carbine, and at the same instant, with a second loud report, the tire of my back wheel abruptly collapsed. It was a good shot if he had aimed for it, and what's more it came unpleasantly near doing the trick. The old bike swerved violently, but with a wild wrench I just succeeded in righting her. For a second I heard him shouting and running behind me, and then, working like a maniac, I bumped up the rest of the slope, and disappeared over the protecting dip at the top.

Of my progress for the next mile or so I have only the most confused recollection. It was like one of those ghastly things that occasionally happen to one in a nightmare. I just remember pedalling blindly along, with the back wheel grinding and jolting beneath me and the moonlit road rising and falling ahead. It must have been more instinct than anything else that kept me going, for I was in the last stages of hunger and weariness, and most of the time I scarcely knew what I was doing.

At last, after wobbling feebly up a long slope, I found I had reached the extreme edge of the Moor. Right below me the road dropped down for several hundred feet into a broad level expanse of fields and woods. Six or seven miles away the lights of Plymouth and Devonport threw up a yellow glare into the sky, and beyond that again I could just see the glint of the moonlight shining on the sea.

It was no good stopping, for I knew that in an hour or so the mounted warders would be again on my track. So clapping on both brakes, I started off down the long descent, being careful not to let the machine get away with me as it had done on the previous hill.

At the bottom, which I somehow reached in safety, I found a sign-post with two hands, one marked Plymouth and the other Devonport. I took the latter road, why I can hardly say, and summoning up my almost spent energies I pedalled off shakily between its high hedges.

How I got as far as I did remains a mystery to me to this day. I fell off twice from sheer weakness, but on each occasion I managed to drag myself back into the saddle again, and it was not until my third tumble, that I decided I could go no farther.

I was in a dark stretch of road bounded on each side by thick plantations. It was a good place to lie up in, but unfortunately there was another and more pressing problem in front of me. Half delirious as I was, I realized that unless I could find something to eat that night my career as an escaped convict was pretty near its end.

I picked myself up, and with a great effort managed to drag the bicycle to the side of the road. Then, clutching the rail that bounded the plantation, I began to stagger slowly forward along the slightly raised path. I think I had a sort of vague notion that there might be something to eat round the next corner.

I had progressed in this fashion for perhaps forty yards, when quite unexpectedly both the trees and the railings came to an end. I remained swaying and half incredulous for a moment: then I began to realize that I was standing in front of an open gate looking up an exceedingly ill-kept drive. At the end of this drive was a house, and the moonlight shining full on the front of it showed me that the whole place had about as forlorn and neglected an appearance as an inhabited building could very well possess. That it was inhabited there could be no doubt, for in the small glass square above the hall door I could see a feeble glimmer of light.

No one could have called it an inviting-looking place, but then I wasn't exactly waiting for invitations where a chance of food was concerned. I just slipped in at the gate, and keeping well in the shadow of the bushes that bounded the drive, I crept slowly and unsteadily forward until I reached a point opposite the front door. I crouched there for a moment, peering up at the house. Except for that flickering gas jet there was no sign of life anywhere; all the windows were shuttered or else in complete darkness.

At first I had a wild idea of ringing the bell and pretending to be a starving tramp. Then I remembered that my description had no doubt been circulated all round the neighbourhood, and that if there was any one in the place they would probably recognize me at once as the missing convict. This choked me off, for though as a rule I have no objection to a slight scuffle, I felt that in my present condition the average housemaid could knock me over with the flick of a duster.

The only alternative scheme that suggested itself to my numbed mind was to commit another burglary. There was a path running down the side of the house, which apparently led round to the back, and it struck me that if I followed this I might possibly come across an unfastened window. Anyhow, it was no good waiting about till I collapsed from exhaustion, so, getting on my feet, I slunk along the laurels as far as the end of the drive, and then crept across in the shadow of an overhanging tree.

I made my way slowly down the path, keeping one hand against the wall, and came out into a small square yard, paved with cobbles, where I found myself looking up at the back of the house. There was a door in the middle with two windows on either side of it, and above these several other rooms—all apparently in complete darkness.

I was beginning to feel horribly like fainting, but by sheer will-power I managed to pull myself together. Going up to the nearest window I peered through the pane. I could see the dim outline of a table with some plates on it just inside, and putting my hand against the bottom sash I gave it a gentle push. It yielded instantly, sliding up several inches with a wheezy rattle that brought my heart into my mouth.

For a moment or two I waited, listening intently for any sound of movement within the house. Then, as nothing happened, I carefully raised the sash a little higher, and poked my head in through the empty window-frame.

It was the kitchen all right: there could be no doubt about that. A strong smell of stale cooking pervaded the warm darkness, and that musty odour brought tears of joy into my eyes. I took one long luxurious sniff, and then with a last effort I hoisted myself up and scrambled in over the low sill.

As my feet touched the floor there was a sharp click. A blinding flash of light shot out from the darkness, striking me full in the face, and at the same instant a voice remarked quietly but firmly: "Put up your hands."

I put them up.

There was a short pause: then from the other end of the room a man in a dressing-gown advanced slowly to the table in the centre. He was holding a small electric torch in one hand and a revolver in the other. He laid down the former with the light still pointing straight at my face.

"If you attempt to move," he remarked pleasantly, "I shall blow your brains out."

With this he walked to the side of the room, struck a match against the wall, and reaching up turned on the gas.

I was much too dazed to do anything, even if I had had the chance. I just stood there with my hands up, rocking slightly from side to side, and wondering how long it would be before I tumbled over.

My captor remained for a moment under the light, peering at me in silence. He seemed to be a man of about sixty—a thin, frail man with white hair and a sharp, deeply lined face. He wore gold-rimmed pince-nez, behind which a pair of hard grey eyes gleamed at me in malicious amusement.

At last he took a step forward, still holding the revolver in his hand.

"A stranger!" he observed. "Dear me—what a disappointment! I hope Mr. Latimer is not ill?"

I had no idea what he was talking about, but his voice sounded very far away.

"If you keep me standing like this much longer," I managed to jerk out, "I shall most certainly faint."

I saw him raise his eyebrows in a sort of half-mocking smile.

"Indeed," he said, "I thought—"

What he thought I never heard, for the whole room suddenly went dim, and with a quick lurch the floor seemed to get up and spin round beneath my feet. I suppose I must have pitched forward, for the last thing I remember is clutching wildly but vainly at the corner of the kitchen table.

* * * * *

My first sensation on coming round was a burning feeling in my lips and throat. Then I suddenly realized that my mouth was full of brandy, and with a surprised gulp I swallowed it down and opened my eyes.

I was lying back in a low chair with a cushion under my head. Standing in front of me was the gentleman in the dressing-gown, only instead of a revolver he now held an empty wine-glass in his hand. When he saw that I was recovering he stepped back and placed it on the table. There was a short pause.

"Well, Mr. Lyndon," he said slowly, "and how are you feeling now?"

A hasty glance down showed me that the jacket of my overalls had been unbuttoned at the neck, exposing the soaked and mud-stained prison clothes beneath. I saw that the game was up, but for the moment I was too exhausted to care.

My captor leaned against the end of the table watching me closely.

"Are you feeling any better?" he repeated.

I made a feeble attempt to raise myself in the chair. "I don't know," I said weakly; "I'm feeling devilish hungry."

He stepped forward at once, his lined face breaking into something like a smile.

"Don't sit up. Lie quite still where you are, and I will get you something to eat. Have you had any food today?"

I shook my head. "Only rain-water," I said.

"You had better start with some bread and milk, then. You have been starving too long to eat a big meal straight away."

Crossing the room, he pushed open a door which apparently led into the larder, and then paused for a moment on the threshold.

"You needn't try to escape," he added, turning back to me. "I am not going to send for the police."

"I don't care what you do," I whispered, "as long as you hurry up with some grub."

Lying there in the sort of semi-stupor that comes from utter exhaustion, I listened to him moving about in the larder apparently getting things ready. For the moment all thoughts of danger or recapture had ceased to disturb me. Even the unexpected fashion in which I was being treated did not strike me as particularly interesting or surprising: my whole being was steeped in a sense of approaching food.

I saw him re-enter the room, carrying a saucepan, which he placed on a small stove alongside the fireplace. There was the scratching of a match followed by the pop of a gas-ring, and half-closing my eyes I lay back in serene and silent contentment.

I was aroused by the chink of a spoon, and the splash of something liquid being poured out. Then I saw my host coming towards me, carrying a large steaming china bowl in his hand.

"Here you are," he said. "Do you think you can manage to feed yourself?"

I didn't trouble to answer. I just seized the cup and spoon, and the next moment I was wolfing down a huge mouthful of warm bread and milk that seemed to me the most perfect thing I had ever tasted. It was followed rapidly by another and another, all equally beautiful.

My host stood by watching me with a sort of half-amused interest.

"I shouldn't eat it quite so fast," he observed. "It will do you more good if you take it slowly."

The first few spoonfuls had already partly deadened my worst pangs, so following his advice I slackened down the pace to a somewhat more normal level. Even then I emptied the bowl in what I think must have been a record time, and with a deep sigh I handed it to him to replenish.

I was feeling better—distinctly better. The food, the rest in the chair, and the comparative warmth of the room were all doing me good in their various ways, and for the first time I was beginning to realize clearly where I was and what had happened.

I suppose my host noticed the change, for he looked at me in an approving fashion as he gave me my second helping.

"There you are," he said in that curious dry voice of his. "Eat that up, and then we'll have a little conversation. Meanwhile—" he paused and looked round—"well, if you have no objection I think I will shut that window. I daresay you have had enough fresh air for today."

I nodded—my mouth was too full for any more elaborate reply—and crossing the room he closed the sash and pulled down the blind.

"That's better," he observed, gently rubbing his hands together; "now we are more comfortable and more private. By the way, I don't think I have introduced myself yet. My name is McMurtrie—Doctor McMurtrie."

"I am charmed to meet you," I said, swallowing down a large chunk of bread.

He nodded his head, smiling. "The pleasure is a mutual one, Mr. Lyndon—quite a mutual one."

The words were simple and smooth enough in themselves, but somehow or other the tone in which they were uttered was not altogether to my taste. It seemed to carry with it the faint suggestion of a cat purring over a mouse. Still I was hardly in a position to be too fastidious, so I accepted his compliment, and went on calmly with my bread and milk.

With the same rather catlike smile Dr. McMurtrie drew up a chair and sat down opposite to me. He kept his right hand in his pocket, presumably on the revolver.

"And now," he said, "perhaps you have sufficiently recovered to be able to tell me a little about yourself. At present my knowledge of your adventures is confined to the account of your escape in this morning's *Daily Mail*."

I slowly finished the last spoonful of my second helping, and placed the cup beside me on the floor. It was a clumsy device to gain time, for now that the full consciousness of my surroundings had returned to me, I was beginning to think that Dr. McMurtrie's methods of receiving an escaped convict were, to say the least, a trifle unusual. Was his apparent friendliness merely a blind, or did it hide some still deeper purpose, of which at present I knew nothing?

He must have guessed my thoughts, for leaning back in his chair he remarked half-mockingly: "Come, Mr. Lyndon, it doesn't pay to be too suspicious. If it will relieve your mind, I can assure you I have no immediate intention of turning policeman, even for the magnificent sum of—how much is it—five pounds, I believe? On mere business grounds I think it would be underrating your market value."

The slight but distinct change in his voice in the last remark invested it with a special significance. I felt a sudden conviction that for some reason of his own Dr. McMurtrie did not intend to give me up—at all events for the present.

"I will tell you anything you want to know with pleasure," I said. "Where did the *Daily Mail* leave off?"

He laughed curtly, and thrusting the other hand into his pocket pulled out a silver cigarette-case.

"If I remember rightly," he said, "you had just taken advantage of the fog to commit a brutal and quite unprovoked assault upon a warder." He held out the case.

"But try one of these before you start," he added. "They are a special brand from St. Petersburg, and I think you will enjoy them. There is nothing like a little abstinence to make one appreciate a good tobacco."

With a shaking hand I pressed the spring. It was three years since I had smoked my last cigarette—a cigarette handed me by the inspector in that stuffy little room below the dock, where I was waiting to be sentenced to death.

If I live to be a hundred I shall never forget my sensations as I struck the match which my host handed me and took in that first fragrant mouthful. It was so delicious that for a moment I remained motionless from sheer pleasure; then lying back again in my chair with a little gasp I drew another great cloud of smoke deep down into my lungs.

The doctor waited, watching me with a kind of cynical amusement.

"Don't hurry yourself, Mr. Lyndon," he observed, "pray don't hurry yourself. It is a pleasure to witness such appreciation."

I took him at his word, and for perhaps a couple of minutes we sat there in silence while the blue wreaths of smoke slowly mounted and circled round us. Then at last, with a delightful feeling of half-drugged contentment, I sat up and began my story.

I told it him quite simply—making no attempt to conceal or exaggerate anything. I described how the idea of making a bolt had come suddenly into my mind, and how I had acted on it without reflection or hesitation. Step by step I went quietly through my adventures, from the time when the fog had rolled down to the moment when, half fainting with hunger and exhaustion, I had climbed in through his kitchen window.

Leaning on the arm of his chair, he listened to me in silence. As far as any movement or change of expression was concerned a statue could scarcely have betrayed less interest, but all the time the steady gleam of his eyes never shifted from my face.

When I had finished he remained there for several seconds in the same attitude. Then at last he gave a short mirthless laugh.

"It must be pleasant to be as strong as you are," he said. "I should have been dead long ago."

I shrugged my shoulders. "Well, I don't exactly feel like going to a dance," I answered.

He got up and walked slowly as far as the window, where he turned round and stood staring at me thoughtfully. At last he appeared to make up his mind.

"You had better go to bed," he said, "and we will talk things over in the morning. You are not fit for anything more tonight."

"No, I'm not," I admitted frankly; "but before I go to bed I should like to feel a little more certain where I'm going to wake up."

There was a faint sound outside and I saw him raise his head. It was the distant but unmistakable hum of a motor, drawing nearer and nearer every moment. For a few seconds we both stood there listening: then with a sudden shock I realized that the car had reached the house and was turning in at the drive.

Weak as I was I sprang from my chair, scarcely feeling the thrill of pain that ran through me at the effort.

"By God!" I cried fiercely, "you've sold me!"

He whipped out the revolver, pointing it full at my face.

"Sit down, you fool," he said. "It's not the police."

CHAPTER IV
ECHOES OF A FAMOUS CASE

Whatever my intentions may have been—and they were pretty venomous when I jumped up—the revolver was really an unnecessary precaution. Directly I was on my feet I went as giddy as a kite, and it was only by clutching the chair that I saved myself from toppling over. I was evidently in a worse way than I imagined.

Lowering his weapon the doctor repeated his order.

"Sit down, man, sit down. No one means you any harm here."

"Who is it in the car?" I demanded, fighting hard against the accursed feeling of faintness that was again stealing through me.

"They are friends of mine. They have nothing to do with the police. You will see in a minute."

I sat down, more from necessity than by choice, and as I did so I heard the car draw up outside the back door.

Crossing to the window the doctor threw up the sash.

"Savaroff!" he called out.

There came an answer in a man's voice which I was unable to catch.

"Come in here," went on McMurtrie. "Don't bother about the car." He turned back to me. "Drink this," he added, pouring out some more brandy into the wine-glass. I gulped it down and lay back again in my chair, tingling all through.

He took my wrist and felt my pulse for a moment. "I know you are feeling bad," he said, "but we'll get your wet clothes off and put you to bed in a minute. You will be a different man in the morning."

"That will be very convenient," I observed faintly.

There was a noise of footsteps outside, the handle of the door turned, and a man—a huge bear of a man in a long Astrachan coat—strode heavily into the room. He was followed by a girl whose face was almost hidden behind a partly-turned-back motor veil. When they caught sight of me they both stopped abruptly.

"Who's this?" demanded the man.

Dr. McMurtrie made a graceful gesture towards me with his hand. "Allow me," he said, "to introduce you. Monsieur and Mademoiselle Savaroff—our distinguished and much-sought-after friend Mr. Neil Lyndon."

The big man gave a violent start, and with a little exclamation the girl stepped forward, turning back her veil. I saw then that she was remarkably handsome, in a dark, rather sullen-looking sort of way.

"You will excuse my getting up," I said weakly. "It doesn't seem to agree with me."

"Mr. Lyndon," explained the doctor, "is fatigued. I was just proposing that he should go to bed when I heard the car."

"How in the name of Satan did he get here?" demanded the other man, still staring at me in obvious amazement.

"He came in through the window with the intention of borrowing a little food. I had happened to see him in the garden, and being under the natural impression that he was—er—well, another friend of ours, I ventured to detain him."

Savaroff gave a short laugh. "But it's incredible," he muttered.

The girl was watching me curiously. "Poor man," she exclaimed, "he must be starving!"

"My dear Sonia," said McMurtrie, "you reflect upon my hospitality. Mr. Lyndon has been faring sumptuously on bread and milk."

"But he looks so wet and ill."

"He is wet and ill," rejoined the doctor agreeably. "That is just the reason why I am going to ask you to heat some water and light a fire in the spare bedroom. We don't want to disturb Mrs. Weston at this time of night. I suppose the bed is made up?"

Sonia nodded. "I think so. I'll go up and see anyhow."

With a last glance at me she left the room, and Savaroff, taking off his coat, threw it across the back of a chair. Then he came up to where I was sitting.

"You don't look much like your pictures, my friend," he said, unwinding the scarf that he was wearing round his neck.

"Under the circumstances," I replied, "that's just as well."

He laughed again, showing a set of strong white teeth. "Yes, yes. But the clothes and the short hair—eh? They would take a lot of explaining away. It was fortunate for you you chose this house—very fortunate. You find yourself amongst friends here."

I nodded.

I didn't like the man—there was too great a suggestion of the bully about him, but for all that I preferred him to McMurtrie.

It was the latter who interrupted. "Come, Savaroff, you take Mr. Lyndon's other arm and we'll help him upstairs. It is quite time he got out of those wet things."

With their joint assistance I hoisted myself out of the chair and, leaning heavily on the pair of them, hobbled across to the door. Every step I took sent a thrill of pain through me, for I was as stiff and sore as though I had been beaten all over with a walking-stick. The stairs were a bit of a job too, but they managed to get me up somehow or other, and I found myself in a large sparsely furnished hall lit by one ill-burning gas jet. There was a door half open on the left, and through the vacant space I could see the flicker of a freshly lighted fire.

They helped me inside, where we found the girl Sonia standing beside a long yellow bath-tub which she had set out on a blanket.

"I thought Mr. Lyndon might like a hot bath," she said. "It won't take very long to warm up the water."

"Like it!" I echoed gratefully; and then, finding no other words to express my emotions, I sank down in an easy chair which had been pushed in front of the fire.

I think the brandy that McMurtrie had given me must have gone to my head, or perhaps it was merely the sudden sense of warmth and comfort coming on top of my utter fatigue. Anyhow I know I fell gradually into a sort of blissful trance, in which things happened to me very much as they do in a dream.

I have a dim recollection of being helped to pull off my soaked and filthy clothes, and later on of lying back with indescribable felicity in a heavenly tub of hot water.

Then I was in bed and somebody was rubbing me, rubbing me all over with some warm pungent stuff that seemed to take away the pain in my limbs and leave me just a tingling mass of drowsy contentment.

After that—well, after that I suppose I fell asleep.

* * * * *

I base this last idea upon the fact that the next thing I remember is hearing some one say in a rather subdued voice: "Don't wake him up. Let him sleep as long as he likes—it's the best thing for him."

Whereupon, as was only natural, I promptly opened my eyes.

Dr. McMurtrie and the dark girl were standing by my bedside, looking down at me.

I blinked at them for a moment, wondering in my half-awake state where the devil I had got to. Then suddenly it all came back to me.

"Well," said the doctor smoothly, "and how is the patient today?"

I stretched myself with some care. I was still pretty stiff, and my throat felt as if some one had been scraping it with sand-paper, but all the same I knew that I was better—much better.

"I don't think there's any serious damage," I said hoarsely. "How long have I been asleep?"

He looked at his watch. "As far as I remember, you went to sleep in your bath soon after midnight. It's now four o'clock in the afternoon."

I started up in bed. "Four o'clock!" I exclaimed. "Good Lord! I must get up—I—"

He laid his hand on my shoulder. "Don't be foolish, my friend," he said. "You will get up when you are fit to get up. At the present moment you are going to have something to eat." He turned to the girl. "What are you thinking of giving him?" he asked.

"There are plenty of eggs," she said, "and there's some of that fish we had for breakfast." She answered curtly, almost rudely, looking at me while she spoke. Her manner gave me the impression that for some reason or other she and McMurtrie were not exactly on the best of terms.

If that was so, he himself betrayed no sign of it. "Either will do excellently," he said in his usual suave way, "or perhaps our young friend could manage both. I believe the Dartmoor air is most stimulating."

"I shall be vastly grateful for anything," I said, addressing the girl. "Whatever is the least trouble to cook."

She nodded and left the room without further remark—McMurtrie looking after her with what seemed like a faint gleam of malicious amusement.

"I have brought you yesterday's *Daily Mail*," he said; "I thought it would amuse you to read the description of your escape. It is quite entertaining; and besides that there is a masterly little summary of your distinguished career prior to its unfortunate interruption." He laid the paper on the bed. "First of all, though," he added, "I will just look you over. I couldn't find much the matter with you last night, but we may as well make certain."

He made a short examination of my throat, and then, after feeling my pulse, tapped me vigorously all over the chest.

"Well," he said finally, "you have been through enough to kill two ordinary men, but except for giving you a slight cold in the head it seems to have done you good."

I sat up in bed. "Dr. McMurtrie," I said bluntly, "what does all this mean? Who are you, and why are you hiding me from the police?"

He looked down on me, with that curious baffling smile of his. "A natural and healthy curiosity, Mr. Lyndon," he said drily. "I hope to satisfy it after you have had something to eat. Till then—" he shrugged his shoulders—"well, I think you will find the *Daily Mail* excellent company."

He left the room, closing the door behind him, and for a moment I lay there with an uncomfortable sense of being tangled up in some exceedingly mysterious adventure. Even such unusual people as Dr. McMurtrie and his friends do not as a rule take in and shelter escaped convicts purely out of kindness of heart. There must be a strong motive for them to run such a risk in my case, but what that motive could possibly be was a matter which left me utterly puzzled. So far as I could remember I had never seen any of the three before in my life.

I glanced round the room. It was a big airy apartment, with ugly old-fashioned furniture, and two windows, both of which looked out in the same direction. The pictures on the wall included an oleograph portrait of the late King Edward in the costume of an Admiral, a large engraving of Mr. Landseer's inevitable stag, and several coloured and illuminated texts. One of the latter struck me as being topical if a little inaccurate. It ran as follows:

THE WICKED FLEE WHEN NO MAN PURSUETH

Over the mantelpiece was a mirror in a mahogany frame. I gazed at it idly for a second, and then a sudden impulse seized me to get up and see what I looked like. I turned back the clothes and crawled out of bed. I felt shaky when I stood up, but my legs seemed to bear me all right, and very carefully I made my way across to the fireplace.

The first glance I took in the mirror gave me a shock that nearly knocked me over. A cropped head and three days' growth of beard will make an extraordinary difference in any one, but I would never have believed they could have transformed me into quite such an unholy-looking ruffian as the one I saw staring back at me out of the glass. If I had ever been conceited about my personal appearance, that moment would have cured me for good.

Satisfied with a fairly brief inspection I returned to the bed, and arranging the pillow so as to fit the small of my back, picked up the *Daily Mail*. I happened to open it at the centre page, and the big heavily leaded headlines caught my eyes straight away.

ESCAPE OF NEIL LYNDON FAMOUS PRISONER BREAKS OUT OF DARTMOOR SENSATIONAL CASE RECALLED

With a pleasant feeling of anticipation I settled down to read.

From our own Correspondent. Princetown.

Neil Lyndon, perhaps the most famous convict at present serving his sentence, succeeded yesterday in escaping from Princetown. At the moment of writing he is still at large.

He formed one of a band of prisoners who were returning from the quarries late in the afternoon. As the men reached the road which leads through the plantation to the main gate of the prison, one of the warders in charge was overcome by an attack of faintness. In the ensuing confusion, a convict of the name of Cairns, who was walking at the head of the gang, made a sudden bolt for freedom. He was immediately challenged and fired at by the Civil Guard.

The shot took partial effect, but failed for the moment to stop the runaway, who succeeded in scrambling off into the wood. He was pursued by the Civil Guard, and it was at that moment that Lyndon, who was in the rear of the gang, also made a dash for liberty.

He seems to have jumped the low wall which bounds the plantation, and although fired at in turn by another of the warders, apparently escaped injury.

Running up the hill through the trees, he reached the open slope of moor on the farther side which divides the plantation from the main wood. While he was crossing this he was seen from the roadway by that well-known horse-dealer and pigeon-shot, Mr. Alfred Smith of Shepherd's Bush, who happened to be on a walking tour in the district.

Mr. Smith, with characteristic sportsmanship, made a plucky attempt to stop him; but Lyndon, who had picked up a heavy stick in the plantation, dealt him a terrific blow on the head that temporarily stunned him. He then jumped the railings and took refuge in the wood.

The pursuing warders came up a few minutes later, but by this time a heavy mist was beginning to settle down over the moor, rendering the prospect of a successful search more than doubtful. The warders therefore surrounded the wood with the idea of preventing Lyndon's escape.

Taking advantage of the fog, however, the latter succeeded in slipping out on the opposite side. He was heard climbing the railings by Assistant-warder Conway, who immediately gave the alarm and closed with the fugitive. The other warders came running up, but just before they could reach the scene of the struggle Lyndon managed to free himself by means of a brutal kick, and darting into the fog disappeared from sight.

It is thought that he has made his way over North Hessary and is lying up in the Walkham Woods. In any case it is practically certain that he will not be at liberty much longer. It is impossible for him to get food except by stealing it from a cottage or farm, and directly he shows himself he is bound to be recaptured.

Considerable excitement prevails in the district, where all the inhabitants are keenly on the alert.

THE MARKS MURDER ECHOES OF A FAMOUS CASE

The escape of Neil Lyndon recalls one of the most famous crimes of modern days.

On the third of October four years ago, as most of our readers will remember, a gentleman named Mr. Seton Marks was found brutally murdered in his luxurious flat on the Chelsea Embankment. It was thought at first that the crime was the work of burglars, for Mr. Marks's rooms contained many art treasures of considerable value. A further examination, however, revealed the fact that nothing had been tampered with, and the next day the whole country was startled and amazed to learn that Neil Lyndon had been arrested on suspicion.

At the trial it was proved beyond question that the accused was the last person in the company of the murdered man. He had gone round to Mr. Marks's flat at four o'clock in the afternoon, and had apparently been admitted by the owner. Two hours later Mr. Marks's servant returning to the flat was horrified to find his master's dead body lying in the sitting-room. Death had been inflicted by means of a heavy blow on the back of the head, but the state of the dead man's face showed that he had been brutally mishandled before being killed.

The accused, while maintaining his innocence of the murder, did not deny either his visit to the flat, or the fact that he had inflicted the other injuries on the deceased. He declined to state the cause of their quarrel, but the defending counsel produced a witness in the person of Miss Joyce Aylmer, a young girl of sixteen, who was able to throw some light on the matter.

Miss Aylmer, a young lady of considerable beauty, stated that for about a year she had been working as an art student in Chelsea, and used occasionally to sit to artists for the head. On the afternoon before the murder she had had a professional engagement of this kind with Mr. Marks. There had been a visitor in the flat when she arrived, but he had left as soon as she came in. Subsequently, according to her statement, the deceased had acted towards her in an outrageous and disgraceful manner. She had escaped from his flat with difficulty, and had subsequently informed Mr. Lyndon of what had taken place.

In his re-examination, the accused admitted that it was on account of Miss Aylmer's statement he had visited the flat. Up till then, he declared, he had had no quarrel with the deceased.

This statement, however, was directly contradicted by Lyndon's partner, Mr. George Marwood. Giving his evidence with extreme reluctance, Mr. Marwood stated that for some time bad blood had undoubtedly existed between Mr. Marks and the accused. He added that in his own hearing on two separate occasions the latter had threatened to kill the deceased.

Pressed still further, he admitted meeting Mr. Lyndon in Chelsea on the night of the murder, when the latter had to all intents and purposes acknowledged his guilt.

On the evidence there could naturally be only one verdict, and Lyndon was found guilty and sentenced to death by Mr. Justice Owen.

A tremendous agitation in favour of his reprieve broke out at once. Apart from the peculiar circumstances under which the crime was committed, it was urged that Mr. Lyndon's services to the country as an inventor should be taken into consideration. Within twenty-four hours over a million people had signed a petition in his favour, and the following day His Majesty was pleased to commute the sentence to one of penal servitude for life.

There is little doubt, however, that Lyndon would have been released at the end of ten or twelve years.

THE ESCAPED CONVICT'S CAREER

Neil Lyndon is the only son of the well-known explorer Colonel Grant Lyndon, who perished on the Upper Amazon some fifteen years ago. He was educated at Haileybury, and Oriel College, Oxford, where he took the highest honours in chemistry and mathematics. Coming down, he entered into partnership with his cousin Mr. George Marwood, and between them the two young inventors met with early and remarkable success. Their greatest achievement was of course the construction of the Lyndon-Marwood automatic torpedo, which was taken up four years ago, after exhaustive tests, by the British Government.

Lyndon is a man of exceptionally powerful physique. He successfully represented Oxford as a heavy-weight boxer in his last term, and the following year was runner up in the Amateur Championship. He is also a fine long-distance swimmer, and a well-known single-handed yachtsman.

Mr. George Marwood, whose painful position in connection with the trial aroused considerable sympathy, has carried on the business alone since his partner's conviction. Quite recently, as our readers will recall, he was the victim of a remarkable outrage at his offices in Victoria Street. While he was working there by himself late at night, a couple of masked men broke into the building, bound and gagged him, and proceeded to ransack the safe. It is said that they secured plans and documents of considerable value, but owing to the non-arrest of the thieves the exact details have never come to light.

So ended the *Daily Mail.*

I finished reading, and taking a long breath, laid down the paper. Up till then I had heard nothing about the news contained in the last paragraph, and it sent my memory back at once to the big well-lighted room in Victoria Street where George and I had spent so many hours together. I wondered what the valuable "plans and documents" might be which the thieves were supposed to have secured. In my day we had always been pretty careful about what we left at the office, and any really important plans—such as those of the Lyndon-Marwood torpedo—were invariably kept at the safe deposit across the street.

From George and the office my thoughts drifted away over the whole of that crowded time referred to in the paper. Brief and bald as the narrative was, it brought up before me a dozen vivid memories, which jostled each other simultaneously in my mind. I saw again poor little Joyce's tear-stained face, and remembered the shuddering relief with which she had clung to me as she sobbed out her story. I could recall the cold rage in which I had set out for Marks's flat, and that first savage blow of mine that sent him reeling and crashing into one of his own cabinets.

Then I was in court again, and George was giving his evidence—the lying evidence that had been meant to send me to the gallows. I remembered the cleverly assumed reluctance with which he had apparently allowed his statements to be dragged from him, and my blood rose hot in my throat as I thought of his treachery.

Above all I seemed to see the fat red face of Mr. Justice Owen, with the ridiculous little three-cornered black cap above it. He had been very cut up about sentencing me to death, had poor old Owen, and I could almost hear the broken tones in which he had faltered out the words:

"... taken from the place where you now stand to the place whence you came—hanged by the neck until your body be dead—and may God have mercy on your soul."

At this cheerful point in my reminiscences I was suddenly interrupted by a sharp knock at the door.

CHAPTER V
AN OFFER WITHOUT AN ALTERNATIVE

With a big effort I pulled myself together. "Come in," I called out.

The door opened, and the girl, Sonia, entered the room. She was carrying a tray, which she set down on the top of the chest of drawers.

"I don't know the least how to thank you for all this," I said.

She turned round and looked at me curiously from under her dark eyebrows.

"For all what?" she asked.

"This," I repeated, waving my hand towards the tray, "and the hot bath last night, and incidentally my life. If it hadn't been for you and Dr. McMurtrie I think my 'career,' as the *Daily Mail* calls it, would be pretty well finished by now."

She stood where she was, her hand on her hip, her eyes fixed on my face.

"Do you know why we are helping you?" she asked.

I shook my head. "I haven't the faintest notion," I answered frankly. "It certainly can't be on account of the charm of my appearance. I've just been looking at myself in the glass."

She shrugged her shoulders half impatiently. "What does a man's appearance matter? You can't expect to break out of Dartmoor in a frock-coat."

"No," I replied gravely; "there must always be a certain lack of dignity about such a proceeding. Still, when one looks like—well, like an escaped murderer, it's all the more surprising that one should be so hospitably received."

She picked up the tray again, and brought it to my bedside.

"Oh!" she said; "I shouldn't build too much upon our hospitality if I were you."

I took the tray from her hands. "I would build upon yours to any extent," I said; "but I am under no illusion whatever about Dr. McMurtrie's disinterestedness. He and your father—it is your father, isn't it?—are coming up to explain matters as soon as I have had something to eat."

She stood silent for a moment, her brows knitted in a frown.

"They mean you no harm," she said at last, "as long as you will do what they want." Then she paused. "Did you murder that man Marks?" she asked abruptly.

I swallowed down my first mouthful of fish. "No," I said; "I only knocked him about a bit. He wasn't worth murdering."

She stared at me as if she was trying to read my thoughts.

"Is that true?" she said.

"Well," I replied, "he was alive enough when I left him, judging from his language."

"Then why did your partner—Mr. Marwood—why did he say that you had done it?"

"That," I said softly, "is a little question which George and I have got to discuss together some day."

She walked to the door and then turned.

"If a man I had trusted and worked with behaved like that to me," she said slowly, "I should kill him."

I nodded my approval of the sentiment. "I daresay it will come to that," I said; "the only thing is one gets rather tired of being sentenced to death."

She gave me another long, curious glance out of those dark brown eyes of hers, and then going out, closed the door behind her.

For an exceedingly busy and agreeable quarter of an hour I occupied myself with the contents of the tray. There was some very nicely grilled whiting, a really fresh boiled egg, a jar of honey, and a large plate of brown bread and butter cut in sturdy slices. Best of all, on the edge of the tray were a couple of McMurtrie's cigarettes. Whether he or Sonia was responsible for this last attention I could not say. I hoped it was Sonia: somehow or other I did not want to be too much indebted to Dr. McMurtrie.

I finished my meal—finished it in the most complete sense of the phrase—and then, putting down my tray on the floor, reverently lighted up. I found that my first essay in smoking on the previous evening had in no way dulled the freshness of my enjoyment, and for a few minutes I was content to lie there pleasantly indifferent to everything except the flavour of the tobacco.

Then my mind began to work. Sonia's questions had once again started a train of thought which ever since the trial had been running through my brain with maddening persistence. If I had not killed Marks, who had? How often had I asked myself that during the past three years, and how often had I abandoned the problem in utter weariness! Sometimes, indeed, I had been almost tempted to think the jury must have been right—that I must have struck the brute on the back of the head without realizing in my anger what I was doing. Then, when I remembered how I had left him crouching against the wall, spitting out curses at me through his cut and bleeding lips, I knew that the idea was nonsense. The wound which they found in his head must have killed him instantly. No man who had received a blow like that would ever speak or move again.

The one thing I felt certain of was that in some mysterious way or other George was mixed up in the business. It was incredible that he could have acted as he did at the trial unless he had had some stronger reason than mere dislike for me. That he did dislike me I knew well, but my six years' association with him had taught me that he would never allow any personal motive to interfere with a chance of making money. By sending me to the gallows or into penal servitude he was practically ruining himself, for with all his acuteness and business knowledge he was quite deficient in any sort of inventive power. And yet he had not hesitated to do it, and to do it by a piece of lying sufficiently cold-blooded and deliberate to make Judas pale with envy.

If there had been any apparent chance of his being able to rob me by the proceeding, I could have understood it. But my business interests as far as past inventions went were safe in the hands of my lawyers, and although I had told him a certain amount about the new explosive which I had been working at, it was quite impossible for him to turn it to any practical use.

No, George must have had some other reason for perjuring his unpleasant soul, and the only one I could think of was that he had purposely turned the case against me in order to shield the real murderer. He had been fairly well acquainted with the dead man, I knew—their tastes indeed ran on somewhat similar lines—and it was just possible that he was aware who had committed the crime.

The thought filled me, as it always had filled me, with a bitter fury. Again and again in my cell I had fancied myself escaping from the prison and choking the truth out of my cousin's throat with my fingers, and now that the first part of this picture had come true, I vowed silently to myself that nothing should stop the remainder from following it. Whatever McMurtrie might propose, I would see George once again face to face, even if death or recapture was the price I had to pay.

I had just arrived at this conclusion when I heard the sound of footsteps in the passage outside. Then the handle of the door turned, and McMurtrie appeared on the threshold with Savaroff looming up behind him. There was a moment's silence, while the doctor stood there smiling down on me as blandly as ever.

"May we come in?" he inquired. "We are not interrupting your tea, I hope."

"No, I have done tea, thank you," I said, with a gesture towards the tray.

Why it was so, I can't say, but McMurtrie's politeness always filled me with a feeling of repulsion. There was something curiously sinister about it.

He stepped forward into the room, followed by Savaroff, who closed the door behind him. The latter then lounged across and sat down on the window-sill, McMurtrie remaining standing by my bedside.

"You have read the *Mail*, I see," he said, picking up the paper. "I hope you admired the size of the headlines."

"It's the type of compliment," I replied, "that I have had rather too much of."

Savaroff broke out into a short gruff laugh. "Our friend," he said, "is modest—so modest. He does not thirst for more fame. He would retire into private life if they would let him."

He chuckled to himself, as though enjoying the subtlety of his own humour. Unlike his daughter, he spoke English with a distinctly foreign accent.

"Ah, yes," said Dr. McMurtrie amiably; "but then, Mr. Lyndon is one of those people that we can't afford to spare. Talents such as his are intended for use." He took off his glasses and began to polish them thoughtfully. "One might almost say that he held them in trust—in trust for Providence."

There was a short silence.

"And is it on account of my talents that you have been kind enough to shelter me?" I asked bluntly.

The doctor readjusted his pince-nez, and seated himself with some deliberation on the foot of the bed.

"The instinct to assist a hunted fellow-creature," he observed, "is almost universal." Then he paused. "I take it, Mr. Lyndon, that you are not particularly anxious to rejoin your friends in Princetown?"

I shook my head. "Not if there is a more pleasant alternative."

Savaroff grunted. "No alternative is likely to be more unpleasant for you," he said harshly.

The touch of bullying in his tone put my back up at once. "Indeed!" I said: "I can imagine several."

McMurtrie's smooth voice intervened. "But ours, Mr. Lyndon, is one which I think will make a very special appeal to you. How would you like to keep your freedom and at the same time take up your scientific work again?"

I looked at him closely. For once there was no trace of mockery in his eyes.

"I should like it very much indeed, if it was possible," I answered.

McMurtrie leaned forward a little. "It is possible," he said quietly.

There was a short pause. Savaroff pulled out a cigar, bit off the end, and spat it into the fireplace. Then he reached sideways to the chest of drawers for a match.

"Explain to him," he said, jerking his head towards me.

McMurtrie glanced at him—it seemed to me a shade impatiently. Then he turned back to me.

"For some time before Mr. Marks's unfortunate death," he said slowly, "you had been experimenting with a new explosive."

I nodded my head. I had no idea how he had got his information, for as far as I was aware George was the only person who had any knowledge of my secret.

"And I believe you were just on the point of success when you were arrested?"

"Theoretically I was," I said. "These matters don't always work out quite so well when you put them to a practical test."

"Still, you yourself were quite satisfied with the prospects?"

I nodded again.

"And unless I am wrong, this new explosive will be immensely more powerful than anything now in use?"

"Immensely," I repeated; "in fact, there would be no practical comparison between them."

"Can you give me any idea as to its strength?"

I hesitated. "According to my calculations," I said slowly, "it ought to prove at least twenty times as powerful as gun-cotton."

Savaroff uttered a hoarse exclamation and sat upright in his seat.

"Are you speaking the truth?" he asked roughly.

I stared him full in the face, and then without answering turned back to McMurtrie.

The latter made a gesture with his hand. "Leave the matter to me, Savaroff," he said sharply. "I understand Mr. Lyndon better than you do." Then addressing me: "Supposing you had all the things that you required, how long would it take you to manufacture some of this powder—or whatever it is?"

"It's difficult to say," I answered. "Perhaps a week; perhaps a couple of months. I could make the actual stuff at once provided I had the materials, but it's a question of doing it in such a way that one can handle it safely for practical purposes. I was experimenting on that very point at the time of my arrest."

McMurtrie nodded his head slowly. "You have been candid with us," he said, "and now I will be equally candid with you. My friend M. Savaroff and myself are very largely interested in the manufacture of high explosives. The appearance of an invention like yours on the market would be a very serious matter indeed for us. On the other hand, if we had control of it, we should, I imagine, be in a position to dictate our own terms."

"You certainly would," I said; "there is no question about that. My explosive would be no more expensive to manufacture than cordite."

"So you see when some exceedingly convenient chance brought you in through our kitchen window it naturally occurred to me to invite you to stay and discuss the matter. You happen to be in a position in which you could be useful to us, and I think that we, on the other hand, might be of some assistance to you."

He leant back and watched me with that cold smile of his.

"What do you say, Mr. Lyndon?" he added.

I did some rapid but necessary thinking. It was quite true that the new explosive would knock the bottom out of the present methods of manufacture, and McMurtrie's interests in the matter might well be large enough to make him run the risk of helping me. There seemed no reason to doubt that he was speaking the truth—and yet, somehow or other I mistrusted him—mistrusted him from my soul.

"How did you know about my experiments?" I asked quietly.

He shrugged his shoulders. "There are such things as trade secrets. It is necessary for a business man to keep in touch with anything that may threaten his interests."

I hesitated a second. "What is it that you propose—exactly?" I inquired.

I saw—or thought I saw—the faintest possible gleam of satisfaction steal into his eyes.

"I propose that you should finish your experiments as soon as possible, make some of this explosive, and hand the actual stuff and the full secret of its manufacture over to us. In return I will guarantee you your freedom, and let you have a quarter interest in all profits we make out of your invention."

He brought out these somewhat startling terms as coolly as though it were an every-day custom of his to do business with escaped convicts. I bent down from the bed, and under cover of picking up my second cigarette from the tray, secured a few useful moments for considering the situation.

"I have no objection to the bargain," I said slowly, helping myself to a match off the table; "the only question is whether it is possible to carry it out. My experiments aren't the kind that can be conducted in a back bedroom. I should want a large shed of some kind, and the farther away it was from any houses the better. There is always the chance of blowing oneself up at this sort of business, and in that case an explosive like mine would probably wreck everything within a couple of miles."

"You shall work under any conditions you please," said McMurtrie amiably. "If it suits you we will fix you up a hut and some sheds down on the Thames marshes, and you can live there till the experiments are finished."

"But I should be recognized," I objected. "I am bound to be recognized. I am fairly well known as it is, and with my picture and description placarded all over England, I shouldn't stand a dog's chance. However lonely a place it was, some one would be bound to see me and give me away sooner or later."

McMurtrie shook his head. "You may be seen," he said, "but there is no reason why you should be recognized."

I paused in the act of lighting my cigarette. "What do you mean?" I asked with some curiosity.

"My dear Mr. Lyndon," said McMurtrie, courteously, "as a scientist yourself you don't imagine that it's beyond the art of an intelligent surgeon to cope with a little difficulty like that?"

"But in what way?" I objected. "A disguise? Any one can see through a disguise except in novels."

The doctor smiled. "I am not suggesting a wig and a pair of spectacles," he observed. "It is rather too late in the world's history for that sort of thing." Then he stopped and studied me for an instant attentively. "In a fortnight, and practically without hurting you," he added, "I can make you as safe from the police as if you were dead and buried."

I sat up in bed. "Under the circumstances," I said, "you'll excuse my being a little inquisitive."

"Oh, there is no secret about it. Any surgeon could do it. I have only to alter the shape of your nose a trifle, and make your forehead rather higher and wider. A stain of some sort will do the rest."

"Yes," I said; "but what about the first part of the programme?"

He shrugged his shoulders. "Child's play," he answered. "Merely a question of paraffin injections and the X-rays."

He spoke with such careless confidence that for once it was impossible to doubt his sincerity.

I lay back again and drew in a large exulting lungful of cigarette smoke. I had suddenly realized that if McMurtrie's offer was genuine, and he could really do what he promised, there were no longer any difficulties in the way of my getting at George. The idea of meeting him, and perhaps even speaking to him, without his being able to recognize me filled me with a wicked satisfaction that no words can do justice to.

I don't think I betrayed my emotion, however, for McMurtrie's keen eyes were on me, and I was not in the least anxious to take him into my confidence. I blew out the smoke in a grey cloud, and then, raising myself on my elbow carefully flicked the ash off my cigarette.

"How am I to know that you will keep your promise?" I asked.

Savaroff made an angry movement, but before he could speak, McMurtrie had broken in.

"You forget what an embarrassing position we shall be putting ourselves in, Mr. Lyndon," he said with perfect good temper. "Shielding a runaway convict is an indictable offence—to say nothing of altering his appearance. As for the money"—he made a little gesture of contempt—

"well, do you think it would pay us to cheat you? There is always the chance that a gentleman who can invent things like this explosive and the Lyndon-Marwood torpedo may have other equally satisfactory notions."

"Very well," I said quietly. "I will accept the offer on one condition — that I can have a week in London before beginning work."

With an oath Savaroff started up from the window-sill.

"Gott in Himmel! and who are you to make terms?" he exclaimed roughly. "Why, we have only to send you back to the prison and you will be flogged like a dog!"

"In which distressing event," I observed, "you would not get your explosive."

"My dear Savaroff," interrupted McMurtrie, soothingly, "there is no need to threaten Mr. Lyndon. I am sure that he appreciates the situation." Then he turned to me. "I suppose you have some reason for making this condition?"

Silently in my heart I invoked the shade of Ananias.

"If you had been in Dartmoor three years," I said, with a rather well-forced laugh, "you would find several excellent reasons for wanting a week in London."

My acting must have been good, for I could have sworn I saw a faint expression of relieved contempt flicker across McMurtrie's face.

"I see. A little holiday—a brief taste of the pleasures of liberty! Well, that seems to me a very natural and reasonable request. What do you think, Savaroff?"

That gentleman contented himself with a singularly ungracious grunt.

"I don't think there would be much risk about it," I said boldly. "If you can change my appearance as completely as you say you can, no one would be the least likely to recognize me. After three years of that dog's life up there I can't settle down in a hut on the Thames marshes without having a few days' fun first. I should be very careful what I did naturally. I have had quite enough of the prison to appreciate being outside."

McMurtrie nodded. "Very well," he said slowly. "I see no objection to your having your 'few days' fun' in London if you want them. It would be safer perhaps to get you away from this house as soon as possible. I should think three weeks would be quite enough for our purposes here—and I daresay it will take us a month to fix up a satisfactory place for you to work in." Then he paused. "Of course if you go to town," he added, "you will have to stay at some address we shall arrange for, and you will have to be ready to start work directly we tell you to."

"Naturally," I said; "I only want—"

I was saved from finishing my falsehood by a sudden sound from outside—the sound of a swing gate banging against its post. For a moment I had a horrible feeling that it might be the police.

Savaroff jumped up and looked out of the window. Then with a little guttural exclamation he turned back to McMurtrie.

"Hoffman!" he muttered, apparently in some surprise.

Who Mr. Hoffman might be I had not the faintest notion, but the mention of the name brought the doctor to his feet at once. I think he was rather annoyed with Savaroff for being unnecessarily communicative. When he spoke, however, it was with his usual perfect composure.

"Well, we will leave you at peace now, Mr. Lyndon. I should try to go to sleep again for a little while if I were you. I will come up later and see whether you would like some supper." He stopped and looked round the room. "Is there anything else you want that you haven't got?"

"If you could advance me a box of cigarettes," I said, "it shall be the first charge on the new explosive."

He nodded, smiling. "I will send Sonia up with it," he answered. Then, following Savaroff, he went out into the passage, carefully closing the door after him.

Left alone, I lay back on the pillow in a frame of mind which I believe novelists describe as "chaotic." I had expected something rather unusual from my interview with McMurtrie, but these proposals of his could hardly be classed under such a mild heading as that. For sheer unexpectedness they about took the biscuit.

I had read in books of a man's appearance being altered so completely that even his best friends failed to recognize him, but it had never occurred to me that such a thing could be done in real life—let alone in the simple fashion outlined by the doctor. Of course, if he was speaking the truth, there seemed no reason why his plan, fantastic as it might sound, should not turn out perfectly successful. A private hut on the Thames marshes was about the last place in which you would look for an escaped Dartmoor convict, especially when he had vanished into thin air within a few miles of Devonport.

What worried me most in the matter was my apparent good luck in having fallen on my feet in this amazing fashion. There is a limit to one's belief in coincidences, and the extraordinary combination of chances suggested by McMurtrie's smooth explanations was just a little too stiff for me to swallow. I felt sure that he was lying in some important particulars — but precisely which they were I was unable to guess for certain.

That he wanted the secret of the new explosive, and wanted it badly, there could be no doubt, but neither he nor Savaroff in the least suggested to me a successful manufacturer of cordite or anything else. They seemed to me to belong to a much more interesting if less conventional type, and I couldn't help wondering what on earth such a curious trio as they and Sonia could be doing tucked away in an ill-furnished, deserted-looking country house in a corner of South Devon.

However it was no good worrying, for as far as I was concerned it was painfully clear that there was no alternative. If I declined their offer and refused to let McMurtrie carve my face about, they had only to turn me out, and in a few hours I should probably be back in my cell with the cheerful prospect of chains, a flogging, and six months' semi-starvation in front of me.

Anything was better than that—even the wildest of plunges in the dark. Indeed I am not at all sure that the mystery that surrounded McMurtrie's offer did not lend it a certain charm in my eyes. My life had been so infernally dull for the last three years that the prospect of a little excitement, even of an unpleasant kind, was by no means wholly disagreeable.

At least I had my week's "fun" in London to look forward to, and the thought of that alone would have been quite enough to make me go through with anything. I had lied to McMurtrie about my object, but the falsehood, such as it was, did not sit very heavily on my conscience. The precise meaning of "fun" is purely a matter of opinion, and I was as much entitled to my definition as he was to his. After all, if a convicted murderer can't be a little careless about the exact truth, who the devil can?

CHAPTER VI
THE FACE OF A STRANGER

McMurtrie had left me under the impression that he meant to start work on my face the next day, but as it turned out the impression was a mistaken one. Both the paraffin wax and the X-ray outfit had to be procured from London, and according to Sonia it was to see about these that her father went off to town early the following morning. She told me this when she brought me up my breakfast, just after I had heard the car drive away from the house.

"Well, I suppose I had better get up too," I said. "I can't stop in bed and be waited on by you."

"You've got to," she replied curtly, "unless you would rather I sent up Mrs. Weston."

"Who's Mrs. Weston?" I inquired.

Sonia placed the tray on my bed. "She's our housekeeper. She's deaf and dumb."

"There are worse things," I observed, "in a housekeeper." Then I sat up and pulled my breakfast towards me. "Of course I would much rather you looked after me. I was only thinking of the trouble I'm giving you."

"Oh, it's not much trouble," she said; then after a little pause she added, in a rather curious voice: "Anyway I shouldn't mind if it was."

"But I am feeling perfectly fit this morning," I persisted. "I might just as well get up if your father would lend me some kit. I don't think I could squeeze into McMurtrie's."

She shook her head. "The doctor says you are to stop where you are. He is coming up to see you." Then she hesitated. "One of the prison warders called here last night to warn us that you were probably hiding in the neighbourhood."

"That was kind," I said, "if a little belated. Had they found the bicycle?"

"No," she answered, "and they are not likely to. My father went out and brought it in the night you arrived. It's buried in the back garden."

There was another short silence, and then she seated herself on the foot of the bed. "Tell me," she said, "this girl—Joyce Aylmer—do you love her?"

The question came out so unexpectedly that it took me by utter surprise. I stopped in the middle of conveying a piece of bacon to my mouth and laid it down again on the plate.

"Why, Joyce is only a child," I said; "at least she was when I went to prison. We were all in love with her in a sort of way. Her father had been an artist in Chelsea before he died, and we looked on her as a kind of general trust. She used to run in and out of the various studios just as she pleased. That was the reason I was so furious with Marks. It was impossible to believe that a man who wasn't an absolute fiend could—" I pulled up short in some slight embarrassment.

"But she is not a child now," remarked Sonia calmly. "According to the paper she must be nineteen."

"Yes," I said, "I suppose people grow older even when I'm in prison."

"And she loves you—she must love you. Do you think any woman could help loving a man who had done what you did for her?"

"Oh, I expect she has forgotten all about me long ago," I said with a sudden bitterness. "People who go to prison can't expect to be remembered—except by the police."

I had spoken recklessly, and even while the words were on my tongue a vision of Joyce's honest blue eyes rose reproachfully in my mind. I remembered the terrible heartbroken little note which she had sent me after the trial, and then her other letter which I had received in Dartmoor—almost more pitiful in its brave attempt to keep hope and interest alive in my heart.

Sonia leaned forward, her hands clasped in her lap.

"I thought," she said slowly, "I thought that perhaps you wanted to go to London in order to meet her."

I shook my head. "I am not quite so selfish as that. I have brought her enough trouble and unhappiness already."

"Then it is your cousin that you mean to see," she said softly—"this man, Marwood, who sent you to the prison."

For a second I was silent. It had suddenly occurred to me that in asking these questions Sonia might be acting under the instructions of McMurtrie or her father.

She saw my hesitation and evidently guessed the cause.

"Oh, you needn't think I shall repeat what you tell me," she broke out almost scornfully. "The doctor and my father are quite capable of taking care of themselves. They don't want me to act as their spy."

There was a genuine ring of dislike in her voice as she mentioned their names which made me believe that she was speaking the truth.

"Well," I said frankly, "I was thinking of looking up George just to see how he has been getting on in my absence. But apart from that I have every intention of playing straight with McMurtrie. It seems to me to be my only chance."

A bell tinkled faintly somewhere away in the house, and Sonia got up off the bed.

"It *is* your only chance," she said quietly, "but it may be a better one than you imagine."

And with this encouraging if somewhat obscure remark she went out and left me to my thoughts.

McMurtrie came up about an hour later. Suave and courteous as ever, he knocked at my door before entering the room, and wished me good morning in the friendliest of fashions.

"I have brought you another *Daily Mail*—yesterday's," he said, throwing the paper down on the bed. "It contains the second instalment of your adventures." Then he paused and looked at me with that curious smile that seemed to begin and end with his lips. "Well," he added, "and how are the stiffness and the sore throat this morning?"

"Gone," I said, "both of them. I have no excuse for stopping in bed except lack of clothes."

He nodded and sat down on the window-sill. "I daresay we can find a way out of that difficulty. My friend Savaroff would, I am sure, be delighted to lend you some garments to go on with. You seem to be much of a size."

"Well, I should be delighted to accept them," I said. "Even the joy of being in a real bed again begins to wear off after two days."

"I am afraid you can't expect very much liberty while you are our guest," he said, leaning back against the window. "It would be too dangerous for you to go outside the house, even at night time. I expect Sonia told you about our visitor yesterday."

"Yes," I said; "I should like to have heard the interview."

"It was quite interesting. From what he told me I should say that few prisoners have been more missed than you are. It appears that there are over seventy warders hunting about the neighbourhood, to say nothing of volunteers."

"I seem to be giving a lot of trouble," I said sadly.

The doctor shrugged his shoulders. "Not to us. I am only sorry that we can't offer you a more entertaining visit." He opened his case and helped himself to a cigarette. "On the whole, however, I daresay you won't find the time drag so very much. There will be the business of altering your appearance—I hope to start on that the day after tomorrow—and then I want you to make me out a full list of everything you will need in connection with your experiments. It would be best perhaps to have a drawing of the actual shed—just as you would like it fitted up. You might start on this right away."

"Certainly," I said. "I shall be glad to have something to do."

"And I don't suppose you will mind much if we can't arrange anything very luxurious for you in the way of living accommodation. We shall have to choose as lonely a place as possible, and it will probably involve your feeding chiefly on tinned food, and roughing it a bit generally. It won't be for very long."

"I shan't mind in the least," I said. "Anything will be comfortable after Princetown. As long as you can fix me up with what I want for my work I shan't grumble about the rest."

He nodded again in a satisfied manner. "By the way," he said, "I suppose you never wore a beard or a moustache before you went to prison?"

"Only once in some amateur theatricals," I answered "and then the moustache came off."

"They will make a great difference in your appearance by themselves," he went on, looking at me critically. "I wonder how long they will take to grow."

I passed my hand up my face, which was already covered with a thick stubble about half an inch in length. "At the present rate of progress," I said, "I should think about a week."

McMurtrie smiled. "Another fortnight on top of that will be nearer the mark, I expect," he said, getting up from the bed. "That will just fit in with our arrangements. In three weeks we ought to be able to fix you up with what you want, and by that time there won't be quite so much excitement about your escape. The *Daily Mail* will have become tired of you, even if the police haven't." He stopped to flick the ash off his cigarette. "Of course you will have to be extremely careful when you are in London. I shall change your appearance so that it will be quite impossible for any one to recognize you, but there will always be the danger of somebody remembering your voice."

"I can disguise that to a certain extent," I said. "Besides, it's not likely that I shall run across any one I know well. I only want to amuse myself for two or three evenings, and the West End's a large place as far as amusement goes." Then I paused. "If you really thought it was too risky," I added carelessly, "I would give up the idea."

It was a bold stroke—but it met with the success that it deserved. Any lingering doubts McMurtrie may have had about my intentions were apparently dispersed.

"I think you will work all the better for a short holiday," he said; "and I am sure you are sensible enough to keep out of any trouble."

He walked to the door, and stood for a moment with his hand on the knob. "I will send you up the clothes and some paper and ink," he added. "Then you can get up or write in bed—just as you like."

After three years of granite quarrying—broken only by a short spell of sewing mailsacks—the thought of getting back to a more congenial form of work was a decidedly pleasant one. During the half-hour that elapsed before Sonia came up with my things, I lay in bed, busily pondering over various points in connection with my approaching task. I had often done the same in the long solitary hours in my cell, and worked out innumerable figures and details in connection with it on my prison slate. Most of them, however, I had only retained vaguely in my head, for it is one of the intelligent rules of our cheerful convict system to allow no prisoner to make permanent notes of anything that might be of possible service to him after his release.

There seemed, therefore, every prospect that I should be fully occupied for some time to come. Indeed, it was not until I had dressed myself in Savaroff's clothes (they fitted me excellently) and sat down at the table with a pen and a pile of foolscap in front of me, that I realized what a lengthy task I had taken on.

All my rough notes—those invaluable notes and calculations that I had spent eighteen months over—were packed away in my safe at the Victoria Street office. I had not bothered about them at the time, for when you are being tried for your life other matters are apt to assume a certain degree of unimportance. Besides, although I had told George of their existence, I knew very well that, being jotted down in a private cypher, no one except myself would be able to make head or tail of what they were about.

Still they would naturally have been of immense help to me now if I could have got hold of them. Clear as the main details were in my mind, I saw I should have to go over a good bit of old ground before I could make out the exact list of my requirements which McMurtrie needed.

All that afternoon and the whole of the following day I stuck steadily to my task. I had little to interrupt me, for with the exception of Sonia who brought me up my meals, and the old deaf-and-dumb housekeeper who came to do my room about midday, I saw or heard nobody. McMurtrie did not appear again, and Savaroff, as I knew, was away in London.

I took an hour off in the evening for the purpose of studying the *Daily Mail*, which proved to be quite as entertaining as the previous issue. There were two and a half columns about me altogether, the first consisting of a powerful if slightly inaccurate description of how I had stolen the bicycle, and the remainder dealing with various features of my crime and my escape. It was headed:

STILL AT LARGE NEIL LYNDON'S FIGHT FOR LIBERTY

and I settled myself down to read with a feeling of enjoyment that would doubtless have gratified Lord Northcliffe had he been fortunate enough to know about it.

"Neil Lyndon," it began, "whose daring escape from Princetown was fully described in yesterday's *Daily Mail*, has so far successfully baffled his pursuers. Not only is he still at liberty, but having possessed himself of a bicycle and a change of clothes by means of an amazingly audacious burglary, it is quite possible that he has managed to get clear away from the immediate neighbourhood."

This opening paragraph was followed by a full and vivid description of my raid on the bicycle house. It appeared that the machine which I had borrowed was the property of a certain Major Hammond, who, when interviewed by the representative of the *Mail*, expressed himself of the opinion that I was a dangerous character and that I ought to be recaptured without delay.

The narrative then shifted to my dramatic appearance on the bicycle, as witnessed by the surprised eyes of Assistant-warder Marshfield. According to that gentleman I had flashed past him at a terrific speed, hurling a handful of gravel in his face, which had temporarily blinded him. With amazing pluck and presence of mind he had recovered himself in time to puncture my back wheel, a feat of marksmanship which, as the *Daily Mail* observed, was "highly creditable under the circumstances."

From that point it seemed that all traces of me had ceased. Both I and the bicycle had vanished into space as completely as Elijah and his fiery chariot, and not all the united brains of Carmelite House appeared able to suggest a wholly satisfactory solution.

"Lyndon," said the *Mail*, "may have succeeded in reaching Plymouth on the stolen machine, and there obtained the food and shelter of which by that time he must have been sorely in need. On the other hand it is possible that, starved, frozen, and most likely wounded, he is crouching in some remote coppice, grimly determined to perish rather than to surrender himself to the warders."

It was "possible," certainly, but as a guess at the truth that was about all that could be said for it.

The thing that pleased me most in the whole paper, however, was the interview with George in the third column. It was quite short—only a six-line paragraph headed "Mr. Marwood and the Escape," but brief as it was, it filled me with a rich delight.

"Interviewed by our Special Correspondent at his residence on the Chelsea Embankment, Mr. George Marwood was reluctant to express any opinion on the escape. 'The whole thing,' he said, 'is naturally extremely distasteful to me. I can only hope that the unhappy man may be recaptured before he succumbs to exposure, and before he has the chance to commit any further acts of robbery and violence.'"

In regard to the last sentiment I had not the faintest doubt that George was speaking the truth from the bottom of his heart. As long as I was at liberty his days and nights would be consumed by an acute and painful anxiety. He was no doubt haunted by the idea that I had broken prison largely for the purpose of renewing our old acquaintance, and the thought that I might possibly succeed in my object must have been an extremely uncomfortable one. I laughed softly to myself as I sat and pictured his misgivings. It cheered me to think that whatever happened later he would be left in this gnawing suspense for at least another three weeks. After that I might perhaps see my way to relieve it.

There were other people, I reflected, who must have read the *Mail* with an equally deep if rather different interest. I tried to fancy how the news of my escape had affected Joyce. For all my cynical outburst in the morning, I knew well that no truer or more honest little heart ever beat in a girl's breast, and that the uncertainty about my fate must even now be causing her the utmost distress.

Then there was Tommy Morrison. Somehow or other I didn't think Tommy would be quite as anxious as Joyce. I could almost see him slapping his leg and laughing that great laugh of his, as he read about my theft of the bicycle and my wild dash down the hill past the warder. He was a great believer in me, was Tommy—and I felt sure that nothing but the news of my recapture would shake his faith in my ability to survive.

It was good to know that, whatever the rest of the world might be thinking, these two at least would be following my escape with a passionate hope that I should pull through.

Just about six o'clock in the evening of the next day Savaroff returned. I heard the car drive up to the house, and then came the sound of voices and footsteps, followed by the banging of a door. After that there was silence for perhaps twenty minutes while my two hosts were presumably talking together in one of the rooms below. Whether Sonia was with them or not I could not tell.

At last I heard some one mounting the stairs, and a moment later McMurtrie's figure framed itself in the doorway.

"I'm afraid I am interrupting your work," he said, standing on the threshold and looking down at the sheets of foolscap which littered the table in front of me.

"Not a bit," I returned cheerfully. "I've just finished"; and I began to gather up the fruits of my two-days' toil into something like order.

He shut the door and came across to where I was sitting. "Do you mean you have made out the full list of what you want?" he asked, picking up one of the sheets and running his eye rapidly over the notes and calculations.

"I have done it all in the rough," I replied, "except the drawing of the shed. That will only take an hour or so."

"Excellent," he exclaimed. "I can see there won't be much time wasted when we once get to work." Then he laid down the paper. "Tomorrow morning I propose trying the first of our little operations. Savaroff has brought me the things I needed, and I think we can finish the whole business in a couple of days."

"What part of me are you going to start on?" I inquired with some interest.

"I think I shall alter the shape of your nose first," he said. "It's practically a painless operation—just one injection of hot paraffin wax under the skin. After that you have only to keep quiet for a couple of hours so that the wax can set in the right shape."

"What about the X-ray treatment?" I asked.

He shrugged his shoulders. "That's perfectly simple too. Merely a matter of covering up everything except the part that we want exposed. One uses a specially prepared sort of lead sheeting. There is absolutely no danger or difficulty about it."

I thought at first that he might be purposely minimizing both operations in order to put me at my ease, but as it turned out he was telling me nothing except the literal truth.

At half-past ten the next morning he came up to my room with Sonia in attendance, the latter carrying a Primus stove and a small black bag.

At his own suggestion I had stayed in bed, and from between the sheets I viewed their entrance not without a certain whimsical feeling of regret. When one has had a nose of a particular shape for the best part of thirty years it is rather a wrench to feel that one is abandoning it for a stranger. I passed my fingers down it almost affectionately.

McMurtrie, who appeared to be in the best of spirits, wished me good-morning in that silkily polite manner of his which I was getting to dislike more and more. Sonia said nothing. She simply put the things down on the table by my bedside, and then stood there with the air of sullen hostility which she seemed generally to wear in McMurtrie's presence.

"I feel rather like a gladiator," I said. "Morituri te salutant!"

McMurtrie, who had taken a shallow blue saucepan out of the bag and was filling it with hot water, looked up with a smile.

"It will be all over in a minute," he said, reassuringly. "The only trouble is keeping the wax liquid while one is actually injecting it. One has to stand it in boiling water until the last second."

He put the saucepan on the stove, and then produced out of the bag a little china-clay cup, which he stood in the water. Into this he dropped a small lump of transparent wax.

We waited for a minute until the latter melted, McMurtrie filling up the time by carefully sponging the bridge of my nose with some liquid antiseptic. Then, picking up what seemed like an ordinary hypodermic syringe, he warmed it carefully by holding it close to the Primus.

"Now," he said; "all you have to do is to keep perfectly still. You will just feel the prick of the needle and the smart of the hot wax, but it won't really hurt. If you move you will probably spoil the operation."

"Go ahead," I answered encouragingly.

He dipped the syringe in the cup, and then with a quick movement of his hand brought it across my face. I felt a sharp stab, followed instantly by a stinging sensation all along the bridge of the nose. McMurtrie dropped the syringe at once, and taking the skin between his fingers began to pinch and mould it with swift, deft touches into the required shape. I lay as motionless as possible, hoping that things were prospering.

It seemed to me a long time before the job was finished, though I daresay it was in reality only a matter of forty-five seconds. I know I felt vastly relieved when, with a quick intake of his breath, McMurtrie suddenly sat back and began to contemplate his work.

"Well?" I inquired anxiously.

He nodded his head, with every appearance of satisfaction.

"I think we can call it a complete success," he said. Then he stepped back and looked at me critically from a couple of paces away. "What do you think, Sonia?" he asked.

"I suppose it's what you wanted," she said, in a rather grudging, ungracious sort of fashion.

"If you won't think me vain," I observed, "I should like to have a look at myself in the glass."

McMurtrie walked to the fireplace and unhooked the small mirror which hung above the mantelpiece.

"I would rather you waited for a couple of days if you don't mind," he said. "You know what you used to look like better than any one else, and it will be a good test if you see yourself quite suddenly when the whole thing is finished. I will borrow this—and keep you out of temptation."

"Just as you like," I returned. "It will at least give me time to train myself for the shock."

Quick and easy as the first operation had been, the second proved equally simple. The only apparatus it involved was an ordinary X-ray machine, with a large glass globe attached to it, which McMurtrie brought up the next morning and arranged carefully by my bedside. On his pressing down a switch, which he did for my benefit, the whole interior of this globe became flooded with those curious lambent violet rays, which have altered so many of our previous notions on the subject of light and its power.

McMurtrie placed me in position, and then producing a large sheet of finely-beaten-out lead, proceeded to bend and twist it into a sort of weird-looking helmet. When I put this on it covered my head and face almost completely, leaving only an inch of hair along the forehead and perhaps a little more over each temple exposed to the light.

Thus equipped, I sat for perhaps an hour in the full glare of the machine. It was dull work, and as McMurtrie made no attempt to enliven it by conversation I was not sorry when he eventually flicked off the switch, and relieved me of my headgear.

I had expected my hair to tumble out in a lump, but as a matter of fact it was over two days in accomplishing the task. There was no discomfort about the process: it just came off gradually all along my forehead, leaving a smooth bare line which I could feel with my fingers. As soon as it was all gone, McMurtrie proceeded to decorate me with some kind of stain that he had specially prepared for my face and neck—a composition which according to him would remain practically unaffected either by washing or exposure. It smelt damnably in the pot, but directly it was rubbed in this slight drawback disappeared.

I was naturally anxious to see what result all these attentions had had upon my personal appearance, but McMurtrie insisted on my waiting until my hair and beard had grown to something like a tolerable length. I can well remember the little thrill of excitement that ran through me when, on the fourth day after my first operation, he brought me back the looking-glass.

"I think we might introduce you to yourself today," he said, smiling. "Of course another fortnight will make a considerable difference still, but even now you will be able to get a good idea of what you will look like. I am curious to hear your opinion."

He handed me the glass, and the next moment, with an involuntary cry of amazement, I was staring at my reflection.

Instead of my usual features I saw a rough-looking, bearded man of about forty-five, with an aquiline nose, a high forehead, and a dark sunburned skin. It was the face of a complete stranger: at the best that of a hard-bitten war correspondent or explorer; at the worst—well, I don't know what it mightn't have been at the worst.

I stared and stared in a kind of incredulous fascination, until McMurtrie's voice abruptly recalled me to my surroundings.

"Well, Mr. Neil Lyndon," he said, "do you recognize yourself?"

I laid down the glass.

"Don't call me that," I replied quietly. "Neil Lyndon is dead."

CHAPTER VII
A KISS AND A CONFESSION

One would hardly expect an escaped murderer to complain of being dull—especially when the whole country is still ringing with the story of his disappearance. Yet I must confess that, when I had once got used to the strangeness of my position, the next two weeks dragged intolerably.

I was accustomed to confinement, but in the prison at all events I had had plenty of hard work and exercise, while here, cooped up entirely in one room, I was able to do nothing but pace restlessly up and down most of the day like a caged bear. I had finished my lists and drawings for McMurtrie, and my only resources were two or three sensational novels which Sonia brought me back one day after a visit to Plymouth. I cannot say I found them very entertaining. I had been rather too deeply into life in that line myself to have much use for the second-hand imaginings of other people.

Of the doctor and Savaroff I saw comparatively little. Both of them were away from the house a good deal of the time, often returning in the car late at night, and then sitting up talking till some unholy hour in the morning. I used to lie awake in bed, and listen to the dull rumble of their voices in the room below.

That there was something mysterious going on which I knew nothing about I became more convinced every day, but what it could be I was unable to guess. Once or twice I tried to sound Sonia on the matter, but although she would talk freely about my own affairs, on any point connected with herself or the curious household to which she belonged she maintained an obstinate silence.

The girl puzzled me strangely. At times it almost seemed as though she were being forced against her will to take part in some business that she thoroughly disliked; but then the obvious way in which the two men trusted her scarcely bore out this idea. She showed no particular affection for her father, and it was plain that she detested McMurtrie, yet there was evidently some bond between them strong enough to keep all three together.

To me she behaved from the first with a sort of sullen friendliness. She would come and sit in my room, and with her chin resting on her hand

and her big dark eyes fixed on mine, she would ask me questions about myself or listen to the stories I told her of the prison. Once, when I had been describing some peculiarly mean little persecution which one of the warders (who objected on principle to what he called "gen'lemen lags") had amused himself by practising on me, she had jumped up and with a quick, almost savage gesture, laid her hand on my arm.

"Never mind," she said; "it's over now, and you shall make them pay for what they have done to you. We can promise you that at least," and she laughed with a curious bitterness I failed to understand.

Of the mysterious Mr. Hoffman, who had turned up at the house on the second day after my arrival, I saw or heard nothing more. I asked Sonia about him one day, but she only replied curtly that he was a business friend of the doctor's, and with this meagre information I had to remain content.

The point that I felt perhaps most inquisitive about was whom McMurtrie could have mistaken me for when I had crawled in through the kitchen window. I had a distinct recollection of his having mentioned some name just before I had collapsed, but it had gone out of my head and for the life of me I couldn't recall it. You know the maddening way a name will hang about the tip of one's tongue, just avoiding every effort at recapture.

Apart from my talks with Sonia, my chief entertainment was reading the *Daily Mail*. Not a day passed but some one seemed to discover a fresh clue to my hiding-place. I was seen and recognized at Manchester, Yarmouth, London, and Edinburgh; while one gentleman wrote to inform the editor he had trustworthy information I was actually in St. Petersburg, having been engaged by the Russian Government to effect certain improvements in their torpedo service. All this was quite pleasing, for, in addition to showing me that the police were still utterly at sea as to my whereabouts, I knew that each fresh report would help to keep George in an acute state of nervous tension.

Just as my imprisonment was becoming almost unbearably irksome, the end arrived with an unexpected abruptness. I was sitting at the window one morning smoking an after-breakfast pipe—a pipe which Sonia had brought me back from Plymouth at the same time as the books—when I heard a loud ring at the front door-bell, followed by a couple of sharp knocks. Despite my three years' absence from worldly affairs, I recognized the unmistakable touch of a telegraph-boy.

Since it was hardly likely that the wire was for me, I continued to smoke with undisturbed serenity. Perhaps ten minutes passed, and I was just wondering whether the message had anything to do with the arrangements which McMurtrie was making on my behalf, when a door slammed and I heard someone coming up the stairs. I knew from the sound that it was the doctor himself.

He entered the room, and looked round with his usual suave smile. To all outward appearance he was as composed as ever, but I had a curious presentiment that something unexpected had happened. However, I thought it best to show no sign of any such impression.

"Good-morning," I said, knocking out my pipe and stuffing it away in my pocket—or rather Savaroff's pocket. "A grand day, isn't it!"

"Beautiful," he answered genially—"quite beautiful." Then he walked across and sat down on the end of the bed. "As a matter of fact, I came up to see whether you felt like taking advantage of it."

"Do you mean that it's safe for me to go out?" I asked with some eagerness.

He shrugged his shoulders. "It's as safe as it ever will be; but I meant rather more than that."

There was a pause.

"Yes?" I said encouragingly.

"I meant that our preparations are going on so well, that as far as I can see there is nothing to be gained by keeping you here any longer. I have just had a wire to say that the cottage and shed we have been arranging for near Tilbury are practically finished. If you want your week in London I think you had better go up this afternoon."

His proposal took me so completely by surprise that for a moment I hardly knew what to say. Somehow or other, I had a suspicion that he was keeping something back. I knew that he had intended me to stay where I was for at least another three days, and he was not the sort of man to change his plans without an uncommonly good reason.

Still, the last thing I wanted was to let him think that I in any way doubted his good faith, so pulling myself together, I forced a really creditable laugh.

"Right you are," I said. "It's rather short notice, but I'm game to start any time. The only thing is, what am I to do about clothes?"

"You can keep those you're wearing to go up in," he answered. "When you get to London you must buy yourself an outfit. Get what you want at different shops and pay for them in cash. I will advance you fifty pounds, which ought to be enough to last you the week."

"One can do quite a lot of dressing and dissipation on fifty pounds," I replied cheerfully. "Where am I going to stay?"

He put his hand in his pocket and pulled out an envelope. "Here's the address," he said. "It's a lodging-house near Victoria Station, kept by a sister of Mrs. Weston. You will find it comfortable and quiet, and you needn't worry about the landlady having any suspicions. I have told her that you have just come back from abroad and that you want to be in London for several days on business. You will pass under the name of Nicholson—James Nicholson."

He handed me the envelope, and I read the address.

Mrs. Oldbury,

3, Edith Terrace,

S.W.

Nr. Victoria Station.

"Very well," I said, getting up from my seat; "I understand I am to stop with Mrs. Oldbury and amuse myself spending the fifty pounds until I hear from you."

He nodded. "Directly things are ready we shall let you know. Till then you are free to do as you like." He opened a small leather case and handed me a bundle of bank-notes. "Here is the money," he added with a smile. "You see, we trust you absolutely. If you choose to make a bolt to America, there will be nothing to stop you."

It was said with such apparent frankness that it ought to have carried conviction; but as a matter of fact it did nothing of the kind. I felt certain that it would not be McMurtrie's fault if he failed to keep himself informed about my movements while I was in London. Too much trustfulness in human nature did not seem likely to be one of his besetting weaknesses.

However, I pocketed the notes cheerfully enough; indeed the mere touch of them in my hand gave me a pleasant feeling of confidence. It is always nice to handle money in comparative bulk, but being absolutely without it for thirty-six months invests the operation with a peculiar charm.

"You had better be ready to start from here about half-past one," said McMurtrie. "Savaroff will take you into Plymouth in the car, and there is a fast train up at two-five. It gets you into London just before seven."

"Good!" I said. "That will give me time to buy what I want when I arrive. It would spoil my dinner if I had to shop afterwards."

McMurtrie, who had crossed to the door, looked back at me with a sort of half-envious, half-contemptuous smile.

"You are a curious fellow, Lyndon," he said. "At times you might be a boy of twenty."

"Well, I am only twenty-nine," I protested; "and one can't always remember that one's an escaped murderer."

I was sitting on the window-sill when I made the last remark; but as soon as he had gone I jumped to my feet and began to pace restlessly up and down the room. Now that the moment of my release was really at hand, a fierce excitement had gripped hold of me. Although I had had plenty of time to get used to my new position, the amazing possibilities of it had never seemed to come fully home to me till that minute. I suddenly realized that I was stepping into an experience such as probably no other human being had ever tasted. I was like a man coming back from the dead, safe against recognition, and with all the record of my past life scarred and burnt into my memory.

I walked to the glass and once again stared long and closely at my reflection. There could be no question about the completeness of my disguise. Between Neil Lyndon as the world had known him, and the grim, bearded, sunburned face that looked back at me out of the mirror, there was a difference sufficiently remarkable to worry the recording angel. People's wits may be sharpened both by fear and affection, but I felt that unless I betrayed myself deliberately, not even those who knew me best, such as George or Tommy, would have the remotest suspicion of my real identity. Anyhow, I intended to put my opinion to the test before very many hours had passed.

I was pondering over this agreeable prospect, and still inspecting myself in the glass, when I heard a soft knock at the door. I opened it, and found Sonia standing outside. She was holding a bag in her hand—a good-sized Gladstone that had evidently seen some hard work in its time, and she came into the room and shut the door behind her before speaking.

"Well," she said, in her curious, half-sullen way, "are you pleased you are going to London?"

"Why, yes," I said; "I'm pleased enough."

As a matter of fact the word "pleased" seemed rather too simple to sum up my emotions altogether adequately.

She placed the bag on the floor and sat down on the bed. Then, leaning her face against the bottom rail, she stared up at me for a moment without speaking.

"What did the doctor tell you?" she asked at last.

"He told me I could go up to London by the two-five," I said.

"Is that all?"

"Dr. McMurtrie," I reminded her, "is never recklessly communicative." Then I paused. "Still I should like to know the reason for the change of programme," I added.

She raised her head and glanced half nervously, half defiantly at the door.

"We are going to give up this house tomorrow—that's the reason," she said, speaking low and rather quickly. "Our work here is finished, and it will be best for us to leave as soon as possible."

"I wish," I said regretfully, "that I inspired just a little more confidence."

Sonia hesitated. Then she sat up, and with a characteristic gesture of hers pushed back her hair from her forehead.

"Come here," she said slowly; "come quite close to me."

I walked towards her, wondering at the sudden change in her voice. As I approached she straightened her arms out each side of her, and half-closing her eyes, raised her face to mine.

"Kiss me," she said, almost in a whisper; "kiss my lips."

I could hardly have declined such an invitation even if I had wished to, but as a matter of fact I felt no such prompting. It was over three years since I had kissed anybody, and with her eyes half-closed and her breast softly rising and falling, Sonia looked decidedly attractive. I bent down till my mouth was almost touching hers. Then with a little sigh she put her arms round my neck, and slowly and deliberately our lips met.

It was at this exceedingly inopportune moment that Savaroff's guttural voice came grating up the stairs from the hall below.

"Sonia!" he shouted—"Sonia! Where are you? I want you."

She quietly disengaged her arms, and drawing back, paused for a moment with her hands on my shoulders.

"Now you understand," she said, looking straight into my eyes. "They are nothing to me, my father and the doctor—I hate them both. It is you I am thinking of—you only." She leaned forward and swiftly, almost fiercely again kissed my mouth. "When the time comes," she whispered—

"Sonia! Sonia!" Once more Savaroff's voice rose impatiently from the hall.

In a moment Sonia had crossed the room. I had one rapid vision of her looking back at me—her lips parted her dark eyes shining passionately, and then the door closed and I was alone.

I sat down on the bed and took a long breath. There was a time when an unexpected incident of this sort would merely have left me in a state of comfortable optimism, but a prolonged residence in Dartmoor had evidently shaken my nerve.

I soon collected myself, however, and lighting a cigarette with some care, got up and walked to the open window. If Sonia was really in love with me—and there seemed to be rather sound evidence that she was—I had apparently, succeeded in making a highly useful ally. This may appear to have been rather a cold-blooded way of regarding the matter, but to tell the truth the whole thing had taken me so utterly by surprise that I could scarcely realize as yet that I had been personally concerned in it. I had kissed her certainly—under the circumstances I could hardly have done otherwise—but of any deliberate attempt to make her fond of me I was beautifully and entirely innocent, it had never struck me that an escaped murderer with an artificial and rather forbidding countenance was in danger of inspiring affection, especially in a girl whose manner had always been slightly suggestive of a merely sullen tolerance. Still, having succeeded in doing so, I felt no qualms in making the best of the situation. I needed friends rather badly, especially friends who had an intimate working acquaintance with the eminent firm of Messrs. McMurtrie and Savaroff. If the not wholly disagreeable task of returning Sonia's proffered affection was all that was necessary, I felt that it would be flying in the face of Providence to decline such an opportunity. I was not the least in love with her—except by a very generous interpretation of the word, but I did not think that this unfortunate fact would seriously disturb my conscience. A life sentence for what you haven't done is apt to rob one's sense of honour of some of its more delicate points.

With a pleasant feeling that things were working for the best, I got up again; and hoisting the Gladstone bag on to the bed began to collect the books, the tooth-brush, and the few other articles which made up my present earthly possessions.

CHAPTER VIII
RT. HON. SIR GEORGE FRINTON, P.C.

That journey of mine to London stands out in my memory with extraordinary vividness. I don't think I shall ever forget the smallest and most unimportant detail of it. The truth is, I suppose, that my whole mind and senses were in an acutely impressionable state after lying fallow, as they practically had, for over three years. Besides, the sheer pleasure of being out in the world again seemed to invest everything with an amazing interest and wonder.

It was just half-past one when Savaroff brought the car round to the front door. I was standing in the hall talking to McMurtrie, who had decided not to accompany us into Plymouth. Of Sonia I had seen nothing since our unfortunately interrupted interview in the morning.

"Well," said the doctor, as with a grinding of brakes the car pulled up outside, "we can look on this as the real beginning of our little enterprise."

I picked up my Gladstone. "Let's hope," I said, "that the end will be equally satisfactory."

McMurtrie nodded. "I fancy," he said, "that we need have no apprehensions. Providence is with us, Mr. Lyndon—Providence or some equally effective power."

There was a note of irony in his voice which left one in no doubt as to his own private opinion of our guiding agency.

I stepped out into the drive carrying my bag. Savaroff, who was sitting in the driving seat of the car, turned half round towards me.

"Put it on the floor at the back under the rug," he said. "You will sit in front with me."

He spoke in his usual surly fashion, but by this time I had become accustomed to it. So contenting myself with a genial observation to the effect that I should be charmed, I tucked the bag away out of sight and clambered up beside him into the left-hand seat. McMurtrie stood in the doorway, that mirthless smile of his fixed upon his lips.

"Good-bye," I said; "we shall meet at Tilbury, I suppose—if not before?"

He nodded. "At Tilbury certainly. Au revoir, Mr. Nicholson."

And with this last reminder of my future identity echoing in my ears, we slid off down the drive.

All the way into Plymouth Savaroff maintained a grumpy silence. He was naturally a taciturn sort of person, and I think, besides that, he had taken a strong dislike to me from the night we had first seen each other. If this were so I had certainly not done much to modify it. I felt that the man was naturally a bully, and it always pleases and amuses me to be disliked by bullies. Indeed, if I had had no other reason for responding to Sonia's proffered affection I should have done so just because Savaroff was her father.

My companion's sulks, however, in no way interfered with my enjoyment of the drive. It was a perfect day on which to regain one's liberty. The sun shone down from a blue sky flecked here and there with fleecy white clouds, and on each side of the road the hedges and trees were just beginning to break into an almost shrill green. The very air seemed to be filled with a delicious sense of freedom and adventure.

As we got nearer to Plymouth I found a fresh source of interest and pleasure in the people that we passed walking along the road or driving in traps and cars. After my long surfeit of warders and convicts the mere sight of ordinarily-dressed human beings laughing and talking filled me with the most intense satisfaction. On several occasions I had a feeling that I should like to jump out of the car and join some group of cheerful-looking strangers who turned to watch us flash past. This feeling became doubly intense when we actually entered Plymouth, where the streets seemed to be almost inconveniently crowded with an extraordinary number of attractive-looking girls.

I was afforded no opportunity, however, for indulging in any such pleasant interlude. We drove straight through the town at a rapid pace, avoiding the main thoroughfares as much as possible, and not slackening until we pulled up outside Millbay station. We left the car in charge of a tired-looking loafer who was standing in the gutter, and taking out my bag, I followed Savaroff into the booking office.

"You had better wait there," he muttered, pointing to the corner. "I will get the ticket."

I followed his suggestion, and while he took his place in the small queue in front of the window I amused myself watching my fellow passengers hurrying up and down the platform. They looked peaceful enough, but I couldn't help picturing what a splendid disturbance there would be if it suddenly came out that Neil Lyndon was somewhere on the premises. The last time I had been in this station was on my way up to Princetown two and a half years before.

At last Savaroff emerged from the throng with my ticket in his hand.

"I have taken you a first-class," he said rather grudgingly. "You will probably have the carriage to yourself. It is better so."

I nodded. "I shouldn't like to infect any of these good people with homicidal mania," I said cheerfully.

He looked at me rather suspiciously—I think he always had a sort of vague feeling that I was laughing at him—and then without further remark led the way out on to the platform.

McMurtrie had given me a sovereign and some loose silver for immediate expenses, and I stopped at the bookstall to buy myself some papers. I selected a *Mail*, a *Sportsman*, *Punch*, and the *Saturday Review*. I lingered over the business because it seemed to annoy Savaroff: indeed it was not until he had twice jogged my elbow that I made my final selection. Then, grasping my bag, I marched up the platform behind him, coming to a halt outside an empty first-class carriage.

"This will do," he said, and finding no sound reason for contradicting him I stepped in and put my bag upon the rack.

"Good-bye, Savaroff," I said cheerfully. "I shall have the pleasure of seeing you too at Tilbury, I suppose?"

He closed the door, and thrust his head in through the open window.

"You will," he said in his guttural voice; "and let me give you a little word of advice, my friend. We have treated you well—eh, but if you think you can in any way break your agreement with us you make a very bad mistake."

I took out my cigarette case. "My dear Savaroff," I said coldly, "why on earth should I want to break my agreement with you? It is the only possible chance I have of a new start."

He looked at me closely, and then nodded his head. "It is well. So long as you remember we are not people to be played with, no harm will come to you."

He let this off with such a dramatic air that I very nearly burst out laughing.

"I shan't forget it," I said gravely. "I've got a very good memory."

There was a shrill whistle from the engine, followed by a warning shout of "Stand back there, please; stand back, sir!" I had a last glimpse of Savaroff's unpleasant face, as he hurriedly withdrew his head, and then with a slight jerk the train began to move slowly out of the station.

I didn't open my papers at once. For some time I just sat where I was in the corner and stared out contentedly over the passing landscape. There is nothing like prison to broaden one's ideas about pleasure. Up till the time of my trial I had never looked on a railway journey as a particularly fascinating experience; now it seemed to me to be simply chock-full of delightful sensations. The very names of the stations—Totnes, Newton Abbot, Teignmouth—filled me with a sort of curious pleasure: they were part of the world that I had once belonged to—the gay, free, jolly world of work and laughter that I had thought lost to me for ever. I felt so absurdly contented that for a little while I almost forgot about George.

The only stop we made was at Exeter. There were not many people on the platform, and I had just decided that I was not going to be disturbed, when suddenly a fussy-looking little old gentleman emerged from the booking office, followed by a porter carrying his bag. They came straight for my carriage.

The old gentleman reached it first, and puckering up his face, peered in at me through the window. Apparently the inspection was a success.

"This will do," he observed. "Leave my bag on the seat, and go and see that my portmanteau is safely in the van. Then if you come back here I will give you threepence for your trouble."

Dazzled by the prospect, the porter hurried off on his errand, and with a little grunt the old gentleman began to hoist himself in through the door. I put out my hand to assist him.

"Thank you, sir, thank you," he remarked breathlessly. "I am extremely obliged to you, sir."

Then, gathering up his bag, he shuffled along the carriage, and settled himself down in the opposite corner.

I was quite pleased with the prospect of a fellow passenger, unexciting as this particular one promised to be. I have either read or heard it stated that when people first come out of prison they feel so shy and so lost that their chief object is to avoid any sort of society at all. I can only say that in my case this was certainly not true. I wanted to talk to every one: I felt as if whole volumes of conversation had been accumulating inside me during the long speechless months of my imprisonment.

It was the old gentleman, however, who first broke our silence. Lowering his copy of the *Times*, he looked up at me over the top of his gold-rimmed spectacles.

"I wonder, sir," he said, "whether you would object to having that window closed; I am extremely susceptible to draughts."

"Why, of course not," I replied cheerfully, and suiting my action to my words I jerked up the sash.

This prompt attention to his wishes evidently pleased him; for he thanked me civilly, and then, after a short pause, added some becoming reflection on the subject of the English spring.

It was not exactly an inspiring opening, but I made the most of it. Without appearing intrusive I managed to keep the conversation going, and in a few minutes we were in the middle of a brisk meteorological discussion of the most approved pattern.

"I daresay you find these sudden changes especially trying," commented my companion. Then, with a sort of apology in his voice, he added: "One can hardly help seeing that you have been accustomed to a warmer climate."

I smiled. "I have been out of England," I said, "for some time"; and if this was not true in the letter, I don't think that even George Washington could have found much fault with it in the spirit.

"Indeed, sir, indeed," said the old gentleman. "I envy you, sir. I only wish my own duties permitted me to winter entirely abroad."

"It has its advantages," I admitted, "but in some ways I am quite pleased to be back again."

My companion nodded his head. "For one thing," he said, "one gets terribly behindhand with English news. I find that even the best of the foreign papers are painfully ill-informed."

A sudden mischievous thought came into my head. "I have hardly seen a paper of any kind for a fortnight!" I said. "Is there any particular news? The last interesting thing I saw was about that young fellow's escape from Dartmoor—that young inventor—what was his name?—who was in for murder."

The old gentleman looked up sharply. "Ah! Lyndon," he said, "Neil Lyndon you mean. He is still at large."

"From what I read of the case," I went on carelessly, "it seems rather difficult to help sympathizing with him—to a certain extent. The man he murdered doesn't appear to have been any great loss to the community."

My companion opened his mouth as if to speak, and then hesitated. "Well, as a matter of fact I am scarcely in a position to discuss the subject," he said courteously. "Perhaps, sir, you are unaware who I am?"

He asked the question with a slight touch of self-conscious dignity, which showed me that in his own opinion at all events he was a person of considerable importance. I looked at him again more carefully. There seemed to be something familiar about his face, but beyond that I was utterly at sea.

"The fact is, I have been so much abroad," I began apologetically —

He cut me short by producing a little silver case from his pocket and handing me one of his cards.

"Permit me, sir," he said indulgently.

I took it and read the following inscription:

RT. HON. SIR GEORGE FRINTON, P.C. *The Reform Club.*

I remembered him at once. He was a fairly well known politician — an old-fashioned member of the Liberal Party, with whose name I had been more or less acquainted all my life. I had never actually met him in the old days, but I had seen one or two photographs and caricatures of him, and this no doubt explained my vague recollection of his features.

For just a moment I remained silent, struggling against a strong impulse to laugh. There was something delightfully humorous in the thought of my sitting in a first-class carriage exchanging cheerful confidences with a distinguished politician, while Scotland Yard and the Home Office were racking their brains over my disappearance. It seemed such a pity I couldn't hand him back a card of my own just for the fun of watching his face while he read it.

MR. NEIL LYNDON *Late of His Majesty's Prison, Princetown.*

Collecting myself with an effort, I covered my apparent confusion with a slight bow.

"It was very stupid of me not to have recognized you from your pictures," I said.

This compliment evidently pleased the old boy, for he beamed at me in the most gracious fashion.

"You see now, sir," he said, "why it would be quite impossible for me to discuss the matter in question."

I bowed again. I didn't see in the least, but he spoke as if the point was so obvious that I thought it better to let the subject drop. I could only imagine that he must be holding some official position, the importance of which he probably overrated.

We drifted off into the discussion of one or two other topics; settling down eventually to our respective newspapers. I can't say I followed mine with any keen attention. My brain was too much occupied with my own affairs to allow me to take in very much of what I read. I just noticed that we were engaged in a rather heated discussion with Germany over the future of Servia, and that a well-meaning but short-sighted Anarchist had made an unsuccessful effort to shoot the President of the American Steel Trust.

Of my own affairs I could find no mention, beyond a brief statement to the effect that I was still at liberty. There was not even the usual letter from somebody claiming to have discovered my hiding-place, and for the first time since my escape I began to feel a little neglected. It was evident that as a news topic I was losing something of my first freshness.

The last bit of the journey from Maidenhead onwards seemed to take us an unconscionably long time. A kind of fierce restlessness had begun to get hold of me as we drew nearer to London, and I watched the fields and houses flying past with an impatience I could hardly control.

We rushed through Hanwell and Acton, and then suddenly the huge bulk of Wormwood Scrubbs Prison loomed up in the growing dusk away to the right of the line. It was there that I had served my "separates" — those first ghastly six months of solitary confinement which make even Princetown or Portland a welcome and agreeable change.

At the sight of that poisonous place all the old bitterness welled up in me afresh. For a moment even my freedom seemed to have lost its sweetness, and I sat there with my hands clenched and black resentment in my heart, staring out of those grim unlovely walls. It was lucky for George that he was not with me in the carriage just then, for I think I should have wrung his neck without troubling about any explanations.

I was awakened from these pleasant reflections by a sudden blare of light and noise on each side of the train. I sat up abruptly, with a sort of guilty feeling that I had been on the verge of betraying myself, and letting down the window, found that we were steaming slowly into Paddington Station. In the farther corner of the carriage my distinguished friend Sir George Frinton was beginning to collect his belongings.

I just had time to pull myself together when the train stopped, and out of the waiting line of porters a man stepped forward and flung open the carriage door. He was about to possess himself of my fellow passenger's bag when the latter waved him aside.

"You can attend to this gentleman," he said. "My own servant is somewhere on the platform." Then turning to me, he added courteously: "I wish you good-day, sir. I am pleased to have made your acquaintance. I trust that we shall have the mutual pleasure of meeting again."

I shook hands with him gravely. "I hope we shall," I replied. "It will be a distinction that I shall vastly appreciate."

And of all unconscious prophecies that were ever launched, I fancy this one was about the most accurate.

Preceded by the porter carrying my bag, I crossed the platform and stepped into a waiting taxi.

"Where to, sir?" inquired the man.

I had a sudden wild impulse to say: "Drive me to George," but I checked it just in time.

"You had better drive me slowly along Oxford Street," I said. "I want to stop at one or two shops."

The man started the engine and, climbing back into his seat, set off with a jerk up the slope. I lay back in the corner, and took in a long, deep, exulting breath. I was in London—in London at last—and if those words don't convey to you the kind of savage satisfaction that filled my soul you must be as deficient in imagination as a prison governor.

CHAPTER IX
THE MAN WITH THE SCAR

My shopping took me quite a little while. There were a lot of things I wanted to get, and I saw no reason for hurrying—especially as McMurtrie was paying for the taxi. I stopped at Selfridge's and laid in a small but nicely chosen supply of shirts, socks, collars, and other undergarments, and then, drifting slowly on, picked up at intervals some cigars, a couple of pairs of boots, and a presentable Homburg hat.

The question of a suit of clothes was the only problem that offered any real difficulties. Apart from the fact that Savaroff's suit was by no means in its first youth, I had a strong objection to wearing his infernal things a moment longer than I could help. I was determined to have a decently cut suit as soon as possible, but I knew that it would be a week at least before any West End tailor would finish the job. In the meantime I wanted something to go on with, and in my extremity I suddenly remembered a place in Wardour Street where four or five years before I had once hired a costume for a Covent Garden ball.

I told the man to drive me there, and much to my relief found the shop still in existence. There was no difficulty about getting what I wanted. The proprietor had a large selection of what he called "West End Misfits," amongst which were several tweeds and blue serge suits big enough even for my somewhat unreasonable proportions. I chose the two that fitted me best, and then bought a second-hand suit-case to pack them away in.

I had spent about fifteen pounds, which seemed to me as much as a fifty-pound capitalist had any right to squander on necessities. I therefore returned to the taxi and, arranging my parcels on the front seat, instructed the man to drive me down to the address that McMurtrie had given me.

Pimlico was a part of London that I had not patronized extensively in the days of my freedom, and I was rather in the dark about the precise situation of Edith Terrace. The taxi-man, however, seemed to suffer under no such handicap. He drove me straight to Victoria, and then, taking the road to the left of the station, turned off into a neighbourhood of dreary-looking streets and squares, all bearing a dismal aspect of having seen better days.

Edith Terrace was, if anything, slightly more depressing than the rest. It consisted of a double row of gaunt, untidy houses, from which most of the original stucco had long since peeled away. Quiet enough it certainly was, for along its whole length we passed only one man, who was standing under a street lamp, lighting a cigarette. He looked up as we went by, and for just one instant I had a clear view of his face. Except for a scar on the cheek he was curiously like one of the warders at Princetown, and for that reason I suppose this otherwise trifling incident fixed itself in my mind. It is funny on what queer chances one's fate sometimes hangs.

We pulled up at Number 3 and, mounting some not very recently cleaned steps, I gave a brisk tug at a dilapidated bell-handle. After a minute I heard the sound of shuffling footsteps; then the door opened and a funny-looking little old woman stood blinking and peering at me from the threshold.

"How do you do?" I said cheerfully. "Are you Mrs. Oldbury?"

She gave a kind of spasmodic jerk, that may have been intended for a curtsey.

"Yes, sir," she said. "I'm Mrs. Oldbury; and you'd be the gentleman I'm expectin'—Dr. McMurtrie's gentleman?"

This seemed an accurate if not altogether flattering description of me, so I nodded my head.

"That's right," I said. "I'm Mr. Nicholson." Then, as the heavily laden taxi-man staggered up the steps, I added: "And these are my belongings."

With another bob she turned round, and leading the way into the house opened a door on the right-hand side of the passage.

"This will be your sitting-room, sir," she said, turning up the gas. "It's a nice hairy room, and I give it a proper cleaning out this morning."

I looked round, and saw that I was in a typical "ground-floor front," with the usual cheap lace curtains, hideous wall paper, and slightly stuffy smell. At the back of the room, away from the window, were two folding doors.

My landlady shuffled across and pushed one of them open. "And this is the bedroom, sir. It's what you might call 'andy—and quiet too. You'll find that a nice comfortable bed, sir. It's the one my late 'usband died in."

"It sounds restful," I said. Then walking to the doorway I paid off the taxi-man, who had deposited his numerous burdens and was waiting patiently for his fare.

As soon as he had gone, Mrs. Oldbury, who had meanwhile occupied herself in pulling down the blinds and drawing the curtains, inquired whether I should like anything to eat.

"I don't think I'll trouble you," I said. "I have got to go out in any case."

"Oh, it's no trouble, sir—no trouble at all. I can put you on a nice little bit o' steak as easy as anything if you 'appen to fancy it."

I shook my head. A few weeks ago "a nice little bit o' steak" would have seemed like Heaven to me, but since then I had become more luxurious. I was determined that my first dinner in London should be worthy of the occasion. Besides, I had other business to attend to.

"No, thanks," I said firmly. "I don't want anything except some hot water and a latchkey, if you have such a thing to spare. I don't know what time you go to bed here, but I may be a little late getting back."

She fumbled in her pocket and produced a purse, from which she extricated the required article.

"I'm not gen'rally in bed—not much before midnight, sir," she said. "If you should be later per'aps you'd be kind enough to turn out the gas in the 'all. I'll send you up some 'ot water by the girl."

She went off, closing the door behind her; and picking up my parcels and bags I carried them into the bedroom and started to unpack. I decided that the blue suit was most in keeping with my mood, so I laid this out on the bed together with a complete change of underclothes. I was eyeing the latter with some satisfaction, when there came a knock at the door, and in answer to my summons the "girl" entered with the hot water. She was the typical lodging-house drudge, a poor little object of about sixteen, with a dirty face and her hair twisted up in a knot at the back of her head.

"If yer please, sir," she said, with a sniff, "Mrs. Oldbury wants ter know if yer'll be likin' a barf in the mornin'."

"You can tell Mrs. Oldbury that the answer is yes," I said gravely. Then I paused. "What's your name?" I asked.

She sniffed again, and looked at me with round, wondering eyes. "Gertie, sir. Gertie 'Uggins."

I felt in my pocket and found a couple of half-crowns.

"Take these, Gertie," I said, "and go and have a damned good dinner the first chance you get."

She clasped the money in her grubby little hand.

"Thank you, sir," she murmured awkwardly.

"You needn't thank me, Gertie," I said; "it was a purely selfish action. There are some emotions which have to be shared before they can be properly appreciated. My dinner tonight happens to be one of them."

She shifted from one leg to the other. "Yes, sir," she said. Then with a little giggle she turned and scuttled out of the room.

I washed and dressed myself slowly, revelling in the sensation of being once more in clean garments of my own. I was determined not to spoil my evening by allowing any bitter or unpleasant thoughts to disturb me until I had dined; after that, I reflected, it would be quite time enough to map out my dealings with George.

Lighting a cigarette I left the house, and set off at a leisurely pace along Edith Terrace. It was my intention to walk to Victoria, and then take a taxi from there to whatever restaurant I decided to dine at. The latter question was not a point to be determined lightly, and as I strolled along I debated pleasantly in my mind the attractions of two or three of my old haunts.

By the time I reached Victoria I had decided in favour of Gaultier's—if Gaultier's was still in existence. It was a place that, in my time at all events, had been chiefly frequented by artists and foreigners, but the food, of its kind, was as good there as anywhere in London.

I beckoned to a passing taxi, and waving his arm in response the driver swerved across the street and drew up at the kerb.

"Where to, guv'nor?" he inquired.

I gave him the direction, and then turned to open the door. As I did so I noticed a man standing on the pavement close beside me looking vacantly across the street. For an instant I wondered where I had seen him before; then quite suddenly I remembered. He was the man we had passed in Edith Terrace, lighting a cigarette under the street lamp—the man who had reminded me of one of the prison warders. I knew I was not mistaken because I could see the scar on his face.

With a sudden vague sense of uneasiness I got into the taxi and shut the door. The gentleman on the pavement paid no attention to me at all. He continued to stand there staring aimlessly at the traffic, until we had jerked forward and turned off round the corner of Victoria Street.

All the same the incident had left a kind of uncomfortable feeling behind it. I suppose an escaped convict is naturally inclined to be suspicious, and somehow or other I couldn't shake off the impression that I was being watched and followed. If so, I had not much doubt whom I was indebted to for the honour. It had never seemed to me likely that McMurtrie would leave me entirely to my own sweet devices while I was in London—not, at all events, until he had satisfied himself that I had been speaking the truth about my intentions.

Still, even if my suspicions were right, there seemed no reason for being seriously worried. The gentleman on the pavement might have overheard me give the address to the driver, but that after all was exactly what I should have liked him to hear. Dinner at Gaultier's sounded a most natural preliminary to an evening's dissipation, and unless I was being actually followed to the restaurant I had nothing to fear. It was quite possible that my friend with the scar was only anxious to discover whether I was really setting out for the West End.

All the same I determined to be devilish careful about my future movements. If McMurtrie wanted a report he should have it, but I would take particular pains to see that it contained nothing which would in any way disturb his belief in me.

We pulled up at Gaultier's, and I saw with a sort of sentimental pleasure that, outside at all events, it had not altered in the least during my three years' exile. There was the same discreet-looking little window, the same big electric light over the door, and, unless I was much mistaken, the same uniformed porter standing on the mat.

When I entered I found M. Gaultier himself, as fat and bland as ever, presiding over the scene. He came forward, bowing low after his usual custom, and motioned me towards a vacant table in the corner. I felt an absurd inclination to slap him on the back and ask him how he had been getting on in my absence.

It seemed highly improbable that he would remember my voice, but, as I had no intention of running any unnecessary risks, I was careful to alter it a little when I spoke to him.

"Good-evening," I began; "are you M. Gaultier?"

He bowed and beamed.

"Well, M. Gaultier," I said, "I want a good dinner—a quite exceptionally good dinner. I have been waiting for it for some time."

He regarded me keenly, with a mixture of sympathy and professional interest.

"Monsieur is hungry?" he inquired.

"Monsieur," I replied, "is both hungry and greedy. You have full scope for your art."

He straightened himself, and for an inspired moment gazed at the ceiling. Then he slapped his forehead.

"Monsieur," he said, "with your permission I go to consult the chef."

"Go," I replied. "And Heaven attend your council."

He hurried off, and I beckoned to the head waiter.

"Fetch me," I said, "a Virginian cigarette and a sherry and bitters."

A true gourmet would probably shudder at such a first course, but it must be remembered that for three years my taste had had no opportunity of becoming over-trained. Besides, in matters of this sort I always act on the principle that it's better to enjoy oneself than to be artistically correct.

Lying back in my chair I looked out over the little restaurant with a sensation of beautiful complacency. The soft rose-shaded lamps threw a warm glamour over everything, and through the delicate blue spirals of my cigarette I could just see the laughing face of a charmingly pretty girl who was dining with an elderly man at the opposite table. I glanced at the clock on the mantelpiece. It was close on eight—the hour when the cell lights at Princetown are turned out, and another dragging night of horror and darkness begins. Slowly and luxuriously I sipped my sherry and bitters.

I was aroused from my reverie by the approach of M. Gaultier, who carried a menu in his hand.

He handed me the card with another bow, and then stepped back as though to watch the result. This was the dinner:

Clear soup.

Grilled salmon.

Lamb. New potatoes.

Woodcock.

Pêche Melba.

Marrow on Toast.

I read it through, enjoying each separate word, and then, with a faint sigh, handed it back to him.

"Heaven," I said, "was undoubtedly at the conference."

M. Gaultier picked up a wine list from the table. "And what will Monsieur drink?" he inquired reverently.

"Monsieur," I replied, "has perfect faith in your judgment. He will drink everything you choose to give him."

Half an hour later I again lay back in my chair, and lapped in a superb contentment gently murmured to myself those two delightful lines of Sydney Smith's—

"Serenely calm, the epicure may say:
Fate cannot harm me, I have dined today."

I sipped my Turkish coffee, lighted the fragrant Cabana which M. Gaultier had selected for me, and debated cheerfully with myself what I should do next. I had had so many unpleasant evenings since my trial that I was determined that this one at all events should be a complete success.

My first impulse of course was to visit George. There was something very engaging in the thought of being ushered into his presence by a respectable butler, and making my excuses for having called at such an unreasonable hour. I pictured to myself how he would look as I gradually dropped my assumed voice, and very slowly the almost incredible truth began to dawn on him.

So charming was the idea that it was only with some reluctance I was able to abandon it. I didn't want to waste George: he had to last me at least three days, and I felt that if I went down there now, warmed and exhilarated with wine and food, I should be almost certain to give myself away. I had no intention of doing that until the last possible moment. I still had a sort of faint irrational hope that by watching George without betraying my identity, I might discover something which would throw a little light on his behaviour to me.

But if I didn't go to Cheyne Walk, what was I to do? I put the question to myself as I slowly lifted the glass of old brandy which the waiter had set down in front of me, and before the fine spirit touched my lips the answer had flashed into my mind. I would go and see Tommy!

It was the perfect solution of the difficulty; and as I put down the glass again I laughed softly in sheer happiness. The prospect of interviewing Tommy without his recognizing me was only a degree less attractive than the thought of a similar experience with George. I knew that the mere sight of his velvet coat and his dear old burly carcase would fill me with the most delightful emotions—emotions which now, amongst all my one-time friends, he and perhaps poor little Joyce would alone have the power to provoke. The others seemed to me as dead as the past to which they belonged.

One thing I was determined on, and that was that I wouldn't give away my secret. It would be difficult not to, for there were naturally a hundred things I wanted to say to Tommy; but, however much I might be tempted, I was resolved to play the game. It was not the thought of my promise to McMurtrie (that sat very easily on my conscience), but the possibility of getting Tommy himself into trouble. I knew that for me he would run any risk in the world with the utmost cheerfulness, but I had no intention of letting him do it. He had done more than enough for me at the time of the trial.

I called for the waiter and paid my bill. It seemed absurdly cheap for such a delightful evening, and I said as much to M. Gaultier, who insisted on accompanying me to the door. He received the remark with a protesting gesture of his hands.

"Most people," he said, "feed. Monsieur eats. To such we do not wish to overcharge. It is a pleasure to provide a dinner which is appreciated."

The porter outside volunteered to call me a taxi, and while he was engaged in that operation I had a sharp look up and down the street to see whether my friend with the scar was hanging about anywhere. I could discern no sign of him, but all the same, when the taxi came up, I took the precaution of directing the man in a fairly audible voice to drive me to the Pavilion, in Piccadilly Circus. It was not until we were within a few yards of that instructive institution that I whistled through the tube and told him to take me on to Chelsea.

I knew Tommy was in the same studio, for Joyce had told me so in her second letter. It was one of a fairly new block of four or five at the bottom of Beaufort Street, about half a mile along the embankment from George's house. All the way down I was debating with myself what excuse I could offer for calling at such a late hour, and finally I decided that the best thing would be to pretend that I was a travelling American artist who had seen and admired some of Tommy's work. Under such circumstances it would be difficult for the latter not to ask me in for a short chat.

I stopped the cab in the King's Road, and getting out, had another good look round to see that I was not being followed. Satisfied on this point, I lighted a second cigar and started off down Beaufort Street.

The stretch of embankment at the bottom seemed to have altered very little since I had last seen it. One or two of the older houses had been done up, but Florence Court, the block of studios in which Tommy lived, was exactly as I remembered it. The front door was open, after the usual casual fashion that prevails in Chelsea, and I walked into the square stone hall, which was lighted by a flickering gas jet.

There was a board on the right, containing the addresses of the various tenants. Opposite No. 3 I saw the name of Mr. T.G. Morrison, and with a slight quickening of the pulse I advanced along the corridor to Tommy's door.

As I reached it I saw that there was a card tied to the knocker. I knew that this was a favourite trick of Tommy's when he was away, and with a sharp sense of disappointment I bent down to read what was written on it. With some difficulty, for the light was damnable, I made out the following words, roughly scribbled in pencil:

"Out of Town. Please leave any telegrams or urgent letters at No. 4. T.M."

I dropped the card and stood wondering what to do. If Tommy had some pal living next door, as seemed probable from his notice, the latter would most likely know what time he was expected to return. For a moment I hesitated: then retracing my steps, I walked back into the hall and glanced at the board to see who might be the tenant of No. 4.

To my surprise I found it was a woman—a "Miss Vivien."

At first I thought I must be wrong, for women had always been the one agreeable feature of life for which Tommy had no manner of use. There it was, however, as plain as a pikestaff, and with a feeling of lively interest I turned back towards the flat. Whoever Miss Vivien might be, I was determined to have a look at her. I felt that the girl whom Tommy would leave in charge of his more important correspondence must be distinctly worth looking at.

I rang the bell, and after a short wait the door was opened by a little maid about the size and age of Gertie 'Uggins, dressed in a cap and a print frock.

"Is Miss Vivien in?" I asked boldly.

She shook her head. "Miss Vivien's out. 'Ave you got an appointment?"

"No," I said. "I only want to know where Mr. Morrison is, and when he's coming back. There's a notice on his door asking that any letters or telegrams should be left here, so I thought Miss Vivien might know."

She looked me up and down, with a faint air of suspicion.

"'E's away in 'is boat," she said shortly. "'E won't be back not till Thursday."

So Tommy still kept up his sailing! This at least was news, and news which had a rather special interest for me. I wondered whether the "boat" was the same little seven-tonner, the *Betty*, in which we had spent so many cheerful hours together off the Crouch and the Blackwater.

"Thanks," I said; and then after a moment's pause I added, "I suppose if I addressed a letter here it would be forwarded?"

"I s'pose so," she admitted a little grudgingly.

There seemed to be nothing more to say, so bidding the damsel good-night, I walked off down the passage and out on to the embankment. If I had drawn a blank as far as seeing Tommy was concerned, my evening had not been altogether fruitless. I felt vastly curious as to who Miss Vivien might be. Somehow or other I couldn't picture Tommy with a woman in his life. In the old days, partly from shyness and partly, I think, because they honestly bored him, he had always avoided girls with a determination that at times bordered on rudeness. And yet, unless all the signs were misleading, it was evident that he and his next-door neighbour were on fairly intimate terms. The most probable explanation seemed to me that she was some elderly lady artist who darned his socks for him, and shed tears in secret over the state of his wardrobe. There was a magnificent uncouthness about Tommy which would appeal irresistibly to a certain type of motherly woman.

I strolled up the embankment in the direction of Chelsea Bridge, smiling to myself over the idea. Whether it was right or not, it presented such a pleasing picture that I had walked several hundred yards before I quite woke up to my surroundings. Then with a sudden start I realized that I was quite close to George's house.

It was a big red-brick affair, standing back from the embankment facing the river. As I came opposite I could see that there was a light on the first floor, in the room which I knew George used as a study. I stopped for a minute, leaning back against the low wall and staring up at the window.

I wondered what my cousin was doing. Perhaps he was sitting there, looking through the evening paper in the vain hope of finding news of my capture. I could almost see the lines on his forehead and the nervous, jerky way in which he would be biting his fingers—a trick of his that had always annoyed me intensely. He would bite harder than ever if he only knew that

I was standing outside in the darkness not more than twenty yards away from him!

I waited for a little while in the hope that he might come to the window, but this luxury was denied me.

"Good-night, George," I said softly; "we'll meet in the morning," and then, with a last affectionate look at the lighted blind, I continued my way along the embankment.

I was not sure which turning I ought to take for Edith Terrace, but an obliging policeman who was on duty outside the Tate Gallery put me on the right track. There was something delicately pleasing to my sense of humour in appealing to a constable, and altogether it was in a most contented frame of mind that I inserted my latch-key into Mrs. Oldbury's door and let myself into the house. My first day's holiday seemed to me to have been quite a success.

CHAPTER X
MADEMOISELLE VIVIEN, PALMIST

I woke next morning at seven, or perhaps I should say I was awakened by Gertie 'Uggins, who to judge from the noise was apparently engaged in wrecking the sitting-room. I looked at my watch, and then halloed to her through the door. The tumult ceased, and a head, elaborately festooned with curl-papers, was inserted into the room.

"Yer want yer barf?" it asked.

"I do, Gertrude," I said; "and after that I want my breakfast. I have a lot to do today."

The head withdrew itself, tittering; and a moment later I heard a shrill voice calling down the kitchen stairs.

"Grahnd floor wants 'is 'ot water quick."

Within about five minutes the ground floor's wish was gratified, Mrs. Oldbury herself arriving with a large steaming can which she placed inside a hip bath. She asked me in a mournful voice whether I thought I could eat some eggs and bacon, and having received a favourable reply left me to my toilet.

It was about a quarter to eight when I sat down to breakfast. Considering that for three years I had been obliged to rise at painfully unseasonable hours, this may appear to have been unnecessarily energetic, but as a matter of fact I was not acting without good reasons.

To start with, it was my purpose to spend a pleasant morning with George. I wanted to be outside his house so that I could see his face when he came out. I felt sure that as long as I was at liberty he would be looking worried and depressed, and I had no wish to postpone my enjoyment of such a congenial spectacle.

Then, provided that I could restrain myself from breaking his head, I intended to follow him to Victoria Street or wherever else he happened to go. Beyond this I had no plan at the moment, but at the back of my mind there was a curious irrational feeling that sooner or later I should stumble across some explanation of the mystery of Marks' death.

I knew that as a rule George didn't start for business until nine-thirty or ten. I was anxious to get out of the house as soon as possible, however, just in case I was correct in my idea that the gentleman with the scar was keeping a kindly eye on my movements. In that case I thought that by departing before half-past eight I should be almost certain to forestall him. If, as I believed, he was under the impression that I had been indulging in a night's dissipation, it was unlikely that he would credit me with sufficient energy to get up before ten or eleven. As to waiting for George—well, I had no objection to that. It was a nice sunny morning, and I could buy a paper and sit on one of the embankment seats.

This, indeed, was exactly what I did. I slipped out of the house as unobtrusively as possible, and, stopping at a little newspaper and tobacco shop round the first corner, invested in a *Telegraph* and a *Sportsman*. Then, after making sure that I was not being followed, I set off for the embankment.

Some of the seats were already occupied by gentlemen and ladies who had apparently been using them in preference to an hotel, but as luck would have it the one opposite George's house was empty. I seated myself in the corner, and after cutting and lighting a cigar with the care that such an excellent brand deserved, I prepared to beguile my wait by reading the *D.T.*

Nothing particularly thrilling seemed to have been happening in the world, but I can't say I felt any sense of disappointment. Just at present my own life afforded me all the excitement my system needed. The only important item of news that I could find was a rather offensive speech by the German Chancellor with reference to the dispute with England. It was a surprising utterance for a statesman in his position, and the *Telegraph* had improved the occasion by writing one of its longest and stateliest leaders on provocative politicians.

I had just finished reading this effort when George appeared. He came out of the front door and down the steps of his house, dressed as usual in a well-fitting frock-coat and tall hat, such as he had always affected in the old days. I stared at him with a sort of hungry satisfaction. He looked pale and harassed, and he carried his head bent forward like a man whose mind was unpleasantly preoccupied. It warmed my heart to see him.

When he had gone some little way along the pavement, I got up from my seat and began to keep pace with him on the other side of the roadway. It was easy work, for he walked slowly, and stared at the ground as though fully taken up with his own thoughts. I was not the least frightened of his recognizing me, but as a matter of fact he never even looked across in my direction.

We marched along in this fashion as far as Vauxhall Bridge Road, where George turned up to the left in the direction of Victoria Street. I walked on a bit, so as to allow him to get about a hundred yards ahead, and then coming back followed in his track. As he drew nearer to the station I began to close up the gap, and all the way along Victoria Street I was only about ten yards behind him. It was tantalizing work, for he was just the right distance for a running kick.

The offices of our firm, which I had originally chosen myself, are on the first floor, close to the Army and Navy Stores. George turned in at the doorway and went straight up, and for a moment I stood in the entrance, contemplating the big brass plate with "Lyndon and Marwood" on it, and wondering what to do next. It seemed odd to think of all that had happened since I had last climbed those stairs.

Exactly across the road was a restaurant. It was new since my time, but I could see that there was a table in the window on the first floor, which must command a fair view of the houses opposite, so I determined to adopt it as a temporary scouting ground. I walked over and pushed open the swinging doors. Inside was a sleepy-looking waiter in his shirt-sleeves engaged in the leisurely pursuit of rolling up napkins.

"Good-morning," I said; "can I have some coffee and something to eat upstairs?"

He regarded me for a moment with a rather startled air, and then pulled himself together.

"Yes, saire. Too early for lunch, saire. 'Am-an'-eggs, saire?"

I nodded. I had had eggs and bacon for breakfast, and on the excellent principle of not mixing one's drinks, 'am an'-eggs sounded a most happy suggestion.

"Very well," I said; "and I wonder if you could let me have such a thing as a sheet of paper, and a pen and ink? I want to write a letter afterwards."

This, I regret to say, was not strictly true, but it seemed to offer an ingenious excuse for occupying the table for some time without arousing too much curiosity.

The waiter expressed himself as being in a position to gratify me, and leaving him hastily donning his coat I marched up the staircase to the room above.

When I sat down at the table in the window I found that my expectations were quite correct. I was looking right across into the main room of our offices, and I could see a couple of clerks working away at their desks quite clearly enough to distinguish their faces. They were both strangers to me, but I was not surprised at this. I always thought that George had probably sacked most of the old staff, if they had not given him notice on their own account. Of my cousin himself I could see nothing. He was doubtless either in his own sanctum, or in the big inner room where I used to work with Watson, my assistant.

It was of course impossible to eat much of the generous dish of 'am-an'-eggs which the waiter brought me up, but I dallied over it as long as possible, and managed to swallow a cup of rather indifferent coffee. Then I smoked another cigar, and when the things were cleared away and the writing materials had arrived, I made a pretence of beginning my letter.

All this time, of course, I was keeping a strict watch across the street. Nothing interesting seemed to happen, and I was just beginning to think that I was wasting my time in a rather hopeless fashion when suddenly I saw George come out of his private office into the main room opposite, wearing his hat and carrying an umbrella. He spoke to one of the clerks as though giving him some parting instructions, and went out, shutting the door behind him.

I jumped to my feet, and hurrying down the stairs, demanded my bill from the rather surprised waiter. Considering that I had been sitting upstairs for over an hour and a half, I suppose my haste did appear a trifle unreasonable; anyway he took so long making out the bill that at last I threw down five shillings and left him at the process.

Even so, I was only just in time. As I came out into the street George emerged from the doorway opposite. He looked less depressed than before and much more like his usual sleek self, and the sight of him in these apparently recovered spirits whipped up my resentment again to all its old bitterness.

He set off at a brisk pace in the direction of the Houses of Parliament, and crossing the street I took up a tactful position in his rear. In this order we proceeded along Whitehall, across Trafalgar Square, and up Charing Cross Road into Coventry Street. Here George stopped for a moment to buy himself a carnation—he had always had a taste for buttonholes—and then resuming our progress, we crossed the Circus, and started off down Piccadilly.

By this time what is known I believe as "the lust of the chase" had fairly got hold of me. More strongly than ever I had the feeling that something interesting was going to happen, and when George turned up Bond Street

I quickened my steps so as to bring me back to my old if rather tempting position close behind him.

Quite suddenly in the very narrowest part of the pavement he came to a stop, and entered a doorway next to a tobacconist's shop. In a couple of strides I had reached the spot, just in time to see him disappearing up a winding flight of stone stairs.

There were two little brass plates at the side of the door, and I turned to them eagerly to see whom he might be honouring with a visit. One was inscribed "Dr. Rich. Jones, M.D.," and the other "Mlle. Vivien."

The moment I read the last name something curiously familiar about it suddenly struck me. Then in a flash I remembered the pencilled notice on Tommy's door, and the obliging "Miss Vivien" who was willing to receive his telegrams.

The coincidence was a startling one, but I was too anxious to discover what George was doing to waste much time pondering over it. Stepping forward to the foot of the stairs, I peered cautiously up. I could see by his hand, which was resting on the banisters, that he had passed the floor above, where the doctor lived, and was half way up the next flight. Whoever Mlle. Vivien might be, she certainly represented George's destination.

I retreated to the door, wondering what was the best thing to do. My previous effort in Victoria Street had been so successful that I instinctively glanced across the street to see whether there was another convenient restaurant from which I could repeat my tactics. There wasn't a restaurant but there was something else which was even better, and that was a small and very respectable-looking public-house.

If I had to wait, a whisky-and-soda seemed a much more agreeable thing to beguile the time with than a third helping of ham and eggs, so crossing the road with a light heart, I pushed open a door marked "Saloon Bar." I found myself in a square, comfortably fitted apartment where a genial-looking gentleman was dispensing drinks to a couple of chauffeurs.

Along the back of the bar ran a big fitted looking-glass, sloped at an angle which enabled it to reflect the opposite side of the street. This was most convenient, for I could stand at the counter with my back to the window, and yet keep my eye all the time upon the doorway from which George would appear.

"Good-morning, sir: what can I get you?" inquired the landlord pleasantly.

"I'll have a whisky-and-soda, thanks," I said.

As he turned round to get it a sudden happy idea flashed into my mind. I waited until he had placed the glass on the bar and was pouring out the soda, and then inquired carelessly:

"You don't happen to know any one of the name of Vivien about here, I suppose?"

He looked up at once. "Vivien!" he repeated; "well, there's a Mamzelle Vivien across the road. D'you mean her?"

I shrugged my shoulders. "I don't know," I said; then, with a coolness which would have done credit to Ananias, I added: "A friend of mine has picked up a little bag or something with 'Vivien, Bond Street,' on it. He asked me to see if I could find the owner."

The landlord nodded his head with interest. "That'll be her, I expect. Mamzelle Vivien the palmist—just across the way."

"Oh, she's a palmist, is she?" I exclaimed. The thought of George consulting a palmist was decidedly entertaining. Perhaps he wanted to find out whether I was likely to wring his neck.

With a side glance at the chauffeurs, the landlord leaned a little towards me and slightly lowered his voice. "Well, that's what she calls 'erself," he observed. "Palmist and Clairvoyante; and a smart bit o' goods she is too."

"But I thought the police had stopped that sort of thing," I said.

The landlord shook his head. "The police don't interfere with her. She don't advertise or anything like that, and I reckon she has some pretty useful friends. You'd be surprised if I was to tell you some o' the people I seen going in there—Cabinet Ministers and Bishops."

"It sounds like the Athenaeum Club," I said. "Do you know what she charges?"

"No," he replied; "something pretty stiff I guess. With folks like that it's a case of make 'ay while the sun shines."

He was called off at this point to attend to another customer, leaving me to ponder over the information he had given me. I felt that somehow or other I must make Mademoiselle Vivien's acquaintance. A beautiful palmist, for whom George deserted his business at eleven in the morning, was just the sort of person who might prove extremely interesting to me. Besides, the fact that her name was the same as that of the lady who lived next door to Tommy lent an additional spur to my curiosity. It might be a mere coincidence, but if so it was a sufficiently odd one to merit a little further investigation.

I drank up my whisky, and after waiting a minute or two, ordered another. I had just got this and was taking my first sip, when quite suddenly I saw in the mirror the reflection of George emerging from the doorway opposite.

I didn't stop to finish my drink. I put down the tumbler, and nodding to the landlord walked straight out into the street. The pavement was thronged with the usual midday crowd, but pushing my way through I dodged across the road and reached the opposite side-walk just in time to see George stepping into a taxi a few yards farther down the street.

I was not close enough to overhear the directions which he gave to the driver, but unless his habits had changed considerably the chances were that he was off to lunch at his club. Anyhow I felt pretty certain that I could pick up his trail again later on at the office if I wanted to. For the moment I had other plans; it was my intention to follow George's example and pay a short call upon "Mademoiselle Vivien."

I walked back, and throwing away the end of my cigar, entered the doorway again and started off up the stairs. I imagined that by going as an ordinary client I should find no difficulty in getting admitted, but if I did I was fully prepared to bribe or bluff, or adopt any method that might be necessary to achieve my purpose. I would not leave until I had at least seen the gifted object of George's midday rambles.

I reached the second landing, where I was faced by a green door with a quaintly carved electric bell in the shape of an Egyptian girl's head, a red stone in the centre of the forehead forming what appeared to be the button. Anyhow I pressed it and waited, and a moment later the door swung silently open. A small but very alert page-boy who looked like an Italian was standing on the mat.

"Is Mademoiselle at home?" I inquired.

He looked me up and down sharply. "Have you an appointment, sir?"

"No," I said, "but will you be good enough to ask whether I can see her? My name is Mr. James Nicholson. I wish to consult her professionally."

"If you will step in here, sir, I will inquire. Mademoiselle very seldom sees any one without an appointment."

He opened a door on the right and ushered me into a small sitting-room, the chief furniture of which appeared to be a couch, one or two magnificent bowls of growing tulips and hyacinths, and an oak shelf which ran the whole length of the room and was crowded with books.

While the boy was away I amused myself by examining the titles. There were a number of volumes on palmistry and on various branches of occultism, interspersed with several books of poetry and such unlikely works as *My Prison Life*, by Jabez Balfour, and Melville Lee's well-known *History of Police*.

It gave me rather an uncanny feeling for the moment to be confronted by the two latter, and I was just wondering whether a Bond Street palmist's cliéntèle made such works of reference necessary, when the door opened and the page-boy reappeared.

"If you will kindly come this way, sir, Mademoiselle will see you," he announced.

I followed him down the passage and into another room hung with heavy curtains that completely shut out the daylight. A small rose-coloured lamp burning away steadily in the corner threw a warm glow over everything, and lit up the low table of green stone in the centre, on which rested a large crystal ball in a metal frame. Except for two curiously carved chairs, there was no other furniture in the room.

Closing the door noiselessly behind him, the boy went out again. I stood there for a little while looking about me; then pulling up a chair I was just sitting down when a slight sound attracted my attention. A moment later a curtain at the end of the room was drawn slowly aside, and there, standing in the gap, I saw the slim figure of a girl, dressed in a kind of long dark Eastern tunic.

I jumped to my feet, and as I did so an exclamation of amazement broke involuntarily from my lips. For an instant I remained quite still, clutching the back of the chair and staring like a man in a trance. Unless I was mad the girl in front of me was Joyce.

CHAPTER XI
BRIDGING THREE YEARS OF SEPARATION

It was the unexpectedness of the thing that threw me off my guard. With a savage effort I recovered myself almost at once, but it was too late to be of any use. At the sound of my voice all the colour had left Joyce's face. Her hands went up to her breast, and with a low cry she stepped forward and then stood there white and swaying, gazing at me with wide-open, half-incredulous eyes.

"My God!" she whispered; "it's you—Neil!"

I think she would have fallen, but I came to her side, and putting my arm round her shoulders gently forced her into one of the chairs. Then I knelt in front of her and took her hands in mine. I saw it was no good trying to deceive her.

"I didn't know," I said simply; "I followed George here."

"What have they done to you?" she moaned. "What have they done to you, my Neil? And your hands—oh, your poor dear hands!"

She burst out crying, and bending down pressed her face against my fingers.

"Don't, Joyce," I said, a little roughly. "For God's sake don't do that."

Half unconsciously I pulled away my hands, which three years in Dartmoor had certainly done nothing to improve.

My abrupt action seemed to bring Joyce to herself. She left off sobbing, and with a sudden hurried glance round the room jumped up from her chair.

"I must speak to Jack—now at once," she whispered. "He mustn't let any one else into the flat."

She stopped for a moment to dry her eyes, which were still wet with tears, and then walking quickly to the door disappeared into the passage. She was only gone for a few seconds. I just had time to get to my feet when she came back into the room, and shutting the door behind her, turned the key in the lock. Then with a little gasp she leaned against the wall. For the first time I realized what an amazingly beautiful girl she had grown into.

"Neil, Neil," she said, stretching out her hands; "is it really you!"

I came across, and taking her in my arms very gently kissed her forehead.

"My little Joyce," I said. "My dear, brave little Joyce."

She buried her face in my coat, and I felt her hand moving up and down my sleeve.

"Oh," she sobbed, "if I had only known where to find you before! Ever since you escaped I have been hoping and longing that you would come to me." Then she half pushed me back, and gazed up into my face with her blue, tear-stained eyes. "Where have you been? What have they done to you? Oh, tell me—tell me, Neil. It's breaking my heart to see you so different."

For a moment I hesitated. I would have given much if I could have undone the work of the last few minutes, for even to be revenged on George I would not willingly have brought my wretched troubles and dangers into Joyce's life. Now that I had done so, however, there seemed to be no other course except to tell her the truth. It was impossible to leave her in her present agony of bewilderment and doubt.

Pulling up one of the chairs I sat down, drawing her on to my knee.

"If I had known it was you, Joyce," I said, "I should have let George go to the devil before I followed him here."

"But why?" she asked. "Where should you go to if you didn't come to me?"

"Oh, my poor Joyce," I said bitterly; "haven't I brought enough troubles and horrors into your life already?"

She interrupted me with a low, passionate cry. "*You* talk like that! You, who have lost everything for my wretched sake! Can't you understand that every day and night since you went to prison I've loathed and hated myself for ever telling you anything about it? If I'd dreamed what was going to happen I'd have let Marks—"

I stopped her by crushing her in my arms, and for a little while she remained there sobbing bitterly, her cheek resting on my shoulder! For a moment or two I didn't feel exactly like talking myself.

Indeed it was Joyce who spoke first. Raising her head she wiped away her tears, and then sitting up gazed long and searchingly into my face.

"There is nothing of you left," she said, "nothing except your eyes—your dear, splendid eyes. I think I should have known you by those even if you hadn't spoken." Then, taking my hands again and pressing them to her, she added passionately: "Oh, tell me what it means, Neil. Tell me everything that's happened to you from the moment you got away."

"Very well," I said recklessly: "I shall be dragging you into all sorts of dangers, and I shall be breaking my oath to McMurtrie, but after all that's just the sort of thing one would expect from an escaped convict."

Step by step, from the moment when I had jumped over the wall into the plantation, I told her the whole astounding story. She listened to me in silence, her face alone betraying the feverish interest with which she was following every word. When I came to the part about Sonia kissing me (I told her everything just as it had happened) her hands tightened a little on mine, but except for that one movement she remained absolutely still.

It was not until I had finished speaking that she made her first comment. After I stopped she sat on for a moment just as she was; and then quite suddenly her face lighted up, and with a little low laugh that was half a sob she leaned forward and slid her arm round my neck.

"Tommy was right," she whispered. "He said you'd do something wonderful. I knew it too, but oh, Neil dear, I've suffered tortures wondering where you were and what had happened."

Then, sitting up again and pushing back her hair, she began to ask me questions.

"These people—Dr. McMurtrie and the others—do you believe their story?"

"No," I said bluntly. "I am quite certain they were lying to me."

"Why should they have helped you, then?"

"I haven't the remotest idea," I admitted. "I am only quite sure that neither McMurtrie nor Savaroff are what they pretend to be. Besides, you remember the hints that Sonia gave me."

"Ah, Sonia!" Joyce looked down and played with one of the buttons of my coat. "Is she—is she very pretty?" she asked.

"She seems likely to be very useful," I said. Then, stroking Joyce's soft curly hair, which had become all tousled against my shoulder, I added: "But I'm answering questions when all the time I'm dying to ask them. There are a hundred things you've got to tell me. What are you doing here? Why do you call yourself Miss Vivien? Are you really living next door to Tommy? And George—how on earth do you come to be mixed up with George?"

"I'll tell you everything," she said, "only I must know all about you first. Why were you following George? You don't mean to let him know who you are? Oh, Neil, Neil, promise me that you won't do that."

"Joyce," I said slowly, "I want to find out who killed Seton Marks. I don't suppose there is the least chance of my doing so, and if I can't I most certainly mean to wring George's neck. That was chiefly what I broke out of prison for."

"Yes, yes," she said feverishly, "but there *is* a chance. You'll understand when I've explained." She put her hands to her forehead. "Oh, I hardly know where to begin."

"Begin anywhere," I said. "Tell me why you're pretending to be a palmist."

She got up from my knee and, walking slowly to the table, seated herself on the end.

"I wanted money," she said; "and I wanted to meet one or two people who might be useful about you."

"But I left eight hundred pounds for you with Tommy," I exclaimed. "You got that?"

She nodded. "It's in the bank now. I have been keeping it in case anything happened. You don't suppose I was going to spend it? How could I have helped you then even when I got the chance?"

"But, my dear Joyce," I protested, "the money was for you. And you couldn't have helped me with it in any case. I had plenty more waiting for me when my sentence was out."

"When your sentence was out," repeated Joyce fiercely. "Do you think I was going to let you stop in prison till then!" She checked herself with an effort. "I had better tell you everything from the beginning," she said. "I couldn't write any more to you, because I was only allowed to send the two letters, and I knew both of them would be read by somebody."

She paused a moment.

"I went away after the trial. I was very ill, and Tommy took me to a little place called Looe, down in Cornwall. We stayed there nearly six months. When I came back I took the flat next to him and called myself Miss Vivien. I had made up my mind then what I was going to do. You see there were only two possible ways in which I could help you. One was to find out who killed Marks, and the other was to get you out of prison—anyhow. Of course, after the trial, it seemed madness to think about the first, but then I just had three things to go on. I knew that you were innocent, I knew that for some reason of his own George had lied about you, and I knew that there had been some one else in the flat the day of the murder."

"The man who was with Marks when you arrived," I said. "But you saw him go away, and there was nothing to connect him with the murder, except the fact that he didn't turn up at the trial. Sexton himself had to admit that in his speech."

"There was his face," said Joyce quietly. "It was a dreadful face. It looked as if all the goodness had been burned out of it."

"There are about five hundred gentlemen like that in Princetown," I said, "including several of the warders. Did they ever find out anything about him?"

Joyce shook her head. "Mr. Sexton did everything he could, but it was quite useless. Whoever he was, the man never came forward, and you see there was no one except me who even knew what he was like. It was partly that which first gave me the idea of becoming a palmist. I thought that up here in the West End I was more likely to come across him than anywhere else. And then there were other people I meant to meet—men in the Government who might be able to get your sentence shortened. I knew I was beautiful, and with some men you can do anything if you're beautiful, and—and you don't care."

"Joyce!" I cried, "for God's sake don't tell me—"

"No," she broke in passionately: "there's nothing to tell you. But if the chance had come I'd have sold myself a thousand times over to get you out of prison. The only man I've met who could do anything has been Lord Lammersfield, and he...." She paused, then with a little break in her voice she added: "Well, I think Lord Lammersfield is rather like Tommy in some ways."

"I suppose there are still one or two white men about," I said.

"Lord Lammersfield used to be at the Home Office once, so of course his influence would count for a great deal. Well, he did all that was possible for me, but about six months ago he told me that there was no chance of your being let out for another three years. It was then that I made up my mind to get to know George."

I thrust my hand in my pocket and pulled out my cigarette case. "You—you've got rather thorough ideas about friendship, Joyce," I said, a little unsteadily. "Can I smoke?"

She picked up a box of matches from the table, and coming across seated herself on the arm of my chair.

"Have I?" she said simply. "Well, you taught me them."

She struck a match and held it to my cigarette.

"How did you manage it?" I asked.

"Oh, it was easy enough. I asked Lord Lammersfield to bring him here one day. You know what George is like; he would never refuse to do anything a Cabinet Minister suggested. Of course he had no idea who I was until he arrived."

"It must have been quite a pleasant surprise for him," I said grimly. "Did he recognize you at once?"

Joyce shook her head. "He had only seen me at the trial, and I had my hair down then. Besides, two years make a lot of difference."

"They've made a lot of difference in you," I said. "They've turned you from a pretty child into a beautiful woman."

With a little low, contented laugh Joyce again laid her head on my shoulder. "I think," she said, "that that's the only one of George's opinions I'd like you to share."

There was a moment's silence. Then I gently twisted one of her loose curls round my finger.

"My poor Joyce," I said, "you seem to have been wading in some remarkably unpleasant waters for my sake."

She shivered slightly. "Oh, it was hateful in a way, but I didn't care. I knew George was hiding something that might help to get you out of prison, and what did my feelings matter compared with that! Besides—" she smiled mockingly—"for all his cleverness and his wickedness George is a fool—just the usual vain fool that most men are about women. It's been easy enough to manage him."

"He knows who you are now, of course?" I said.

She nodded. "I told him. He would have been almost certain to find out, and then he would probably have been suspicious. As it is he thinks our meeting was just pure chance."

"But surely," I objected, "he must have guessed you were on my side?"

She gave a short, bitter laugh. "Yes," she said, "he guessed that all right. It's what he calls 'a sacred bond between us.' There are times, you know, when George is almost funny."

"There are times," I said, "when he must make Judas Iscariot feel sick."

"I sometimes wonder why I haven't killed him," she went on slowly. "I think I should have if he had ever tried to kiss me. As it is—" she laughed again in the same way—"as it is we are becoming great friends. He is taking me out to dinner at the Savoy tonight."

"But if he doesn't try to make love to you—" I began.

"Oh!" she said, with a little shrug of her shoulders, "that's coming. At present he imagines that he is being clever and diplomatic. Also there's a business side to the matter."

"Yes," I said; "there would be with George."

"He's horribly frightened of you. Of course he tries to hide it from me, but I can see that ever since you escaped from prison he has been living in a state of absolute terror. His one idea at present is a frantic hope that you will be recaptured. That's partly where I come in."

"You?" I repeated.

"Yes. He thinks that sooner or later, when you want help, you will probably write and tell me where you are."

"And then you are to pass the good news on to him?"

She nodded. "He says that if I let him know at once, he will arrange to get you safely out of the country."

I lay back in the chair and laughed out loud.

Joyce, who was still sitting on the arm, looked down happily into my face. "Oh," she said, "I love to hear you laugh again." Then, slipping her hand into mine, she went on: "I suppose he means to arrange it so that it will look as if you had been caught by accident while he was trying to help you."

"I expect so," I said. "I should be out of the way again then, and you would be so overcome by gratitude—Oh, yes, there's quite a Georgian touch about it."

The sharp tinkle of an electric bell broke in on our conversation. Joyce jumped up from the chair, and for a moment both remained listening while "Jack" answered the door.

"I know who it is," whispered Joyce. "It's old Lady Mortimer. She had an appointment for one o'clock."

"But what have you arranged to do?" I asked. "There's no reason you should put all your people off. I can go away for the time, or stop in another room, or something."

"No, no; it's all right," whispered Joyce. "I'll tell you in a minute."

She waited until we heard the front door shut, and then coming back to me sat down again on my knee.

"I told Jack," she said, "not to let any one into the flat till three o'clock. I have an appointment then I ought to keep, but that still gives us nearly two hours. I will send Jack across to Stewart's to fetch us some lunch, and we'll have it in here. What would you like, my Neil?"

"Anything but eggs and bacon," I said, getting out another cigarette.

She jumped up with a laugh, and, after striking me a match, went out into the passage, leaving the door open. I heard her call the page-boy and give him some instructions, and then she came back into the room, her eyes dancing with happiness and excitement.

"Isn't this splendid!" she exclaimed. "Only this morning I was utterly miserable wondering if you were dead, and here we are having lunch together just like the old days in Chelsea."

"Except for your hair, Joyce," I said. "Don't you remember how it was always getting in your eyes?"

"Oh, that!" she cried; "that's easily altered."

She put up her hands, and hastily pulled out two or three hairpins. Then she shook her head, and in a moment a bronze mane was rippling down over her shoulders exactly as it used to in the old days.

"I wish I could do something like that," I said ruefully. "I'm afraid my changes are more permanent."

Joyce came up and thrust her arm into mine. "My poor dear," she said, pressing it to her. "Never mind; you look splendid as you are."

"Won't your boy think there's something odd in our lunching together like this?" I asked. "He seems a pretty acute sort of youth."

"Jack?" she said. "Oh, Jack's all right. He was a model in Chelsea. I took him away from his uncle, who used to beat him with a poker. He doesn't know anything about you, but if he did he would die for you cheerfully. He's by way of being rather grateful to me."

"You always inspired devotion, Joyce," I said, smiling. "Do you remember how Tommy and I used to squabble as to which of us should eventually adopt you?"

She nodded, almost gravely; then with a sudden change back to her former manner, she made a step towards the inner room, pulling me after her.

"Come along," she said. "We'll lunch in there. It's more cheerful than this, and anyway I want to see you in the daylight."

I followed her in through the curtains, and found myself in a small, narrow room with a window which looked out on the back of Burlington Arcade. A couple of chairs, a black oak gate-legged table, and a little green sofa made up the furniture.

Joyce took me to the window, and still holding my arm, made a second and even longer inspection of McMurtrie's handiwork.

"It's wonderful, Neil," she said at last. "You look fifteen years older and absolutely different. No one could possibly recognize you except by the way you speak."

"I've been practising that," I said, altering my voice. "I shouldn't have given myself away if you hadn't taken me by surprise."

She smiled again happily. "It's so good to feel that you're safe, even if it's only for a few days." Then, letting go my arm, she crossed to the sofa. "Come and sit down," she went on. "We've got to decide all sorts of things, and we shan't have too much time."

"I've told you my plans, Joyce," I said, "such as they are. I mean to go through with this business of McMurtrie's, though I'm sure there's something crooked at the bottom of it. As for the rest—" I shrugged my shoulders and sat down on the sofa beside her; "well, I've got the sort of hand one has to play alone."

Joyce looked at me quietly and steadily.

"Neil," she said; "do you remember that you once called me the most pig-headed infant in Chelsea?"

"Did I?" I said. "That was rather rude."

"It was rather right," she answered calmly; "and I haven't changed, Neil. If you think Tommy and I are going to let you play this hand alone, as you call it, you are utterly and absolutely wrong."

"Do you know what the penalties are for helping an escaped convict?" I asked.

She laughed contemptuously. "Listen, Neil. For three years Tommy and I have had no other idea except to get you out of prison. Is it likely we should leave you now?"

"But what can you do, Joyce?" I objected. "You'll only be running yourselves into danger, and—"

"Oh, Neil dear," she interrupted; "it's no good arguing about it. We mean to help you, and you'll have to let us."

"But suppose I refuse?" I said.

"Then as soon as Tommy comes back tomorrow I shall tell him everything that you've told me. I know your address at Pimlico, and I know just about where your hut will be down the Thames. If you think Tommy will rest for a minute till he's found you, you must have forgotten a lot about him in the last three years."

She spoke with a kind of indignant energy, and there was an obstinate look in her blue eyes, which showed me plainly that it would be waste of time trying to reason with her.

I reflected quickly. Perhaps after all it would be best for me to see Tommy myself. He at least would appreciate the danger of dragging Joyce into the business, and between us we might be able to persuade her that I was right.

"Well, what are your ideas, Joyce?" I said. "Except for keeping my eye on George I had no particular plan until I heard from McMurtrie."

Joyce laid her hand on my sleeve. "Tomorrow," she said, "you must go and see Tommy. He is coming back by the midday train, and he will get to the flat about two o'clock. Tell him everything that you have told me. I shan't be able to get away from here till the evening, but I shall be free then, and we three will talk the whole thing over. I shan't make any more appointments here after tomorrow."

"Very well," I said reluctantly. "I will go and look up Tommy, but I can't see that it will do any good. I am only making you and him liable to eighteen months' hard labour." She was going to speak, but I went on. "Don't you see, Joyce dear, there are only two possible courses open to me? I can either wait and carry out my agreement with McMurtrie, or I can go down to Chelsea and force the truth about Marks's death out of George—if he really knows it. Dragging you two into my wretched affairs won't alter them at all."

"Yes, it will," she said obstinately. "There are lots of ways in which we can help you. Suppose these people turn out wrong, for instance; they might even mean to give you up to the police as soon as they've got your secret. And then there's George. If he does know anything about the murder I'm the only person who is the least likely to find it out. Why—"

A discreet knock at the outer door interrupted her, and she got up from the sofa.

"That's Jack with the lunch," she said. "Come along, Neil dear. We won't argue about it any more now. Let's forget everything for an hour,— just be happy together as if we were back in Chelsea."

She held out her hands to me, her lips smiling, her blue eyes just on the verge of tears. I drew her towards me and gently stroked her hair, as I used to do in the old days in Chelsea when she had come to me with some of her childish troubles. I felt an utter brute to think that I could ever have doubted her loyalty, even for an instant.

How long we kept the luckless Jack waiting on the mat I can't say, but at last Joyce detached herself, and crossing the room, opened the door. Jack came in carrying a basket in one hand and a table-cloth in the other. If he felt any surprise at finding Joyce with her hair down he certainly didn't betray it.

"I got what I could, Mademoiselle," he observed, putting down his burdens. "Oyster patties, galatine, cheese-cakes, and a bottle of champagne. I hope that will please Mademoiselle?"

"It sounds distinctly pleasing, Jack," said Joyce gravely. "But then you always do just what I want."

The boy flushed with pleasure, and began to lay the table without even so much as bestowing a glance on me. It was easy enough to see that he adored his young mistress—adored her far beyond questioning any of her actions.

All through lunch—and an excellent lunch it was too—Joyce and I were ridiculously happy. Somehow or other we seemed to drop straight back into our former jolly relations, and for the time I almost forgot that they had ever been interrupted. In spite of all she had been through since, Joyce, at the bottom of her heart, was just the same as she had been in the old days—impulsive, joyous, and utterly unaffected. All her bitterness and sadness seemed to slip away with her grown-up manner; and catching her infectious happiness, I too laughed and joked and talked as cheerfully and unconcernedly as though we were in truth back in Chelsea with no hideous shadow hanging over our lives. I even found myself telling her stories about the prison, and making fun of one of the chaplain's sermons on the beauties of justice. At the time I remembered it had filled me with nothing but a morose fury.

It was the little clock on the mantlepiece striking a quarter to three which brought us back to the realities of the present.

"I must go, Joyce," I said reluctantly, "or I shall be running into some of your Duchesses."

She nodded. "And I've got to do my hair by three, and turn myself back from Joyce into Mademoiselle Vivien—if I can. Oh, Neil, Neil; it's a funny, mad world, isn't it!" She lifted up my hand and moved it softly backwards and forwards against her lips. Then, suddenly jumping up, she went into the next room, and came back with my hat and stick.

"Here are your dear things," she said; "and I shall see you tomorrow evening at Tommy's. I shan't leave him a note—somebody might open it; I shall just let you go and find him yourself. Oh, I should love to be there when he realizes who it is."

"I know just what he'll do," I said. "He'll stare at me for a minute; then he'll say quite quietly, 'Well, I'm damned,' and go and pour himself out a whisky."

She laughed gaily. "Yes, yes," she said. "That's exactly what will happen." Then with a little change in her voice she added: "And you will be careful, won't you, Neil? I know you're quite safe; no one can possibly recognize you; but I'm frightened all the same—horribly frightened. Isn't it silly of me?"

I kissed her tenderly. "My Joyce," I said, "I think you have got the bravest heart in the whole world."

And with this true if rather inadequate remark I left her.

I had plenty to think about during my walk back to Victoria. Exactly what result the sharing of my secret with Tommy and Joyce would have, it was difficult to forecast, but it opened up a disquieting field of possibilities. Rather than get either of them into trouble I would cheerfully have thrown myself in front of the next motor bus, but if such an extreme course could be avoided I certainly had no wish to end my life in that or any other abrupt fashion until I had had the satisfaction of a few minutes' quiet conversation with George.

I blamed myself to a certain extent for having given way to Joyce. Still, I knew her well enough to be sure that if I had persisted in my refusal she would have stuck to her intention of trying to help me against my will. That would only have made matters more dangerous for all of us, so on the whole it was perhaps best that I should go and see Tommy. I had not the fainest doubt he would be anxious enough to help me himself if I would let him, but he would at least see the necessity for keeping Joyce out of the affair. We ought to be able to manage her between us, though when I remembered the obstinate look in her eyes I realized that it wouldn't be exactly a simple matter.

I stopped at a book-shop just outside Victoria, which I had noticed on the previous evening. I wanted to order a copy of a book dealing with a certain branch of high explosives that I had forgotten to ask McMurtrie for, and when I had done that I took the opportunity of buying a couple of novels by Wells which had been published since I went to prison. Wells was a luxury which the prison library didn't run to.

With these tucked under my arm, and still pondering over the unexpected results of my chase after George, I continued my walk to Edith Terrace. As I reached the house and thrust my key into the lock the door suddenly opened from the inside, and I found myself confronted by the apparently rather embarrassed figure of Miss Gertie 'Uggins.

"I 'eard you a-comin'," she observed, rubbing one hand down her leg, "so I opened the door like."

"That was very charming of you, Gertrude," I said gravely.

She tittered, and then began to retreat slowly backwards down the passage. "There's a letter for you in the sittin'-room. Come by the post after you'd gorn. Yer want some tea?"

"I don't mind a cup," I said. "I've been eating and drinking all day; it seems a pity to give it up now."

"I'll mike yer one," she remarked, nodding her head. "Mrs. Oldbury's gorn out shoppin'."

She disappeared down the kitchen stairs, and opening the door of my room I discovered the letter she had referred to stuck up on the mantelpiece. I took it down with some curiosity. It was addressed to James Nicholson, Esq., and stamped with the Strand postmark. I did not recognize the writing, but common-sense told me that it could only be from McMurtrie or one of his crowd.

When I opened the envelope I found that it contained a half-sheet of note-paper, with the following words written in a sloping, foreign-looking hand:

"You will receive either a message or a visitor at five o'clock tomorrow afternoon. Kindly make it convenient to be at home at that hour."

That was all. There was no signature and no address, and it struck me that as an example of polite letter-writing it certainly left something to be desired. Still, the message was clear enough, which was the chief point, so, folding it up, I thrust it back into the envelope and put it away in my pocket. After all, one can't expect a really graceful literary style from a High Explosives Syndicate.

I wondered whether the note meant that the preparations which were being made for me at Tilbury were finally completed. McMurtrie had promised me a week in Town, and so far I had only had two days; still I was hardly in a position to kick if he asked me to go down earlier. Anyhow I should know the next day, so there seemed no use in worrying myself about it unnecessarily.

It was my intention to spend a quiet interval reading one of my books, before going out somewhere to get some dinner. In pursuance of this plan I exchanged my boots for a pair of slippers and settled myself down comfortably in the only easy-chair in the room. In about ten minutes' time, faithful to her word, Gertie 'Uggins brought me up an excellent cup of tea, and stimulated by this and the combined intelligence and amorousness of Mr. Wells's hero, I succeeded in passing two or three very agreeable hours.

At seven o'clock I roused myself rather reluctantly, put on my boots again, and indulged in the luxury of a wash and a clean collar. Then, after ringing the bell and informing Mrs. Oldbury that I should be out to dinner, I left the house with the pleasantly vague intention of wandering up West until I found some really attractive restaurant.

It was a beautiful evening, more like June than the end of April; and with a cigarette alight, I strolled slowly along Victoria Street, my mind busy over the various problems with which Providence had seen fit to surround me. I had got nearly as far as the Stores, when a sudden impulse took me to cross over and walk past our offices. A taxi was coming up the road, so I waited for a moment on the pavement until it had passed. The back part of the vehicle was open, and as it came opposite to me, the light from one of the big electric standards fell clear on the face of the man inside. He was sitting bolt upright, looking straight out ahead, but in spite of his opera hat and his evening dress I recognized him at once. It was the man with the scar—the man I had imagined to be tracking me on the previous evening.

CHAPTER XII
A SCRIBBLED WARNING

I have never been slow to act in moments of sudden emergency, and in rather less than a second I had made up my mind. The mere idea of stalking one's own shadower was a distinctly attractive one; surrounded as I was by a baffling sense of mystery and danger I jumped at the chance with an almost reckless enthusiasm.

Coming up behind was another taxi—an empty one, the driver leaning back in his seat puffing lazily at a pipe. I stepped out into the road and signalled to him to pull up.

"Follow that taxi in front," I said quickly. "If you keep it in sight till it stops I'll give you five shillings for yourself."

All the languor disappeared from the driver's face. Hastily knocking out his pipe, he stuffed it into his pocket, and the next moment we were bowling up Victoria Street hard on the track of our quarry.

I sat back in the seat, filled with a pleasant exhilaration. Of course it was just possible that I was making a fool of myself—that the gentleman in front was as innocent of having spied on my movements as the Bishop of London. Still if that were the case there could be no harm in following him, while if he were really one of McMurtrie's friends a closer acquaintance with his methods of spending the evening seemed eminently desirable.

Half way along Whitehall my driver quickened his pace until we were only a few yards behind the other taxi. I was just going to caution him not to get too near, when I realized that unless we hung on as close as possible we should probably lose it in the traffic at the corner of the Strand. The soundness of this reasoning was apparent a moment later, when we only just succeeded in following it across the Square before a policeman's hand peremptorily barred the way.

Past the Garrick Theatre, across Long Acre, and up Charing Cross Road the chase continued with unabated vigour. At the Palace the other driver turned off sharp to the left, and running a little way along Old Compton Street came to a halt outside Parelli's, the well-known restaurant. As he began to slow down I picked up the speaking tube and instructed my man to go straight past on the other side of the street, an order which he promptly obeyed without changing his pace. I didn't make the mistake of looking round. I just sat still in my seat until we had covered another thirty yards or so, and then gave the signal to stop.

The driver, who seemed to have entered thoroughly into the spirit of the affair, at once clambered out of his seat and came round as though to open the door.

"Gent's standin' on the pavement payin' 'is fare, sir," he observed in a hoarse whisper. "Thought ye might like to know before ye gets out."

"Thanks," I said; "I'll take the chance of lighting a cigarette."

I was about to suit the action to the word, when with a sudden exclamation the man again interrupted me.

"There's another gent just come up in a taxi, sir—proper toff too from 'is looks. 'E's shakin' 'ands with our bloke."

"Is he an old man?" I asked quickly—"an old man with glasses?"

"'E don't look very old, but 'e's got a glass right enough—leastways one o' them bow-winder things in 'is eye." He paused. "They've gone inside now, Guv'nor; they won't spot ye if you want to 'op it."

He opened the door, and stepping out on to the pavement I handed him half a sovereign, which I was holding in readiness.

He touched his cap. "Thank ye, sir. Thank ye very much." Then, fumbling in his pocket, he produced a rather dirty and crumpled card. "I don't rightly know what the game is, Guv'nor," he went on in a lowered tone, "but if you should 'appen to want to call on me for evidence any time, Martyn's Garridge, Walham Green, 'll always find me. Ye only need to ask for Dick 'Arris. They all knows me round there."

I accepted the card, and having assured Mr. Harris that in the event of my needing his testimony I would certainly look him up, I lit my delayed cigarette and started to stroll back towards Parelli's. Whoever my original friend and his pal with the eyeglass might be, I was anxious to give them a few minutes' law before thrusting myself upon their society. I had known Parelli's well in the old days, and remembering the numerous looking-glasses which decorated its walls, I thought it probable that I should be able to find some obscure seat, from which I could obtain a view of their table without being too conspicuous myself. Still, it seemed advisable to give them time to settle down to dinner first, so, stopping at a newspaper shop at the corner, I spun out another minute or two in buying myself a copy of *La Vie Parisienne* and the latest edition of the *Pall Mall*. With these under my arm and a pleasant little tingle of excitement in my heart I walked up to the door of the restaurant, which a uniformed porter immediately swung open.

I found myself in a brightly lit passage, inhabited by a couple of waiters, one of whom came forward to take my hat and stick. The other pushed back the glass door which led into the restaurant, and then stood there bowing politely and waiting for me to pass.

I stopped for a moment on the threshold, and cast a swift glance round the room. It was a large, low-ceilinged apartment, broken up by square pillars, but as luck would have it I spotted my two men at the very first attempt. They were sitting at a table in one of the farther corners, and they seemed to be so interested in each other's company that neither of them had even looked up at my entrance.

I didn't wait for them to do it either. Quickly and unobtrusively I walked to the corner table on the left of the floor, and sat down with my back towards them. I was facing a large mirror which reflected the other side of the room with admirable clearness.

A waiter handed me the menu, and after I had ordered a light dinner I spread out *La Vie Parisienne* on the table, and bending over it made a pretence of admiring its drawings. As a matter of fact I kept my entire attention focused on the looking-glass.

I could only see the back of the man with the scar, but the face of his companion, who was sitting sideways on, was very plainly visible. It was a striking-looking face, too. He seemed to be about thirty-five—a tall, clean-shaven, powerfully built man, with bright blue eyes and a chin like the toe of a boot. His hair was prematurely grey, and this, together with the monocle that he was wearing, gave him a curious air of distinction. He looked like a cross between a successful barrister and a retired prize-fighter.

I watched him with considerable interest. If he was another of McMurtrie's mysterious circle, I certainly preferred him to any of the ones I had previously come across. His face, though strong and hard, had none of Savaroff's brutality in it, and he was quite lacking in that air of sinister malevolence that seemed to hang about the doctor.

As far as I could see, most of the talking was being done by the man with the scar. He also appeared to be the host, for I saw him pick up the wine list, and after consulting his companion's taste give a carefully selected order to the waiter. Then my own dinner began to arrive, and putting aside *La Vie*, I propped up the *Pall Mall* in front of me and started to attack the soup.

All through the meal I divided my attention between the paper and the looking-glass. I was careful how I made use of the latter, for the waiter was hovering about most of the time, and I didn't want him to think that I was spying on some of the other customers. So quite genuinely I waded through the news, keeping on glancing in the mirror over the top of the paper from time to time just to see how things were progressing behind me.

That my two friends were getting along together very well was evident not only from their faces but from the sounds of laughter which at intervals came floating down the room. Indeed, so animated was their conversation, that although I had begun my dinner later, I had finished some little time before they had. I had no intention of leaving first, however, so ordering myself some coffee, I sat back in my chair, and with the aid of a cigar, continued my study of the *Pall Mall*.

I was in the middle of a spirited article on the German trouble, headed "What Does the Kaiser Mean?" when glancing in the mirror I saw a waiter advance to the table behind me, carrying a bottle of port in a basket, with a care that suggested some exceptional vintage. He poured out a couple of glasses, and then placing it reverently on the table, withdrew from the scene.

I watched both men take a sip, and saw them set down their glasses with a thoroughly satisfied air. Then the man with the scar made a sudden remark to the other, who, turning his head, looked away over his shoulder into the restaurant. His attention could only have been withdrawn from the table for a couple of seconds at the most, but in that fraction of time something happened which set my heart beating rapidly in a kind of cold and tense excitement.

So swiftly, that if I had not been looking straight in the mirror I should have missed seeing it, the man with the scar brought his hand down over his companion's glass. Unless my eyes were playing me a trick, I distinctly saw him empty something into the wine.

There are rare occasions in life when one acts instinctively in the right way before one's mind has had time to reason matters out. It was so with me now. Without stopping to think, I whipped out a pencil from my pocket, and snatched away a piece of white paper from underneath the small dish of candied fruit in front of me. Spreading it out on the table I hastily scribbled the following words:

"Don't drink your wine. The man with you has just put something into it."

I folded this up, and beckoned to one of the waiters who was standing by the door. He came forward at once.

"Do you want to earn half a sovereign?" I asked.

"Yes, sir," he answered, without the faintest air of surprise.

"Listen to me, then," I said, "and whatever you do don't look round. In the farther corner behind us there's a gentleman with an eyeglass dining with another man. Go up the centre of the room and give him this note. If he asks you who it's from, say some one handed it you in the hall and told you to deliver it. Then go and get my bill and bring it me here."

The waiter bowed, and taking the note departed on his errand, as casually as though I had instructed him to fetch me a liqueur. All the time I had been speaking I had kept a watchful eye on the mirror, and as far as I could tell neither of the two men had noticed our conversation. They were talking and laughing, the man I had sent the message to lightly fingering the stem of his wine-glass, and blowing thin spirals of cigarette smoke into the air. Even as I looked he raised the glass, and for one harrowing second I thought I was too late. Then, like a messenger from the gods, the waiter suddenly appeared from behind one of the pillars and handed him my note on a small silver tray.

He took it casually with his left hand; at the same time setting down his wine-glass on the table. I saw him make an excuse to his host, and then open it and read it. I don't know exactly what I had expected him to do next, but the result was certainly surprising. Instead of showing any amazement or even questioning the waiter, he made some laughing remark to his companion, and putting his hand in his pocket pulled out a small leather case from which he extracted a card.

Bending over the table he wrote two or three words in pencil, and handed it to the waiter. As he did so the edge of his sleeve just caught the wine-glass. I saw the other man start up and stretch out his hand, but he was too late to save it. Over it went, breaking into pieces against one of the plates, and spilling the wine all across the table-cloth.

It was done so neatly that I could almost have sworn it was an accident. Indeed the exclamation of annoyance with which the culprit greeted his handiwork sounded so perfectly genuine that if I hadn't known what was in the note I should have been completely deceived. I saw the waiter step forward and dab hurriedly at the stain with a napkin, while the author of the damage, coolly pulling up another glass, helped himself to a fresh supply from the bottle. A more beautifully carried out little bit of acting it has never been my good luck to witness.

If the man with the scar suspected anything (which I don't think he did) he was at least intelligent enough to keep the fact to himself. He laughed heartily over the contretemps, and taking out his cigar-case offered his companion a choice of the contents. I saw the latter shake his head, raising his half-finished cigarette as much as to indicate his preference for that branch of smoking. It struck me, however, that his refusal was possibly dictated by other motives.

Full of curiosity as I was, I thought it better at this point not to tempt Fate any further. At any moment the man with the scar might look round, and although I was some distance away, it was quite likely that if he did he would recognize my reflection in the mirror. I was doubly anxious now to avoid any such mischance, so, picking up *La Vie*, I opened its immoral but conveniently spacious pages, and from behind their shelter waited for my bill.

It was not long in coming. Impassive as ever, the waiter reappeared with his little silver tray, which this time contained a white slip folded across in the usual fashion. As I took it up I felt something inside, and opening it I discovered a small visiting card with the following inscription:

MR. BRUCE LATIMER 145 *Jermyn Street*, W.

Scribbled across the top in pencil were the following words:

"Thanks. I shall be still more grateful if you will look me up at the above address."

Quickly and unobtrusively I tucked it away in my waistcoat pocket, and glancing at the total of the bill, which came to about fifteen shillings, put down a couple of my few remaining sovereigns. It pays to be a little extravagant when you have been well served.

A swift inspection of the mirror showed me that neither of the occupants of the end table was looking in my direction, so taking my chance I rose quickly to my feet and stepped forward behind the shelter of the nearest pillar. Here I was met by another waiter who handed me my hat and stick, while his impassive colleague, pocketing the two pounds, advanced to the door and opened it before me with a polite bow. I felt rather like the hero of a melodrama making his exit after the big scene.

Once in the street, the full realization of what I had just been through came to me with a sort of curious shock. It seemed an almost incredible thing that a man should make an attempt to drug or poison another in a public restaurant, but, unless I was going off my head, that was what had actually occurred. Of course I might possibly have been mistaken in what I saw in the glass, but the readiness with which Mr. Latimer (somehow the name seemed vaguely familiar to me) had accepted my hint rather knocked that theory on the head. It showed that he, at all events, had not regarded such a contingency as being the least bit incredible.

I began to try and puzzle out in my mind what bearings this amazing incident could have on my own affairs. I was not even sure as yet whether the man with the scar had been really spying on my movements or whether my seeing him twice on the night of my arrival in Town had been purely a matter of coincidence. If he was a friend of McMurtrie's, it seemed to stand to reason that' Mr. Bruce Latimer was not. Even in such a weird sort of syndicate as I had apparently stumbled against it was hardly probable that the directors would attempt to poison each other in West End restaurants.

The question was should I accept the invitation pencilled across the card? I was anxious enough in all conscience to find out something definite about McMurtrie and his friends, but I certainly had no wish to mix myself up with any mysterious business in which I was not quite sure that they were concerned. For the time being my own affairs provided me with all the interest and excitement that I needed. Besides, even if the man with the scar was one of the gang, and had really tried to poison or drug his companion, I was scarcely in a position to offer the latter my assistance. Apart altogether from the fact that I had given my promise to the doctor, it was obviously impossible for me to explain to a complete stranger how I came to be mixed up with the matter. An escaped convict, however excellent his intentions may be, is bound to be rather handicapped in his choice of action.

With my mind busy over these problems I pursued my way home, only stopping at a small pub opposite Victoria to buy myself a syphon of soda and a bottle of drinkable whisky. With these under my arm (it's extraordinary how penal servitude relieves one of any false pride) I continued my journey, reaching the house just as Big Ben was booming out the stroke of half-past nine.

·   It seemed a bit early to turn in, but I had had such a varied and emotional day that the prospect of a good night's rest rather appealed to me. So, after mixing myself a stiff peg, I undressed and got into bed, soothing my harassed mind with another chapter or two of H.G. Wells before attempting to go to sleep. So successful was this prescription that when I did drop off it was into a deep, dreamless slumber which was only broken by the appearance of Gertie 'Uggins with a cup of tea at eight o'clock the next morning.

Soundly and long as I had slept I didn't hurry about getting up. According to Joyce, Tommy would not be back until somewhere about two, and I had had so many grisly mornings of turning out at five o'clock after a night of sleepless horror that the mere fact of being able to lie in bed between clean sheets was still something of a novelty and a pleasure. Lie in bed I accordingly did, and, in the process of consuming several cigarettes, continued to ponder over the extraordinary events of the previous evening.

When I did roll out, it was to enjoy another nice hot bath and an excellent breakfast. After that I occupied myself for some time by running over the various notes and calculations which I had made while I was with McMurtrie, just in case I found it necessary to start the practical side of my work earlier than I expected. Everything seemed right, and savagely anxious as I was to stay in town till I could find some clue to the mystery of George's treachery, I felt also an intense eagerness to get to grips with my new invention. I was positively hungry for a little work. The utter idleness, from any intelligent point of view, of my three years in prison, had been almost the hardest part of it to bear.

At about a quarter to two I left the house, and making my way down on to the embankment set off for Chelsea. It was a delightful day, warm and sunny as July; and this, combined with the fact that I was on my way to see Tommy, lifted me into a most cheerful frame of mind. Indeed I actually caught myself whistling—a habit which I don't think I had indulged in since my eventful visit to Mr. Marks.

I looked up at George's house as I passed, but except for a black cat sunning herself on the top of the gatepost there was no sign of life about the place. My thoughts went back to Joyce, and I wondered how the dinner party at the Savoy had gone off. I could almost see George sitting at one side of the table with that insufferable air of gallantry and self-satisfaction that he always assumed in the presence of a pretty girl. Poor, brave little Joyce! If the pluck and loyalty of one's friends counted for anything, I was certainly as well off as any one in London.

As I drew near Florence Mansions I felt a sort of absurd inclination to chuckle out loud. Much as I disliked the thought of dragging Tommy into my tangled affairs, the prospect of springing such a gorgeous surprise on him filled me with a mischievous delight. Up till now, except for my arrest and sentence, I had never seen anything upset his superb self-possession in the slightest degree.

A glance at the board in the hall as I turned in showed me that he had arrived. I marched along the passage till I came to his flat, and lifting the knocker gave a couple of sharp raps. There was a short pause; then I heard the sound of footsteps, and a moment later Tommy himself opened the door.

He was wearing the same dressing-gown that I remembered three years ago, and at the sight of his untidy hair and his dear old badly-shaved face I as nearly as possible gave the show away. Pulling myself together with an effort, however, I made him a polite bow.

"Mr. Morrison?" I inquired in my best assumed voice.

"That's me all right," said Tommy.

"My name's Nicholson," I said. "I am an artist. I was asked to look you up by a friend of yours—Delacour of Paris."

I had mentioned a man for whose work I knew Tommy entertained a profound respect.

"Oh, come in," he cried, swinging open the door and gripping my hand; "come in, old chap. Delighted to see you. The place is in a hell of a mess, but you won't mind that. I've only just got back from sailing."

He dragged me into the studio, which was in the same state of picturesque confusion as when I had last seen it, and pulling up a large easy-chair thrust me down into its capacious depths.

"I'm awfully glad I was in," he went on. "I wouldn't have missed you for the world. How's old Delacour? I haven't seen him for ages. I never get over to Paris these days."

"Delacour's all right," I answered—"at least, as far as I know."

Tommy walked across the room to a corner cupboard. "You'll have a drink, won't you?" he asked; "there's whisky and brandy, and Grand Marnier, and I've got a bottle of port somewhere if you'd care for a glass."

There was a short pause. Then in my natural voice I remarked quietly and distinctly: "You were always a drunken old blackguard, Tommy."

The effect was immense. For a moment Tommy remained perfectly still, his mouth open, his eyes almost starting out of his head. Then quite suddenly he sat down heavily on the couch, clutching a bottle of whisky in one hand and a tumbler in the other.

"Well, I'm damned!" he whispered.

"Never mind, Tommy," I said cheerfully; "you'll be in the very best society."

CHAPTER XIII
REGARDING MR. BRUCE LATIMER

For perhaps a second Tommy remained motionless; then sitting up he removed the cork, and poured himself out about a quarter of a tumbler of neat spirit. He drained this off at a gulp, and put down both the glass and the bottle.

"God deliver us!" he observed; "is it really you?"

I nodded. "What's left of me, Tommy."

He jumped to his feet, and the next moment he was crushing my hands with a grip that would have broken some people's fingers. "You old ruffian!" he muttered; "I always said you'd do something like this. Lord alive, it's good to see you, though!" Then, pulling me up out of the chair, he caught me by the shoulders and stared incredulously into my face. "But what the devil's happened? What have you done to yourself?"

"I know what I'm going to do to myself," I replied. "I am going to get outside some of that drink you were talking about—if there's any left."

With something between a laugh and a choke he let me go, and crossing to the couch picked up the whisky and splashed out a generous tot into the glass.

"Here you are—and I'm hanged if I don't have another one myself. I believe I could drink the whole bottle without turning a hair."

"I'm quite sure you could, Tommy," I said, "unless you've deteriorated."

We raised our tumblers and clinked them together with a force that cracked mine from the rim to the bottom. I drained off the contents, however, before they could escape, and flung the broken glass into the fireplace.

"It would have been blasphemous to drink out of it again in any case," I said.

With a big, happy laugh Tommy followed my example. Then he came up again and caught me by the arm, as though to make sure that I was still there.

"Neil, old son," he said, "I'm so glad to see you that I shall start wrecking the blessed studio in a minute. For God's sake tell me what it all means."

"Sit down, then," I said; "sit down and give me a chance. It's—it's a hell of a yarn, Tommy."

He laughed again, and letting go my arm threw himself back into the easy-chair.

"It would be," he said.

I always have a feeling that I can talk better when I am on my feet, and so, while Tommy sat there puffing out great clouds of smoke from a huge cherry-wood pipe, I paced slowly up and down the room giving him my story. Like Joyce, he listened to me without saying a word or interrupting me in any way. I told him everything that had happened from the moment when I had escaped from prison to the time when I had given my promise that I would come and look him up.

"I couldn't help it, Tommy," I finished. "I didn't want to drag you in, but you know what Joyce is when she has once made up her mind about anything. I thought the only way was to come and see you. Between us—"

I got no further, for with a sudden exclamation—it sounded more like a growl than anything else—Tommy had risen from his chair.

"And do you mean to tell me that, if it hadn't been for Joyce, you wouldn't have come! By Gad, Neil, if I wasn't so glad to see you I'd—I'd—" Words failed him, and gripping hold of my hands again he wrung them with a force that made me wince.

Then, suddenly dropping them, he started to stride about the room. "Lord, what a yarn!" he exclaimed. "What a hell of a yarn!"

"Well, I told you it was," I said, nursing my crushed fingers.

"I knew something had happened. I knew at least that you weren't going to be taken alive; but this—" He stopped short in front of me and once more gazed incredulously into my face. "I wouldn't know you from the Angel Gabriel!" he added.

"Except that he's clean shaven," I said. Then I paused. "Look here, Tommy," I went on seriously, "what are we going to do about Joyce? I'm all right, you see. There's nothing to prevent me clearing out of the country directly I've finished with McMurtrie. If I choose to go and break George's neck, that's my own business. I am not going to have you and Joyce mixed up in the affair."

Tommy sat down on the edge of the table. "My dear chap," he said slowly, "do you understand anything about Joyce at all? Do you realize that ever since the trial she has had only one idea in her mind—to get you out of prison? She has lived for nothing else the last three years. All this palmistry business was entirely on your account. She wanted to make money and get to know people who could help her, and she's done it—done it in the most astounding way. When she found it was too soon for your sentence to be altered she even made up some mad plan of taking a cottage near the prison and bribing one of the warders with that eight hundred pounds you left her. It was all I could do to put her off by telling her that you would probably be shot trying to get away. Is it likely she'll chuck the whole thing up now, just when there's really a chance of helping you?"

"But there isn't a chance," I objected. "If we couldn't find out the truth at the trial it's not likely we shall now—unless I choke it out of George. Besides, it's quite possible that even he doesn't know who really killed Marks. He may only have lied about me for some reason of his own."

Tommy nodded impatiently. "That's likely enough, but it's all my eye to say we can't help you. There are a hundred ways in which you'll want friends. To start with, all this business of McMurtrie's, or whatever his name is, sounds devilish queer to me. I don't believe his yarn any more than you do. There's something shady about it, you can be certain. When are you supposed to start work?"

I looked at the clock. "I shall know in about an hour," I said. "I forgot to tell you that when I came back from Joyce's yesterday I found a note—I suppose from them—saying that I should have a message or a visitor at five o'clock today, and would I be good enough to be home at that time. At least it wasn't put quite so politely." Then I paused. "Good Lord!" I exclaimed, "that reminds me. I haven't told you the most amazing part of the whole yarn." I put my hand in my pocket and pulled out the card which had been sent me in the restaurant. "Have you ever heard of a man called Bruce Latimer?" I asked.

To my amazement Tommy nodded his head. "Bruce Latimer," he repeated. "Yes, I know *a* Bruce Latimer?—lives in Jermyn Street. What's he got to do with it?"

"You know him!" I almost shouted.

"Yes, slightly. He belongs to the Athenians. He used to do a lot of sailing at one time, but I haven't seen him down there this year."

"Who is he? What is he?" I demanded eagerly.

"Well, I don't know exactly. He's in some Government office, I believe, but he's not the sort of chap who ever talks about his own affairs. Where on earth did you come across him?"

As quickly as possible I told Tommy the story of my visit to Parelli's, and showed him the card which Latimer had sent me by the waiter. He took it out of my hand, looking at me with a sort of half-sceptical amazement.

"You're not joking?" he said. "This is Gospel truth you're telling me?"

I nodded. "Humour's a bit out of my line nowadays, Tommy," I answered. "The Dartmoor climate doesn't seem to suit it."

"But—but—" he stared for a moment at the card without speaking. "Well, this beats everything," he exclaimed. "What in God's name can Bruce Latimer have to do with your crowd?"

"That," I remarked, "is exactly what I want to find out."

"Find out!" repeated Tommy. "We'll find out right enough. Do you think he guessed who it was that sent the note?"

"Most likely he did," I said. "I was the nearest person, but in any case he only saw my back. You can't recognize a man from his back."

Tommy took two or three steps up and down the studio. "*You* mustn't go and see him," he said at last—"that's quite certain. You can't afford to mix yourself up in a business of this sort."

"No," I said reluctantly, "but all the same I should very much like to know what's at the bottom of it."

"Suppose I take it on, then?" suggested Tommy.

"What could you say?" I asked.

"I should tell him that it was a friend of mine—an artist who was going abroad the next day—who had seen it happen, and that he'd given me the card and asked me to explain. It's just possible Latimer would take me into his confidence. He would either have to do that or else pretend that the whole thing was a joke."

"I'm quite sure there was no joke about it," I said. "Whether the chap with the scar belongs to McMurtrie's crowd or not, I'm as certain as I am that I'm standing here that he drugged that wine. He may not have meant to murder Latimer, but it looks uncommon fishy."

"It looks even fishier than you think," answered Tommy. "I'd forgotten for the moment, when you asked about him, but I remember now that some fellow at the Athenians once told me that Latimer was supposed to be a secret-service man of some kind."

"A secret-service man!" I repeated incredulously. "I didn't know we went in for such luxuries in this country except in novels. Do you believe it?"

"I didn't pay much attention at the time—I thought it was probably all rot—but this business—" He stopped, and thrusting his hands into his pockets, again paced slowly up and down the room.

I gave a thoughtful whistle. "By Jove, Tommy!" I said; "if that's a fact and the gentleman with the scar is really one of our crowd, I seem to have dropped in for a rather promising time—don't I! I knew I was up against the police, but it's a sort of cheerful surprise to find that I'm taking on the secret service as well."

Tommy pulled up short. "Look here, Neil!" he said. "I don't like it; I'm hanged if I do. There's some rotten dirty work going on somewhere; that's as plain as a pikestaff. I believe these people are simply using you as a cats-paw. All they want is to get hold of the secret of this new explosive of yours; then as likely as not they'll hand you over to the police, or else...." he paused. "Well, you've seen the sort of crowd they are. It may be all rot about Latimer being in the secret service, but there's no doubt they tried to poison or drug him last night. Men who will go as far as that wouldn't stick at getting rid of you if it happened to suit their book."

I nodded. "That's all true enough, Tommy," I said; "but what am I to do? I took the bargain on, and I've no choice now except to go through with it. I can't walk up to a policeman and say I think Dr. McMurtrie is a dangerous person engaged on some sort of illegal enterprise."

Tommy came up, and laid his hand on my shoulder. "Drop it, Neil; chuck the whole thing and go to America. Joyce has got that eight hundred pounds of yours; and I can easily let you have another two or three. In six months' time you'll be able to make as much money as you choose. You've had three years of hell; what's the good of running any risks that you can avoid? If there's the least faintest chance of getting at the truth, you can be certain I'll do it. Don't go and smash up all the rest of your life over this cursed business. What does it matter if all the fools in England think you killed Marks? He deserved to be killed anyway—the swine! Leave them to think, and clear off to some country where you can start fresh and fair again. It doesn't matter the least where you go to, you're bound to come to the top."

It was about the longest speech I had ever heard Tommy make, and certainly the most eloquent. For a moment indeed I was almost tempted to take his advice. Then the thought of George and all the complicated suffering that I had been through rose up like a wall across my mind.

"No," I said firmly; "I'm damned if I'll go. I'll see this out if it means the end of everything."

As I spoke there came a sharp "ting" from the clock on the mantelpiece, and looking up I saw that it was half-past four. "By Gad, Tommy," I added, "I must go from here, though. I've got to be back at Edith Terrace by five o'clock, or I shall miss this mysterious visitor."

"You're coming back here afterwards?" he asked.

I nodded. "If I can. I haven't the least notion how long they'll keep me, but I told Joyce I would come round and let you know what had happened."

"Good," said Tommy. "Don't be longer than you can help. I'll get in something to eat, and we'll all have supper together—you and I and Joyce, and then we can have a good jaw afterwards. There are still tons of things I want to know about."

He thrust his arm through mine and walked with me to the door of the flat.

"By the way, Thomas," I said, "I suppose the police aren't watching your place, just on the off-chance of my rolling up. They must remember you were rather a particular pal of mine."

"I don't think so," he answered. "They may have had a man on when you first escaped, but if so he must have got fed up with the job by now. Don't you worry in any case. Your guardian angel wouldn't recognize you in that get up—let alone a policeman."

"If there's any justice," I said, "my guardian angel got the sack three years ago."

With this irreverent remark, I shook his hand, and walking down the passage passed out on to the embankment.

Having a good two miles to cover and only five-and-twenty minutes to do it in, it struck me that driving would be the most agreeable method of getting home. I hesitated for a moment between a taxi and a motor bus, deciding in favour of the latter chiefly from motives of sentiment. I had not been on one since my arrest, and besides that the idea of travelling along the streets in open view of the British public rather appealed to me. Since my interview with Tommy I was beginning to feel the most encouraging confidence in McMurtrie's handiwork.

So, turning up Beaufort Street, I jumped on to a "Red Victoria" at the corner, and making my way upstairs, sat down on one of the front seats. It was the first time I had been down the King's Road by daylight, and the sight of all the old familiar landmarks was as refreshing as rain in the desert. Twice I caught a glimpse of some one whom I had known in the old days — one man was Murgatroyd, the black and white artist, and the other Doctor O'Hara, the good-natured Irish medico who had once set a broken finger for me. The latter was coming out of his house as we passed, and I felt a mischievous longing to jump off the bus and introduce myself to him, just to see what he would do.

At the corner of Sloane Square I had an unexpected and rather dramatic reminder of my celebrity. As we emerged from the King's Road a procession of five or six sandwich-men suddenly appeared from the direction of Symons Street, shuffling dejectedly along at intervals of a few yards. They were carrying double boards, on which, boldly printed in red-and-black letters, stared the following announcement:

MADAME TUSSAUD'S

MARYLEBONE ROAD

NEIL LYNDON

A LIFELIKE PORTRAIT

I gazed down at them with a sort of fascinated interest. Somehow or other it seemed rather like reading one's own tombstone, and I couldn't help wondering whether I was in the main hall or whether I had been dignified with an eligible site in the Chamber of Horrors. If it hadn't been for my appointment I should most certainly have taken a cab straight up to Marylebone Road in order to find out.

Promising myself that treat on the morrow, I stuck to my seat, and at ten minutes to five by the station clock we drew up outside Victoria. I got off and walked briskly along to Edith Terrace. Turning the corner of the street, I observed the figure of Miss Gertie 'Uggins leaning against the front railings, apparently engaged in conversation with an errand boy on the other side of the road. As soon as she recognized me she dived down the area steps, reappearing at the front door just as I reached the house.

"I was watchin' for yer," she remarked in a hoarse whisper. "There's summun wants to see yer in there." She jerked her thumb towards the sitting-room. "It's a lidy," she added.

"A lady!" I said. "What sort of a lady?"

"Ow! A reel lidy. She's got a lovely 'at."

"Is she young and dark and rather nice to look at?" I asked.

Gertie nodded. "That's 'er. She wouldn't give no nime, but that's 'er right enough."

I didn't wait to ask any more questions, but putting down my hat on the hall table, I walked up to the sitting-room and tapped lightly on the door.

"Come in," called out a voice.

I turned the handle, and the next moment I was face to face with Sonia.

CHAPTER XIV
A SUMMONS FROM DR. McMURTRIE

She had risen from the sofa as I entered and was standing in the centre of the room. The neatly cut, close-fitting dress that she was wearing suited her dark beauty to perfection and showed off the lines of her lithe, slender figure. She gave me a curious momentary impression of some sort of graceful wild animal.

"Ah!" she exclaimed softly. "I am glad you weren't late. I have to go away quite soon."

I took the hand she held out to me. "My dear Sonia," I said, "why didn't you let me know that you were going to be the visitor?"

"I didn't know myself," she answered. "The doctor meant to come, but he was called away unexpectedly this afternoon, so he sent me instead. I have got a letter for you from him." She let go my fingers gently, and picking up her bag which was lying on the table, opened it and took out an envelope.

"Shall I read it now?" I asked.

She nodded.

I slit up the flap and pulled out a folded sheet of foolscap from inside. It was in McMurtrie's handwriting, but there was no date and no address.

"DEAR MR. NICHOLSON,

"All the necessary arrangements have now been made with regard to your workshop at Tilbury. It is situated on the marshes close to the river, three miles east of the town and a mile to the west of Cunnock Creek. You can reach it either by the main road which runs half a mile inland, or by walking along the saltings under the sea-wall.

"You cannot mistake the place, as it is an absolutely isolated building, consisting of a small cabin or hut, with a large shed attached for your work. It is not luxurious, but we have at least fitted up the interior of your living-room as comfortably as possible, and you will find in the shed everything that you specified in your list as being necessary for your experiments.

"I should be glad if you would arrange to go down there and start work the day after tomorrow. There is a train from Fenchurch Street to Tilbury at 11.45 in the morning, and if you will catch that I will see that there is a trap to meet you at the station and drive you out along the road as near to the place as it is possible to get. This hardly gives you the full week in London which you wished for, but circumstances have arisen that make it of great importance to us to be able to place your invention on the market as quickly as possible. From your own point of view the sooner the work is done the sooner you will be in possession of funds, and so able to make any use of your liberty you choose.

"Sonia has the keys of the building, and will give them you with this letter.

"While you are working at the hut, it will be better, I think, if you stay entirely on the premises. I believe you will find everything you want in the way of food and cooking materials, and you will, of course, take down your own personal belongings with you. In the event of anything you really need having been forgotten, you can always walk into Tilbury, but I should strongly advise you not to do so, except in a case of absolute necessity. Apart from any danger of your being recognized, we are extremely anxious that no one connected with the powder trade should have the least idea that experiments are being conducted with regard to a new explosive. A large part of the immediate value of your invention will consist in its coming on the market as an absolute surprise.

"I have been unexpectedly called away for a few days, but directly I return I shall come down to Tilbury and see you. Should you wish to communicate with me in the interval, you can do so by writing or wiring to me at the Hotel Russell, London, W.C.

"I hope that you have enjoyed your well-earned if rather long-delayed holiday.

"Your sincere friend,

"L.J. McMURTRIE."

I finished reading and slowly refolded the letter.

"You know what this is about, of course, Sonia?" I said.

She nodded again. "They want you to go down there at once. You must do it; you must do everything you are told just at present."

"I ought to be able to manage that," I said grimly. "I've had plenty of practice the last three years."

With a swift, silent movement she came up to me and put her hands on my arm. "You must trust me," she said, speaking in that low passionate voice of hers. "You know that I love you; you know that I am only waiting for the right time to act. When it comes I will give you a chance such as few men have had—a chance that will mean wealth and freedom and—and—love." She breathed out the last word almost in a whisper, and then, raising her hands to my shoulders, drew down my face and pressed her lips to mine.

I have no dislike to being kissed by a beautiful woman; indeed, on the previous occasion when Sonia had so honoured me I had distinctly enjoyed the experience. This time, however, I felt a trifle uncomfortable. I had a kind of unpleasant sensation that somehow or other I was not quite playing the game.

Still, as I have said elsewhere, an escaped convict cannot afford to be too nice in his emotions, so I returned her kiss with the same readiness and warmth as I had done before. Then, straightening myself, I unlaced her arms from my neck, and looked down smilingly into those strange dark eyes that were turned up to mine.

"I'm a poor sort of host," I said, "but you see I am a little out of training. Won't you have some tea or anything, Sonia?"

"No, no," she answered quickly. "I don't want anything. I must go in a minute; I have to meet my father with the car." Then, taking my hand between hers, she added: "Tell me what you have been doing yourself. Have you seen your cousin—the man who lied about you at the trial? I have been afraid about him; I have been afraid that you would kill him and perhaps be found out."

"There's no hurry about it," I said. "It's rather pleasant to have something to look forward to."

"But you have seen him?"

I nodded. "I had the pleasure of walking behind him for a couple of miles yesterday. He looks a little worried, but quite well otherwise."

She laughed softly. "Ah, you can afford to let him wait. And the girl, Joyce? Have you seen her?"

She asked the question quite dispassionately, and yet in some curious way I had a sudden vague feeling of menace and danger. Anyhow, I lied as readily and instinctively as Ananias.

"No," I said. "George is the only part of my past that interests me now."

I thought I saw the faintest possible expression of satisfaction flicker across her face, but if so it was gone immediately.

"Sonia," I said, "there is a question I want to ask you. Am I developing nerves, or have I really been watched and followed since I came to London?"

She looked at me steadily. "What makes you think so?" she asked.

"Well," I said, "it may be only my imagination, but I have an idea that a gentleman with a scar on his face has been taking a rather affectionate interest in my movements."

For a moment she hesitated; then with a rather scornful little laugh she shrugged her shoulders. "I told them it was unnecessary!" she said.

I crushed down the exclamation that nearly rose to my lips. So the man with the scar *was* one of McMurtrie's emissaries, after all, and his dealings with Mr. Bruce Latimer most certainly did concern me. The feeling that I was entangled in some unknown network of evil and mystery came back to me with redoubled force.

"I hope the report was satisfactory," I said lightly.

Sonia nodded. "They only wanted to make certain that you had gone to Edith Terrace. I don't think you were followed after the first night."

"No," I said, "I don't think I was." Precisely how much the boot had been on the opposite foot it seemed unnecessary to add.

Sonia walked to the table and again opened her bag. "I mustn't stay any longer—now," she said. "I have to meet the car at six o'clock. Here are the keys." She took them out and came across to where I was standing.

"Good-bye, Sonia," I said, taking her hands in mine.

"No, no," she whispered; "don't say that: I hate the word. Listen, Neil. I am coming to you again, down there, when we shall be alone—you and I together. I don't know when it will be, but soon—ah, just as soon as I can. I can't help you, not in the way I mean to, until you have finished your work, but I will come to you, and—and...." Her voice failed, and lowering her head she buried her face in my coat. I bent down, and in a moment her lips met mine in another long, passionate kiss. It was hard to see how I could have acted otherwise, but all the same I didn't feel exactly proud of myself.

Indeed, it was in a state of very mixed emotions that I came back into the house after we had walked together as far as the corner of the street. The mere fact of my having found out for certain that the man with the scar was an agent of McMurtrie's was enough in itself to give me food for pretty considerable thought. Any suspicions I may have had as to the genuineness of the doctor's story were now amply confirmed. I was not intimately acquainted with the working methods of the High Explosives Trade, but it seemed highly improbable that they could involve the drugging or poisoning of Government officials in public restaurants. As Tommy had forcibly expressed it, there was some "damned shady work" going on somewhere or other, and for all Sonia's comforting assurances concerning my own eventual prosperity, I felt that I was mixed up in about as sinister a mystery as even an escaped murderer could very well have dropped into.

The thought of Sonia brought me back to the question of our relations. I could hardly doubt now that she loved me with all the force of her strange, sullen, passionate nature, and that for my sake she was preparing to take some pretty reckless step. What this was remained to be seen, but that it amounted to a practical betrayal of her father and McMurtrie seemed fairly obvious from the way in which she had spoken. From the point of view of my own interests, it was an amazing stroke of luck that she should have fallen in love with me, and yet somehow or other I felt distinctly uncomfortable about it. I seemed to be taking an unfair advantage of her, though how on earth I was to avoid doing so was a question which I was quite unable to solve. I certainly couldn't afford to quarrel with her, and she was hardly the sort of girl to accept anything in the nature of a disappointment to her affections in exactly a philosophic frame of mind.

I was still pondering over this rather delicate problem, when there came a knock at the door, and in answer to my summons Gertie 'Uggins inserted her head.

"The lidy's gorn?" she observed, looking inquiringly round the room.

I nodded. "There is no deception, Gertrude," I said. "You can search the coal-scuttle if you like."

She wriggled the rest of her body in round the doorway. "Mrs. Oldbury sent me up to ask if you'd be wantin' dinner."

"No," I said; "I am going out."

Gertie nodded thoughtfully. "Taikin' 'er, I s'pose?"

"To be quite exact," I said, "I am dining with another lady."

There was a short pause. Then, with an air of some embarrassment Gertie broke the silence. "'Ere," she said: "you know that five bob you give me?"

"Yes," I said.

"Well, I ain't spendin' it on no dinner—see. I'm goin' to buy a 'at wiv it—a 'at like 'ers: d'yer mind?"

"I do mind," I said severely. "That money was intended for your inside, Gertie, not your outside. You have your dinner, and I'll buy you a new hat myself."

She clasped her hands together. "Ow!" she cried. "Yer mean it? Yer reely mean it?"

"I never joke," I said, "on sacred subjects."

Then to my dismay she suddenly began to cry. "You ain't 'alf—'alf bin good to me," she jerked out. "No one ain't never bin good to me like you. I'd—I'd do anyfink for you."

"In that case," I said, "you may give me my hat—and cheer up."

She obeyed both commands, and then, still sniffing, valiantly marched to the front door and opened it for me to go out.

"Goo'-night, sir," she said.

"Good-night, Gertrude," I replied; and leaving her standing on the step I set off down the street. Whatever else prison might have done for me, it certainly seemed to have given me a capacity for making friends.

I reached Florence Court at about a quarter to seven, keeping a sharp lookout along the embankment as I approached for any sign of a loitering detective. Except for one aged gentleman, however, who seemed to be wholly occupied in spitting in the Thames, the stretch in front of the studios was absolutely deserted. Glancing at the board in the hall as I entered, I saw that "Mr. Morrison" and "Miss Vivien" were both "in"—a statement which in Tommy's case was confirmed a moment later by his swift appearance at the door in answer to my knock.

"Mr. Morrison, I believe?" I said.

He seized me by the arm and dragged me inside.

"This is fine. I never thought you'd be back as quick as this. Are things all right?"

"I should hardly go as far as that," I said. "But we seem to be getting along quite nicely."

He nodded. "Good! I just want a wash, and then we'll go right in to Joyce's place. We are going to have supper there, and you can tell us all about it while we're feeding."

He splashed out some water into a basin in the corner of the studio, and made his ablutions with a swiftness that reminded me of some of my own toilets in the grey twilight of a Dartmoor dawn. Tommy was never a man who wasted much trouble over the accessories of life.

"Come along," he said, flinging down the towel on the sofa. "Joyce will be dying to hear what's happened!"

I turned towards the hall, but he suddenly put his hand on my shoulder and pulled me back.

"Not that way. We've a private road now—runs along the back of the studios."

He crossed the room, and opened a door which led out into a narrow stone passage roofed in by glass.

I followed him along this till we came to another door, on which Tommy tapped twice with his knuckles. In a moment we heard a key turn and Joyce was standing on the threshold. When she saw who it was she gave a little cry of welcome and held out both her hands.

"But how nice!" she exclaimed. "I never thought you'd be here so soon."

We had each taken a hand, and talking and laughing at the same time, she pulled us in after her and shut the door.

"At last!" she cried softly; "at last!" And for a second or two we all three stood there just gripping each other's hands and not saying a word. It certainly was rather a good feeling.

Tommy was the first to break the silence. "Damn it," he said huskily, "if Neil didn't look so exactly like a brigand chief I believe I should blubber. Eh, Joyce—how do you feel?"

"I feel all right," said Joyce. "And he doesn't look a bit like a brigand chief. He looks splendid." She stood back and surveyed me with a sort of tender proprietorship.

"I suppose we shall get used to it," remarked Tommy. "It nearly gave me heart disease to begin with." Then, going and locking the side door, he added cheerfully, "I vote we have supper at once. I've had nothing except whisky since I came off the boat."

"Well, there's heaps to eat," said Joyce. "I've been out marketing in the King's Road."

"What have you got?" demanded Tommy hungrily.

Joyce ticked them off with her fingers. "There's a cold chicken and salad, some stuffed olives—those are for you, Neil, you always used to like them—a piece of Stilton cheese and a couple of bottles of champagne. They're all in the kitchen, so come along both of you and help me get them."

"Where's the faithful Clara?" asked Tommy.

"I've sent her out for the evening. I didn't want any one to be here except just us three."

We all trooped into Joyce's tiny kitchen and proceeded to carry back our supper into the studio, where we set it out on the table in the centre. We were so ridiculously happy that for some little time our conversation was inclined to be a trifle incoherent: indeed, it was not until we had settled down round the table and Tommy had knocked the head off the first bottle of champagne with the back of his knife that we in any way got back to our real environment.

It was Joyce who brought about the change. "I keep on feeling I shall wake up in a minute," she said, "and find out that it's all a dream."

"Put it off as long as possible," said Tommy gravely. "It would be rotten for Neil to find himself back in Dartmoor before he'd finished his champagne."

"I don't know when I shall get any more as it is," I said. "I've got to start work the day after tomorrow."

There was a short pause: Joyce pushed away her plate and leaned forward, her eyes fixed on mine; while Tommy stretched out his arm and filled up my glass.

"Go on," he said. "What's happened?"

In as few words as possible I told them about my interview with Sonia, and showed them the letter which she had brought me from McMurtrie. They both read it—Joyce first and then Tommy, the latter tossing it back with a grunt that was more eloquent than any possible comment.

"It's too polite," he said. "It's too damn' polite altogether. You can see they're up to some mischief."

"I am afraid they are, Tommy," I said; "and it strikes me that it must be fairly useful mischief if we're right about Mr. Bruce Latimer. By the way, does Joyce know?"

Tommy nodded. "She's right up to date: I've told her everything. The question is, how much has that affair got to do with us? It's quite possible, if they're the sort of scoundrels they seem to be, that they might be up against the Secret Service in some way quite apart from their dealings with you."

"By Jove, Tommy!" I exclaimed, "I never thought of that. One's inclined to get a bit egotistical when one's an escaped murderer."

"It was Joyce's idea," admitted Tommy modestly, "but it's quite likely there's something in it. Of course we've no proof at present one way or the other. What do you think this girl—what's her name—Sonia—means to do?"

I shrugged my shoulders. "Goodness knows," I said. "It looks as if there was a chance of making a big immediate profit on my invention, and that she intended me to scoop it in instead of her father and McMurtrie. I can't think of anything else."

Tommy pulled up a fresh plate and helped himself to some cheese.

"She must be pretty keen on you," he observed.

"Well, you needn't rub it in, Tommy," I said. "I feel quite enough of a cad as it is."

"You're not," interrupted Joyce indignantly. "If she really loves you, of course she wants to help you whether you love her or not."

"Still, she'll expect a *quid pro quo*," persisted Tommy.

"Then it isn't love," returned Joyce scornfully, "and in that case there's no need to bother about her."

This seemed a most logical point of view, and I determined to adopt it for the future if my conscience would allow me.

"What about your invention?" asked Tommy. "How long will it take you to work it out?"

"Well, as a matter of fact," I said, "it is worked out—as much as any invention can be without being put to a practical test. I was just on that when the smash came. I had actually made some of the powder and proved its power, but I'd never tried it on what one might call a working basis. If they've given me all the things I want, I don't see any reason why I shouldn't fix it up in two or three days. There's no real difficulty in its manufacture. I wasn't too definite with McMurtrie. I thought it best to give myself a little margin."

Tommy nodded. "You've handled the whole thing splendidly up till now," he said. "I rather think it's the ticklish part that's coming, though." Then he paused. "Look here!" he added suddenly. "I've got a great notion. Why shouldn't we run down tomorrow in the *Betty* and have a squint at this place of yours? There's nothing like taking a few soundings when you're not too sure about things."

I drew in a deep breath. "I'd love to, Tommy," I said, "but it's rather asking for trouble, isn't it? Suppose there was still someone about there? If McMurtrie had the faintest idea I'd given away the show—"

"He won't," interrupted Tommy; "he can't. We'll take precious good care of that. Listen here: I've got the whole thing mapped out in my mind. The *Betty's* at Leigh, where I laid her up yesterday. I had a seven-horsepower Kelvin engine put in her last year, so we can get up, whatever the wind is—I know the tide will be about right. Well, my idea is that we three go down to Leigh tomorrow morning and take her up to this place Cunnock Creek, or somewhere near. Then if it's all serene you can land and have a look round; if there seems to be any one about we can just push off again. Joyce and I won't show up at all, anyway: we'll stop on board and let you do the scouting."

"Yes, yes," exclaimed Joyce, her eyes shining eagerly. "Let's go. It can't do any harm, and you might find out all sorts of useful things."

"Besides," added Tommy, "it would be the deuce of a day, and it's a long time since any of us had a good day, eh, Joyce?"

"Three years," said Joyce quietly.

That decided me. "Right you are," I said. "You're—you're something like pals, you two."

We clinched the arrangement with a grip, and then Joyce, jumping up from the table, crossed the room to a small writing-desk. "I've got a time-table somewhere here," she said, "so we can look out the train right away."

"It's all right," said Tommy. "I know 'em backwards. We'll catch the nine-five from Fenchurch Street. It's low water at eight-thirty, so that will get us in about the right time. We can leave the *Betty* at Tilbury or Gravesend afterwards, and come back by train from there. We'll be home for dinner or supper or something."

Joyce nodded. "That will just do," she said. "I am going out again with George in the evening. Oh, I haven't told either of you about last night—have I?"

I shook my head. "No," I said, "but in any case I wish you'd drop that part of it, Joyce dear. I hate to think of you dining with George: it offends my sense of decency."

She took an envelope out of the desk and came back to her place at the table. "I mean to drop it quite soon," she said calmly, "but I must go tomorrow. George is on the point of being rather interesting." She paused a moment. "He told me last night that he was expecting to get a cheque for twelve thousand pounds."

"Twelve thousand pounds!" I echoed in astonishment.

"Where the Devil's he going to get it from?" demanded Tommy.

"That," said Joyce, "is exactly what I mean to find out. You see George is at present under the impression that if he can convince me he is speaking the truth I am coming away with him for a yachting cruise in the Mediterranean. Well, tomorrow I am going to be convinced—and it will have to be done very thoroughly."

Tommy gave a long whistle. "I wonder what dog's trick he's up to now. He can't be getting the money straight: I know they've done nothing there the last year."

"It would be interesting to find out," I admitted. "All the same, Joyce, I don't see why you should do all the dirty work of the firm."

"It's my job for the minute," said Joyce cheerfully, "and none of the firm's work is dirty to me."

She came across, and opening my coat, slipped the envelope which she had taken out of her desk into my inner pocket. "I got those out of the bank today," she said—"twenty five-pound notes. You had better take them before we forget: you're sure to want some money."

Then, before I could speak, she picked up the second bottle of champagne that Tommy had just opened, and filled up all three glasses.

"I like your description of us as the firm," she said; "don't you, Tommy? Let's all drink a health to it!"

Tommy jumped to his feet and held up his glass. "The Firm!" he cried. "And may all the fools who sent Neil to prison live to learn their idiocy!"

I followed his example. "The Firm!" I cried, "and may everyone in trouble have pals like you!"

Joyce thrust her arm through mine and rested her head against my shoulder. "The Firm!" she said softly. Then, with a little break in her voice, she added in a whisper: "And you don't really want Sonia, do you, Neil?"

CHAPTER XV
A HUMAN "CATCH"

It's not often that the weather in England is really appropriate to one's mood, but the sunshine that was streaming down into Edith Terrace as I banged the front door at half-past eight the next morning seemed to fit in exactly with my state of mind. I felt as cheerful as a schoolboy out for a holiday. Apart altogether from the knowledge that I was going to spend a whole delightful day with Tommy and Joyce, the mere idea of getting on the water again was enough in itself to put me into the best of spirits.

I stopped for a moment at the flower-stall outside Victoria Station to buy Joyce a bunch of violets—she had always been fond of violets—and then calling up a taxi instructed the man to drive me to Fenchurch Street.

I found Tommy and Joyce waiting for me on the platform. The former looked superbly disreputable in a very old and rather dirty grey flannel suit, while Joyce, who was wearing a white serge skirt with a kind of green knitted coat, seemed beautifully in keeping with the sunshine outside.

"Hullo!" exclaimed Tommy. "We were just getting the jim-jams about you. Thought you'd eloped with Sonia or something."

I shook my head. "I never elope before midday," I said. "I haven't the necessary stamina."

I offered Joyce the bunch, which she took with a smile, giving my hand a little squeeze by way of gratitude. "You dear!" she said. "Fancy your remembering that."

"Well, come along," said Tommy. "This is the train all right; I've got the tickets and some papers."

He opened the door of a first-class carriage just behind us, and we all three climbed in. "We shall have it to ourselves," he added. "No one ever travels first on this line except the Port of London officials, and they don't get up till the afternoon."

We settled ourselves down, Tommy on one side and Joyce and I on the other, and a minute later the train steamed slowly out of the station. Joyce slipped her hand into mine, and we sat there looking out of the window over the sea of grey roofs and smoking chimney-stacks which make up the dreary landscape of East London.

"Have a paper?" asked Tommy, holding out the *Daily Mail*.

"No, thanks, Tommy," I said. "I'm quite happy as I am. You can tell us the news if there is any."

He opened the sheet and ran his eye down the centre page. "There's nothing much in it," he said, "bar this German business. No one seems to know what's going to happen about that. I wonder what the Kaiser thinks he's playing at. He can't be such a fool as to want to fight half Europe."

"How is the Navy these days?" I asked. "One doesn't worry about trifles like that in Dartmoor."

"Oh, we're all right," replied Tommy cheerfully. "The Germans haven't got a torpedo to touch yours yet, and we're still a long way ahead of 'em in ships. We could wipe them off the sea in a week if they came out to fight."

"Well, that's comforting," I said. "I don't want them sailing up the Thames till I've finished. I've no use for a stray shell in my line of business."

"I tell you what I'm going to do, Neil," said Tommy. "I was thinking it over in bed last night after you'd gone. If there is any possible sort of anchorage for a boat in this Cunnock Creek I shall leave the *Betty* there. It's only a mile from your place, and then either Joyce or I can come down and see you without running the risk of being spotted by your charming pals. Besides, at a pinch it might be precious handy for you. If things got too hot on shore you could always slip away by water. It's not as if you were dependent on the tides. Now I've had this little engine put in her she'll paddle off any old time—provided you can get the blessed thing to start."

"You're a brick, Tommy," I said gratefully. "There's nothing I'd like better. But as for you and Joyce coming down—"

"Of course we shall come down," interrupted Joyce. "I shall come just as soon as I can. Who do you think is going to look after you and do your cooking?"

"Good Lord, Joyce!" I said. "I'm in much too tight a corner to worry about luxuries."

"That's no reason why you should be uncomfortable," said Joyce calmly. "I shan't come near you in the day, while you're working. I shall stay on the *Betty* and cook dinner for you in the evening, and then as soon as it's dark you can shut up the place and slip across to the creek. Oh, it will be great fun—won't it, Tommy?"

Tommy laughed. "I think so," he said; "but I suppose there are people in the world who might hold a different opinion." Then he turned to me. "It's all right, Neil. We'll give you two or three clear days to see how the land lies and shove along with your work. Joyce has got to find out where George is getting that cheque from, and I mean to look up Latimer and sound him about his dinner at Parelli's. You'll be quite glad to see either of us by that time."

"Glad!" I echoed. "I shall be so delighted, I shall probably blow myself up. It's you two I'm thinking of. The more I see of this job the more certain I am there's something queer about it, and if there's going to be any trouble down there I don't want you and Joyce dragged into it."

"We shan't want much dragging," returned Tommy. "As far as the firm's business goes we're all three in the same boat. We settled that last night."

"So there's nothing more to be said," added Joyce complacently.

I looked from one to the other. Then I laughed and shrugged my shoulders. "No," I said, "I suppose there isn't."

Through the interminable slums of Plaistow and East Ham we drew out in the squalid region of Barking Creek, and I looked down on the mud and the dirty brown water with a curious feeling of satisfaction. It was like meeting an old friend again after a long separation. The lower Thames, with its wharves, its warehouses, and its never-ceasing traffic, had always had a strange fascination for me; and in the old days, when I wanted to come to Town from Leigh or Port Victoria, I had frequently sailed my little six-tonner, the *Penguin*, right up as far as the Tower Bridge. I could remember now the utter amazement with which George had always regarded this proceeding.

"Are you feeling pretty strong this morning?" asked Tommy, breaking a long silence. "The *Betty's* lying out in the Ray, and the only way of getting at her will be to tramp across the mud. There's no water for another four hours. We shall have to take turns carrying Joyce."

"You won't," said Joyce. "I shall take off my shoes and stockings and tramp too. I suppose you've got some soap on board."

"You'll shock Leigh terribly if you do," said Tommy. "It's a beautiful respectable place nowadays—all villas and trams and picture palaces—rather like a bit of Upper Tooting."

"It doesn't matter," said Joyce. "I've got very nice feet and ankles, and I'm sure it's much less immoral than being carried in turns. Don't you think so, Neil?"

"Certainly," I said gravely. "No properly-brought-up girl would hesitate for a moment."

We argued over the matter at some length: Tommy maintaining that he was the only one of the three who knew anything about the minds of really respectable people—a contention which Joyce and I indignantly disputed. As far as I can remember, we were still discussing the point when the train ran into Leigh station and pulled up at the platform.

"Here you are," said Tommy, handing me a basket. "You freeze on to this; it's our lunch. I want to get a couple more cans of paraffin before we go on board. There is some, but it's just as well to be on the safe side."

We left the station, and walking a few yards down the hill, pulled up at a large wooden building which bore the dignified title of "Marine and Yachting Stores." Here Tommy invested in the paraffin and one or two other trifles he needed, and then turning off down some slippery stone steps, we came out on the beach. Before us stretched a long bare sweep of mud and sand, while out beyond lay the Ray Channel, with a number of small boats and fishing-smacks anchored along its narrow course.

"There's the *Betty*," said Tommy, pointing to a smart-looking little clinker-built craft away at the end of the line. "I've had her painted since you saw her last."

"And from what I remember, Tommy," I said, "she wanted it—badly."

Joyce seated herself on a baulk of timber and began composedly to take off her shoes and stockings. "How deep does one sink in?" she asked. "I don't want to get this skirt dirtier than I can help."

"You'll be all right if you hold it well up," said Tommy, "unless we happen to strike a quicksand."

"Well, you must go first," said Joyce, "then if we do, Neil and I can step on you."

Tommy chuckled, and sitting down on the bank imitated Joyce's example, rolling his trousers up over the knee. I followed suit, and then, gathering up our various belongings, we started off gingerly across the mud.

Tommy led the way, his shoes slung over his shoulder, and a tin of paraffin in each hand. He evidently knew the lie of the land, for he picked out the firmest patches with remarkable dexterity, keeping on looking back to make sure that Joyce and I were following in his footsteps. It was nasty, sloppy walking at the best, however, for every step one took one went in with a squelch right up to the ankle, and I think we had all had pretty well enough by the time we reached the boat. Poor Joyce, indeed, was so exhausted that she had to sit down on the lunch basket, while Tommy and I, by means of wading out into the channel, managed to get hold of the dinghy.

Our first job on getting aboard was to wash off the mud. We sat in a row along the deck with our feet over the side; Tommy flatly refusing to allow us any farther until we were all properly cleaned. Then, while Joyce was drying herself and putting on her shoes and stockings, he and I went down into the cabin and routed out a bottle of whisky and a siphon of soda from somewhere under the floor.

"What we want," he observed, "is a good stiff peg all round"; and the motion being carried unanimously as far as Joyce and I were concerned, three good stiff pegs were accordingly despatched.

"That's better," said Tommy with a sigh. "Now we're on the safe side. There's many a good yachtsman died of cold through neglecting these simple precautions." Then jumping up and looking round he added cheerfully: "We shall be able to sail the whole way up; the wind's dead east and likely to stay there."

"I suppose you'll take her out on the engine," I said. "This is a nice useful ditch, but there doesn't seem to be much water in it for fancy work."

Tommy nodded. "You go and get in the anchor," he said, "and I'll see if I can persuade her to start. She'll probably break my arm, but that's a detail."

He opened a locker at the back of the well, and squatted down in front of it, while I climbed along the deck to the bows and proceeded to hand in several fathoms of wet and slimy chain. I had scarcely concluded this unpleasant operation, when with a sudden loud hum the engine began working, and the next moment we were slowly throbbing our way forwards down the centre of the channel.

The Ray runs right down to Southend Pier, but there are several narrow openings out of it connecting with the river. Through one of these Tommy steered his course, bringing us into the main stream a few hundred yards down from where we had been lying. Then, turning her round, he handed the tiller over to Joyce, and clambered up alongside of me on to the roof of the cabin.

"Come on, Neil," he said. "I've had enough of this penny steamer business. Let's get out the sails and shove along like gentlemen."

The *Betty's* rig was not a complicated one. It consisted of a mainsail, a jib, and a spinnaker, and in a very few minutes we had set all three of them and were bowling merrily upstream with the dinghy bobbing and dipping behind us. Tommy jumped down and switched off the engine, while Joyce, resigning the tiller to me, climbed up and seated herself on the boom of the mainsail. She had taken off her hat, and her hair gleamed in the sunshine like copper in the firelight.

I don't think we did much talking for the first few miles: at least I know I didn't. There is no feeling in the way of freedom quite so fine as scudding along in a small ship with a good breeze behind you; and after being cooped up for three years in a prison cell I drank in the sensation like a man who has been almost dying of thirst might gulp down his first draught of water. The mere tug of the tiller beneath my hand filled me with a kind of fierce delight, while the splash of the water as it rippled past the sides of the boat seemed to me the bravest and sweetest music I had ever heard.

I think Joyce and Tommy realized something of what I was feeling, for neither of them made any real attempt at conversation. Now and then the latter would jump up to haul in or let out the main sheet a little, and once or twice he pointed out some slight alteration which had been recently made in the buoying of the river. Joyce sat quite still for the most part, either smiling happily at me, or else watching the occasional ships and barges that we passed, most of which were just beginning to get under way.

We had rounded Canvey Island and left Hole Haven some little distance behind us, when Tommy, who was leaning over the side staring out ahead, suddenly turned back to me.

"There's someone coming round the point in a deuce of a hurry," he remarked. "Steam launch from the look of it. Better give 'em a wide berth, or we'll have their wash aboard."

I bent down and took a quick glance under the spinnaker boom. A couple of hundred yards ahead a long, white, vicious-looking craft was racing swiftly towards us, throwing up a wave on either side of her bows that spread out fanwise across the river.

I shoved down the helm, and swung the *Betty* a little off her course so as to give them plenty of room to go by. They came on without slackening speed in the least, and passed us at a pace which I estimated roughly to be about sixteen knots an hour. I caught a momentary glimpse of a square-shouldered man with a close-trimmed auburn beard crouching in the stern, and then the next moment a wave broke right against our bows, drenching all three of us in a cloud of flying spray.

Tommy swore vigorously. "That's the kind of river-hog who ought to be choked," he said. "If I—"

He was interrupted by a sudden exclamation from Joyce. She had jumped up laughing when the spray swept over her, and now, holding on to the rigging, she was pointing excitedly to something just ahead of us.

"Quick, Tommy!" she said. "There's a man in the water—drowning. They've swamped his boat."

In a flash Tommy had leaped to the side. "Keep her going," he shouted to me. "We're heading straight for him." Then scrambing aft he grabbed hold of the tow rope and swiftly hauled the dinghy alongside.

"I'll pick him up, Tommy," I said quietly. "You look after the boat: you know her better than I do."

He nodded, and calling to Joyce to take over the tiller sprang up on to the deck ready to lower the sails. I cast off the painter, all but one turn, and handing the end to Joyce, told her to let it go as soon as I shouted. Then, pulling the dinghy right up against the side of the boat, I waited my chance and dropped down into her.

I was just getting out the sculls, when a sudden shout from Tommy of "There he is!" made me look hurriedly round. About twenty yards away a man was splashing feebly in the water, making vain efforts to reach an oar that was floating close beside him.

"Let her go, Joyce!" I yelled, and the next moment I was tugging furiously across the intervening space with the loose tow rope trailing behind me.

I was only just in time. Almost exactly as I reached the man he suddenly gave up struggling, and with a faint gurgling sort of cry disappeared beneath the water. I leaned out of the boat, and plunging my arm in up to the shoulder, clutched him by the collar.

"No, you don't, Bertie," I said cheerfully. "Not this journey."

It's a ticklish business dragging a half-drowned man into a dinghy without upsetting it, but by getting him down aft, I at last managed to hoist him up over the gunwale. He came in like some great wet fish, and I flopped him down in the stern sheets. Then with a deep breath I sat down myself. I was feeling a bit pumped.

For a moment or two my "catch" lay where he was, blowing, gasping, grunting, and spitting out mouthfuls of dirty water. He was a little weazened man of middle age, with a short grizzled beard. Except for a pair of fairly new sea-boots, he was dressed in old nondescript clothes which could not have taken much harm even from the Thames mud. Indeed, on the whole, I should think their recent immersion had done them good.

"Well," I said encouragingly, "how do you feel?"

With a big effort he raised himself on his elbow. "Right enough, guv'nor," he gasped, "right enough." Then, sinking back again, he added feebly: "If you see them oars o' mine, you might pick 'em up."

There was a practical touch about this that rather appealed to me. I sat up, and, looking round, discovered the *Betty* about forty yards away. Tommy had got the sails down and set the engine going, and he was already turning her round to come back and pick us up. I waved my hand to him — a greeting which he returned with a triumphant hail.

Standing up, I inspected the surrounding water for any sign of my guest's belongings. I immediately discovered both oars, which were drifting upstream quite close to one another and only a few yards away; but except for them there was no sign of wreckage. His boat and everything else in it had vanished as completely as a submarine.

I salvaged the oars, however, and had just got them safely on board, when the *Betty* came throbbing up, and circled neatly round us. Tommy, who was steering, promptly shut down the engine to its slowest pace, and reaching up I grabbed hold of Joyce's hand, which she held out to me, and pulled the dinghy alongside.

"Very nice, Tommy," I said. "Lipton couldn't have done it better."

"How's the poor man?" asked Joyce, looking down pityingly at my prostrate passenger.

At the sound of her voice the latter roused himself from his recumbent position, and made a shaky effort to sit up straight.

"He'll be all right when he's got a little whisky inside him," I said. "Come on, Tommy; you catch hold, and I'll pass him over."

I stooped down, and, taking him round the waist, lifted him right up over the gunwale of the *Betty*, where Tommy received him rather like a man accepting a sack of coals. Then, catching hold of the tow rope, I jumped up myself, and made the dinghy fast to a convenient cleat.

Tommy dumped down his burden on one of the well seats.

"You've had a precious narrow squeak, my friend," he observed pleasantly.

The man nodded. "If you hadn't 'a come along as you did, sir, I'd 'ave bin dead by now—dead as a dog-fish." Then turning round he shook his gnarled fist over the *Betty's* stern in the direction of the vanished launch. "Sunk me wi' their blarsted wash," he quavered; "that's what they done."

"Well, accidents will happen," I said; "but they were certainly going much too fast."

"Accidents!" he repeated bitterly; "this warn't no accident. They done it a purpose—the dirty Dutchmen."

"Sunk you deliberately!" exclaimed Tommy. "What on earth makes you think that?"

A kind of half-cunning, half-cautious look came into our visitor's face.

"Mebbe I knows too much to please 'em," he muttered, shaking his head. "Mebbe they'd be glad to see old Luke Gow under the water."

I thought for a moment that the shock of the accident had made him silly, but before I could speak Joyce came out of the cabin carrying half a tumbler of neat whisky.

"You get that down your neck," said Tommy, "and you'll feel like a two-year-old."

I don't know if whisky is really the correct antidote for Thames water, but at all events our guest accepted the glass and shifted its contents without a quiver. As soon as he had finished Tommy took him by the arm and helped him to his feet.

"Now come along into the cabin," he said, "and I'll see if I can fix you up with some dry kit." Then turning to me he added: "You might get the sails up again while we're dressing, Neil; it's a pity to waste any of this breeze."

I nodded, and resigning the tiller to Joyce, climbed up on to the deck, and proceeded to reset both the mainsail and the spinnaker, which were lying in splendid confusion along the top of the cabin. I had just concluded this operation when Tommy and our visitor reappeared—the latter looking rather comic in a grey jersey, a pair of white flannel trousers, and an old dark blue cricketing blazer and cap.

"I've been telling our friend Mr. Gow that he's got to sue these chaps," said Tommy. "He knows who they are: they're a couple of Germans who've got a bungalow on Sheppey, close to that little creek we used to put in at."

"You make 'em pay," continued Tommy. "They haven't a leg to stand on, rushing past like that. They as near as possible swamped us."

Mr. Gow cast a critical eye round the *Betty*. "Ay! and you'd take a deal o' swampin,' mister. She's a fine manly little ship, an' that's a fact." Then he paused. "It's hard on a man to lose his boat," he added quietly; "specially when 'is livin' depends on 'er."

"What do you do?" I asked. "What's your job?"

Mr. Gow hesitated for a moment. "Well, in a manner o' speakin', I haven't got what you might call no reg'lar perfession, sir. I just picks up what I can outer the river like. I rows folks out to their boats round Tilbury way, and at times I does a bit of eel fishing—or maybe in summer there's a job lookin' arter the yachts at Leigh and Southend. It all comes the same to me, sir."

"Do you know Cunnock Creek?" asked Tommy.

"Cunnock Crick!" repeated Mr. Gow. "Why, I should think I did, sir. My cottage don't lie more than a mile from Cunnock Crick. Is that where you're makin' for?"

Tommy nodded. "We were thinking of putting in there," he said. "Is there enough water?"

"Plenty o' water, sir—leastways there will be by the time we get up. It runs a bit dry at low tide, but there's always a matter o' three to four feet in the middle o' the channel."

This was excellent news, for the *Betty* with her centre-board up only drew about three feet six, so except at the very lowest point the creek would always be navigable.

"Is it a safe place to leave a boat for the night with no one on board?" inquired Tommy.

Mr. Gow shook his head. "I wouldn't go as far as that, sir. None o' the reg'lar boatmen or fishermen wouldn't touch 'er, but they're a thievin' lot o' rascals, some o' them Tilbury folk. If they happened to come across 'er, as like as not they'd strip 'er gear, to say nothin' of the fittings." Then he paused. "But if you was thinkin' o' layin' 'er up there for the night, I'd see no one got monkeyin' around with 'er. I'd sleep aboard meself."

"Well, that's a bright notion," said Tommy, turning to me. "What do you think, Neil?"

"I think it's quite sound," I answered. "Besides, he can help me look after her for the next two or three days. I shall be too busy to get over to the creek much myself." Then putting my hand in my pocket I pulled out Joyce's envelope, and carefully extracted one of the five-pound notes from inside. "Look here, Mr. Gow!" I added, "we'll strike a bargain. If you'll stay with the *Betty* for a day or so, I'll give you this fiver to buy or hire another boat with until you can get your compensation out of our German friends. I shall be living close by, but I shan't have time to keep my eye on her properly."

Mr. Gow accepted the proposal and the note with alacrity. "I'm sure I'm very much obliged to you, sir," he said gratefully. "I'll just run up to my cottage when we land to get some dry clothes, and then I'll come straight back and take 'er over. She won't come to no harm, not with Luke Gow on board; you can reckon on that, sir."

He touched his cap, and climbing up out of the well, made his way forward, as though to signalize the fact that he was adopting the profession of our paid hand.

"I'm so glad," said Joyce quietly. "I shan't feel half so nervous now I know you'll have someone with you."

Tommy nodded. "It's a good egg," he observed. "I think old whiskers is by way of being rather grateful." Then he paused. "But what swine those German beggars must be not to have stopped! They must have seen what had happened."

"I wonder what he meant by hinting that they'd done it purposely," I said.

Tommy laughed. "I don't know. I asked him in the cabin, but he wouldn't say any more. I think he was only talking through his hat."

"I'm not so sure," I said doubtfully. "He seemed to have some idea at the back of his mind. I shall sound him about it later on."

With the wind holding good and a strong tide running, the *Betty* scudded along at such a satisfactory pace that by half-past twelve we were already within sight of Gravesend Reach. There is no more desolate-looking bit of the river than the stretch which immediately precedes that crowded fairway. It is bounded on each side by a low sea wall, behind which a dreary expanse of marsh and salting spreads away into the far distance. Here and there the level monotony is broken by a solitary hut or a disused fishing hulk, but except for the passing traffic and the cloud of gulls perpetually wheeling and screaming overhead there is little sign of life or movement.

"You see them two or three stakes stickin' up in the water?" remarked Mr. Gow suddenly, pointing away towards the right-hand bank.

I nodded.

"Well, you keep 'em in line with that little clump o' trees be'ind, an' you'll just fetch the crick nicely."

He and Tommy went forward to take in the spinnaker, while, following the marks he had indicated, I brought the *Betty* round towards her destination. Approaching the shore I saw that the entrance to the creek was a narrow channel between two mud-flats, both of which were presumably covered at high tide. I called to Joyce to wind up the centre-board to its fullest extent, and then, steering very carefully, edged my way in along this drain, while Mr. Gow leaned over to leeward diligently heaving the lead.

"Plenty o' water," he kept on calling out encouragingly. "Keep 'er goin', sir, keep 'er goin'. Inside that beacon, now up with 'er a bit. That's good!"

He discarded the lead and hurried to the anchor. I swung her round head to wind, Tommy let down the mainsail, and the next moment we brought up with a grace and neatness that would almost have satisfied a Solent skipper.

We were in the very centre of a little muddy creek with high banks on either side of it. There was no other boat within sight; indeed, although we were within three miles of Tilbury, anything more desolate than our surroundings it would be difficult to imagine.

Mr. Gow assisted us to furl the sails and put things straight generally, and then coming aft addressed himself to me.

"I don't know what time you gen'lemen might be thinkin' o' leavin'; but if you could put me ashore now I could be back inside of the hour."

"Right you are," I said. "I'll do that straight away."

We both got into the dinghy, and in a few strokes I pulled him to the bank, where he stepped out on to the mud. Then he straightened himself and touched his cap.

"I haven't never thanked you properly yet, sir, for what you done," he observed. "You saved my life, and Luke Gow ain't the sort o' man to forget a thing like that."

I backed the boat off into the stream. "Well, if you'll save our property from the Tilbury gentlemen," I said, "we'll call it quits."

When I got back to the ship I found Tommy and Joyce making preparations for lunch.

"We thought you'd like something before you pushed off," said Tommy. "One can scout better on a full tummy."

"You needn't apologize for feeding me," I replied cheerfully. "I've a lot of lost time to make up in the eating line."

It was a merry meal, that little banquet of ours in the *Betty's* cabin. The morning's sail had given us a first-rate appetite, and in spite of the somewhat unsettled state of our affairs we were all three in the best of spirits. Indeed, I think the unknown dangers that surrounded us acted as a sort of stimulant to our sense of pleasure. When you are sitting over a powder mine it is best to enjoy every pleasant moment as keenly as possible. You never know when you may get another.

At last I decided that it was time for me to start.

"I tell you what I think I'll do, Tommy," I said. "I'll see if there's any way along outside the sea-wall. I could get right up to the place then without being spotted, if there should happen to be any one there."

Tommy nodded. "That's the idea," he said. "And look here: I brought this along for you. I don't suppose you'll want it, but it's a useful sort of thing to have on the premises."

He pulled out a small pocket revolver, loaded in each chamber, and handed it over to me.

I accepted it rather doubtfully. "Thanks, Tommy," I said, "but I expect I should do a lot more damage with my fists."

"Oh, please take it, Neil," said Joyce simply.

"Very well," I answered, and stuffing it into my side pocket, I buttoned up my coat. "Now, Tommy," I said; "if you'll put me ashore we'll start work."

It was about a hundred yards to the mouth of the creek, and with the tide running hard against us it was quite a stiff little pull. Tommy, however, insisted on taking me the whole way down, just to see whether there was any chance of getting along outside the sea-wall. We landed at the extreme point, and jumping out on to the mud, I picked my way carefully round the corner and stared up the long desolate stretch of river frontage. The tide was still some way out, and although the going was not exactly suited to patent-leather boots, it was evidently quite possible for any one who was not too particular.

I turned round and signalled to Tommy that I was all right; then, keeping in as close as I could to the sea-wall, I set off on my journey. It was slow walking, for every now and then I had to climb up the slope to get out of the way of some hopelessly soft patch of mud. On one of these occasions, when I had covered about three-quarters of a mile, I peered cautiously over the top of the bank. Some little way ahead of me, right out in the middle of the marsh, I saw what I imagined to be my goal. It was a tiny brick building with a large wooden shed alongside, the latter appearing considerably the newer and more sound of the two.

I was inspecting it with the natural interest that one takes in one's future country house, when quite suddenly I saw the door of the building opening. A moment later a man stepped out on to the grass, and looked quickly round as though to make certain that there was no one watching. Although the distance was about three hundred yards I recognized him at once.

It was my friend of the restaurant—Mr. Bruce Latimer.

CHAPTER XVI
CONFRONTING THE INTRUDER

The discovery was a beautifully unexpected one, but I was getting used to surprises by this time. I bobbed down at once behind the sea-wall, and crouched there for a moment wondering what was the best thing to do. After what I had found out it seemed hardly probable that Latimer could be there in the capacity of McMurtrie's caretaker; but if not, how on earth had he hit upon the place, and what was he doing prowling about inside it?

Raising myself up again with extreme care I had another look through the grass. Latimer had left the building and was stooping down in front of the door of the shed, his attention being obviously concentrated on the lock. I was rather a long way off, but as far as I could see he appeared to be trying to slip back the bolt with the aid of a piece of wire.

I think that decided me. However dangerous it might be to show myself, it seemed still more risky to allow some one of whose motives I was at present completely ignorant to inspect my future workshop. Almost before I realized what I was doing I had slipped over the bank and dropped down on to the marsh.

The slight noise I made must have reached Latimer's ears, for he wheeled round with amazing promptness. At the same instant his right hand travelled swiftly into the side pocket of his coat—a gesture which I found sufficiently illuminating in view of what I was carrying myself in a similar place. When he saw how far off I was he seemed to hesitate for a moment; then pulling out a case he coolly and deliberately lit himself a cigarette, and after taking a quick glance round started to stroll slowly towards me. I noticed that he still kept his hand in his side pocket.

My mind was working pretty rapidly as we approached each other. What would happen seemed to me to depend chiefly upon whether Latimer had seen me in the restaurant, and had guessed that it was I who had sent him the message. If not, it struck me that he must be wondering rather badly who I was and what connection I had with the hut.

When we were still twenty yards apart he pulled up and waited for me, smoking his cigarette with every appearance of tranquil enjoyment.

"I beg your pardon, sir," he said in a pleasant, lazy voice, "but I wonder if you could tell me who this building belongs to?"

I came to a halt right in front of him. "Well," I replied boldly, "until I saw you coming out of the door just now I was under the impression that I was the legal tenant."

He smiled, and taking off his hat made me a slight bow.

"I must really beg your pardon," he said. "I was trespassing shamelessly. The fact of the matter is that I am acting on behalf of the District Surveyor, and finding the door open and being unable to get any answer, I took the liberty of looking inside."

If ever in my life I felt confident that a man was telling me a lie it was at that moment, but my belief was certainly due to no fault of Mr. Latimer's. He spoke with a coolness and an apparent candour that would have done credit to a Cabinet Minister.

"The District Surveyor!" I repeated. "And what does that distinguished person want with me?"

Mr. Latimer made a gesture towards the hut with his disengaged hand. "It's nothing of any real importance," he said, "but you appear to have been making some slight alterations here. This wooden building—"

"It's only a temporary structure," I interrupted.

He nodded. "Quite so. Still there are certain bye-laws which we have to see attended to. The Surveyor happened to notice it the other day when he was passing, and he asked me to find out the exact purpose it was intended for. We are bound to make some restrictions about wooden buildings on account of the extra chance of their catching fire."

The idea of the District Surveyor being seriously perturbed over the possibility of my being roasted alive struck me as rather improbable, but I was careful not to give any impression of doubting the statement.

"As a matter of fact," I said, "there is no chance of a tragedy of that sort. I have taken the place to make a few experiments in connection with photography. The stuff I am using is quite uninflammable."

All the time I was speaking I was watching him carefully to see if I could detect the least sign of his recognizing me. For any such indication, however, we might have been utter strangers.

He accepted my falsehood as politely as I had received his.

"Well, in that case," he said, with a smile, "there is really no need for me to bother you any further. I will tell the Surveyor that you are a strictly law-abiding citizen. Meanwhile"—he stepped back and again raised his hat—"let me apologize once more for having broken into your place."

Whether there was any deliberate irony in his remark I was unable to guess; his manner at all events gave no hint of it.

"You needn't apologize," I returned artlessly. "It was my own fault for leaving the door open."

I thought I saw the faintest possible quiver at the corner of his lips, but if so it was gone again at once.

"Yes," he said gravely. "You will find it safer to keep the place locked up. Good-day, sir."

"Good-day," I replied, and turning deliberately away from him I sauntered off towards the hut.

I did not look round until I had reached the door; and even then I made a pretence of dropping my keys and stooping to pick them up. The precaution, however, seemed a little superfluous. Mr. Latimer was some thirty or forty yards away, walking inland across the marsh in the direction of Tilbury. I couldn't help wondering whether he had noticed the mast of the *Betty*, which was just visible in the distance, sticking up demurely above the bank of the creek.

I stepped inside the hut—it was really little more than a hut—and closed the door. The first impression I received was one of being back in my prison cell. The only light in the place filtered in through a tiny and very dirty window, which looked out in the direction that Latimer had taken. For the rest, as soon as my eyes were used to the gloom, I made out a camp bed with blankets on it, a small wooden table and chair, a jug and basin, and in the farther corner of the room a miscellaneous collection of cooking and eating utensils. There was also a large wooden box which I imagined to contain food.

I took in all this practically at a glance, for my mind was still too occupied with my late visitor to trouble much about anything else.

I sat down on the bed and tried to think out the situation clearly. There could be no doubt that Latimer had been spying on the place, if such an unpleasant word could be applied to a gentleman who was supposed to be in Government service. The question was, what did he suspect? I had pretty good evidence that he was up against McMurtrie and the others in some shape or other, and presumably it was on account of my connection with them that I had been favoured with his attentions. Still, this didn't seem to make the situation any the more cheerful for me. If Latimer was really a secret-service man, as some one had told Tommy, it stood to reason that I must be assisting in some particularly shady and dangerous sort of enterprise. I had no special objection to this from the moral point of view, but on the other hand I certainly didn't want to throw away my hardly-won liberty before I had had the satisfaction of settling accounts with George.

I debated with myself whether it would be best to let McMurtrie know that the place was being watched. To a certain extent his interests in the matter seemed to be identical with mine, but my mistrust of him was still strong enough to make me hesitate. Beyond his bare word and that of Sonia I had no proof as yet that he intended to play straight with me.

One thing appeared certain, and that was that Latimer had failed to recognize me as the man who had sent him the warning at Parelli's. In a way this gave me an advantage, but it was a forlorn enough sort of advantage in view of the unknown dangers by which I was surrounded.

I got up off the bed, feeling anything but comfortable, and going to the door had another look round. Latimer had disappeared behind the thin belt of trees that fringed the Tilbury road, and so far as I could see there was no one else about. Getting out my keys, I walked along to the shed and opened the door.

If my living accommodation was a trifle crude, McMurtrie had certainly made up for it here. He had evidently carried out my instructions with the most minute care and an absolute disregard for expense. Lead tanks, sinks, chemicals, an adequate water supply in the shape of a pump—everything I had asked for seemed to have been provided. I looked round the large, clean, well-lighted place with a sensation of intense satisfaction. The mere sight of all these preparations made me ache to begin work, for I was consumed with the impatience that any inventor would feel who had been compelled to leave a big discovery on the very verge of completion.

Coming out, I closed the door again, and carefully turned the key behind me. Then walking back to the hut I locked that up as well. I hadn't the faintest belief in Latimer's story about finding the place open, and apart from making things safe I certainly didn't want to leave any traces of my surprise visit. From what I knew of McMurtrie I felt sure that he had left somebody in charge, and that in all probability Latimer had merely taken advantage of their temporary absence.

After a last glance all round, to make sure that the coast was still clear, I walked rapidly down to the sea-wall and scrambled up on to the top. The tide had risen a bit, but there was just room to get along, so jumping down I set off on my return journey.

There was something very cheering and reassuring in the sight of the *Betty* riding easily at her anchor, as I made my way round the mouth of the creek. Tommy and Joyce were both on deck: the former in his shirt-sleeves, swabbing down his new paint with a wet mop. Directly he saw me he abandoned the job to Joyce, and with a wave of his hand proceeded to get out the dinghy. A minute later he was pulling for the shore.

"All serene?" he inquired calmly, as he ran the boat up to where I was standing.

"Yes," I said. "We needn't hurry; there's no one chasing me." Then pushing her off the mud I jumped in. "I'll tell you the news," I added, "when we get on board."

We headed off for the *Betty*, and as we came alongside and I handed up the painter to Joyce, I felt rather like the raven must have done when he returned to the Ark. As far as peace and security were concerned, my outside world seemed to be almost as unsatisfactory as his.

"How have you got on?" demanded Joyce eagerly.

I climbed up on to the deck.

"I've had quite an interesting time," I said. Then I paused and looked round the boat. "Is Mr. Gow back?" I inquired.

Tommy shook his head. "Not yet. I expect he's blueing some of that fiver in anticipation."

"Come and sit down, then," I said, "and I'll tell you all about it."

They both seated themselves beside me on the edge of the well, and in as few words as possible I let them have the full story of my adventures. At the first mention of Latimer's name Tommy indulged in a low whistle, but except for that non-committal comment they listened to me in silence.

Joyce was the first to speak when I had finished.

"It's hateful, isn't it?" she said. "I feel as if we were fighting in the dark."

"That's just what we are doing," answered Tommy, "but we're letting in a bit of light by degrees though." Then he turned to me. "McMurtrie's got some game on, evidently, and this chap Latimer's dropped on it. That was why they tried to put him out of the way."

"Yes," I said, "and if Latimer is really in the secret service, it must be a precious queer sort of game too."

Tommy nodded. "I wonder if they're anarchists," he said, after a short pause. "Perhaps they want your powder to blow up the Houses of Parliament or the Law Courts with."

I laughed shortly. "No," I said. "Whatever McMurtrie's after, it's nothing so useful and unselfish as that. If I thought it was I shouldn't worry."

"Well, there's only one thing to do," observed Tommy, after a pause, "and that's to go and look up Latimer, as I suggested. You're sure he didn't recognize you?"

I shrugged my shoulders. "I'm sure of nothing about him," I replied, "except that he's a superb liar."

"We must risk it anyhow," said Tommy. "He's the only person who knows anything of what's going on, and he evidently wants to find out who sent him that note, or he wouldn't have answered it as he did. He'll have to give me some sort of explanation if I go and see him. I shall rub it into him that my supposed pal is a perfectly sensible, unimaginative sort of chap—and anyway people don't invent a yarn like that."

"Look!" interrupted Joyce suddenly. "Isn't that Mr. Gow coming along by those trees?"

She pointed away down the creek, and following her direction I saw the figure of our trusty retainer trudging back towards the ship, with a bundle over his shoulder. He had exchanged Tommy's picturesque outfit for some garments of his own, more in keeping with his new and dignified position.

"I'll pick him up," I said; "but what are we going to do about getting back? We had better not try Tilbury, or we may run into Latimer; it would put the hat on everything if he saw us together."

Tommy consulted his watch. "It's just half-past three now," he said. "I vote we run across to Gravesend and catch the train there. Old Whiskers can bring the boat back here after we've gone—if he's still sober."

"Of course he's sober," said Joyce; "look at the beautiful way he's walking."

I should hardly have applied quite such a complimentary adjective to Mr. Gow's gait myself, but all the same Joyce's diagnosis proved to be quite correct. Mr. Gow was sober—most undoubtedly and creditably sober. I rowed to the bank, and brought him on board, and when we told him of our plans he expressed himself as being perfectly competent to manage the return journey single-handed.

"You leave 'er to me," he remarked consolingly. "I shan't want no help—not to bring 'er in here. Some people don't hold with being alone in a boat, but that ain't Luke Gow's way."

He went forward to get up the anchor, while Tommy and I occupied ourselves with the exciting sport of trying to start the engine. It went off at last with its usual vicious kick, and a few minutes later we were throbbing our way out of the creek into the main river.

The tide was right at its highest, and down the centre of the fairway straggled a long procession of big hooting steamers, sluggish brown-sailed barges, and small heavily-burdened tugs, puffing out their usual trails of black smoke. One felt rather like a terrier trying to cross Piccadilly, but by waiting for our chance we dodged through without disaster, and pulled up in a comparatively tranquil spot off the Gravesend landing-stage.

Tommy signalled to one of the boatmen who were hanging about the steps waiting for stray passengers.

"This chap will take us off," he said, turning to Mr. Gow. "You push straight back while the engine's running; she usually stops when we've got about as far as this."

"And I'll come over to the creek some time tomorrow," I added; though in my present circumstances a confident prophecy of any kind seemed a trifle rash.

We went ashore and stood for a moment on the stage watching the *Betty* thread her course back through the traffic. Mr. Gow seemed to handle her with perfect confidence, and relieved on this point we turned round and set off for the station.

We found ourselves in luck's way. An unusually obliging train was due to start in ten minutes' time, and as before we managed to secure an empty compartment.

"I tell you what I want you to do when we get back to town, Joyce," I said. "I want you to help me buy a hat."

"What's the matter with the one you're wearing?" demanded Tommy. "It just suits your savage style of beauty."

"Oh, this new one isn't for me," I explained. "It's for a lady—a lady friend, as we say."

"I didn't know you had any," said Joyce, "except me and Sonia."

I smiled arrogantly. "You underrate my attractions," I replied. "Haven't I told you about Miss Gertie 'Uggins?" Then I proceeded to sketch in Gertrude as well as I could, finishing up with the story of her spirited determination to spend the five shillings I had given her on a really fashionable head-dress.

Tommy slapped his leg and chuckled. "I believe any woman would starve herself to death for something new to wear," he remarked.

"Of course she would," said Joyce with spirit—"any decent woman." Then she turned to me. "I think it's sweet, Neil; I shall give her a new hat myself, just because she loves you."

Tommy laughed again. "You'll find that an expensive hobby to keep up, Joyce," he said. "You'll have to start a bonnet-shop."

All the way back to town we talked and joked in much the same strain, as cheerfully as though none of us had a care in the world. If there had been a stranger in the carriage listening to us, he would, I think, have found it impossible to believe that I was Neil Lyndon, the much-wanted convict, and that Tommy and Joyce were engaged in the criminal pursuit of helping me avoid the police. No doubt, as I said before, the very danger and excitement of our position accounted to some extent for our high spirits, but in my case they were due even more to a natural reaction from the misery of the last three years. Ever since I had met Tommy and Joyce again I seemed to have been shedding flakes off the crust of bitterness and hatred which had built itself up round my soul.

Even my feelings towards George were slowly becoming less murderous. I was still as determined as ever to get at the truth of his amazing treachery if I could; but the savage loathing that I had previously cherished for him was gradually giving place to a more healthy sensation of contempt. I felt now that, whatever his motives may have been, there would be far more satisfaction in kicking him than in killing him. Besides, the former process was one that under favourable circumstances could be repeated indefinitely.

"You're spending the evening with me, Neil, of course," observed Tommy, as we drew into Charing Cross.

I nodded. "We'll take a taxi and buy the hat somewhere, and then drop Joyce at Chelsea. After that I am open to any dissipation."

"Only keep away from the Savoy," said Joyce. "I am making my great surrender there, and it would hamper me to have you and Tommy about."

We promised to respect her privacy, and then, getting out of the train, which had drawn up in the station, we hailed a taxi and climbed quickly into it. Charing Cross is the last place to dawdle in if you have any objection to being recognized.

"Shall we be able to write to you?" asked Joyce. "I shall want to tell you about George, and Tommy will want to let you know how he gets on with

Latimer. Of course I'm coming down to the boat in a day or two; but all sorts of things may happen before then."

I thought rapidly for a moment. "Write to me at the Tilbury post-office," I said. "Only don't make a mistake and address the letter to Neil Lyndon. Too much excitement isn't good for a Government official."

Tommy laughed. "It's just the sort of damn silly thing I should probably have done," he said. "Can't you imagine the postmaster's face when he read the envelope? I should like to paint it as a Christmas supplement to the *Graphic*."

"Where did you tell the man to stop, Joyce?" I asked.

"Holland's," said Joyce. "I am going to buy Gertie a really splendid hat—something with birds and flowers on it. I am sure I know just what she'll think beautiful. I suppose I had better tell them to send it round to you at Edith Terrace. You won't want to carry it about London."

"Not unless Tommy likes to wear it," I said. "I think I'm disguised enough as it is."

We pulled up outside Mr. Holland's imposing shop-front, and Joyce, who was sitting next the door, got up from her seat. Then she leaned forward and kissed me.

"Good-bye, Neil," she said. "I shall come down on Tuesday and go straight to the *Betty*, unless I hear anything special from you before then." She paused. "And oh, dear Neil," she added, "you will be careful, won't you? If anything was to happen now, I believe I should kill George and jump into the Thames."

"In that case," I said, "I shall be discretion itself. I couldn't allow George anything like so charming an end; it would be quite wasted on him."

Joyce smiled happily and, opening the door, jumped out on to the pavement. "You keep the taxi on," she said. "I shall take a bus home. I can't be hurried over buying a hat—even if it's for Gertie. Where shall I tell the man to go to?"

"Better say the Studio," answered Tommy. "We both want a wash and a drink before we start dissipating."

For an escaped murderer and his guilty accessory, I am afraid that our dissipation proved to be rather a colourless affair. Tommy had always had simple tastes in the way of amusement, and even if it had been safe for us to parade the West End in each other's company, I certainly had no wish to waste my time over a theatre or anything of that sort. I found that real life supplied me with all the drama I needed just at present.

What we actually did was to dine quietly in a little out-of-the-way restaurant just off Sloane Square, and then play billiards for the remainder of the evening in a room above a neighbouring tavern. We had several most exciting games. In old days I had been able to beat Tommy easily, but owing to a regrettable oversight on the part of the Government there is no table at Princetown, and in consequence I was rather short of practice.

Afterwards Tommy walked with me as far as Victoria, where we discussed such arrangements for the future as we were in a position to make.

"I'll write to you, anyway, Neil," he said, "as soon as I've tackled Latimer; and I'll probably come down with Joyce on Tuesday. If you want me any time before, send me a wire."

I nodded. "You'll be more useful to me in London, Tommy," I said. "All the threads of the business are up here. McMurtrie—Latimer— George"—I paused—"I'd give something to know what those three do between them," I added regretfully.

Tommy gripped my hand. "It's all right, old son," he said. "I'm not much of a believer in inspirations and all that sort of rot, but somehow or other I'm dead certain we're going to win out. I've had a feeling like that ever since the trial—and so has Joyce."

"Thanks, Tommy," I said briefly. "You'd give a jellyfish a backbone— you two."

And with a last squeeze of the hand I left him standing there, and set off across the station for Edith Terrace.

It was close on midnight when I got back, and every one in the house seemed to have gone to bed. The light had been put out in the hall, but the door of my sitting-room was partly open, and a small jet of gas was flickering away over the fireplace. I turned this up and, looking round, discovered a large box with Holland's label on it, a note, and a half-sheet of paper—all decorating the table in the centre of the room.

I examined the half-sheet of paper first. It contained several dirty thumb-marks and the following message, roughly scrawled in pencil:

"sir the lady with the hat cum for you about for aclock i told her as you was out and she rote this leter gerty."

Hastily picking up the envelope, I slit open the flap, and pulled out the "leter" from inside. It covered two sides, and was written in Sonia's curious, sloping, foreign-looking hand.

"I have to go away with my father until the end of next week. By that time, if you have succeeded with your invention, there will be nothing to stop our plans. I would have explained everything to you today if you had been here. As it is, *on no account give your secret to any one* until I have seen you. I shall come down to Tilbury either on Friday or Saturday, and within a few hours we can be utterly beyond the reach of any further danger or difficulties. Until then, my lover—SONIA."

I read it through twice, and then slowly folding it up, thrust it back into the envelope.

"It seems to me," I said, "that I'm going to have quite an interesting house-party."

CHAPTER XVII
THE WORKSHOP ON THE MARSHES

I gave Gertie her hat next morning when she brought me up my breakfast. It was a gorgeous thing—rather the shape of a dustman's helmet, with a large scarlet bird nestling on one side of it, sheltered by some heavy undergrowth. Gertie's face, as I pulled it out of the box, was a study in about eight different emotions.

"Oo—er," she gasped faintly. "That ain't never for me."

"Yes, it is, Gertrude," I said. "It was specially chosen for you by a lady of unimpeachable taste."

I held it out to her, and she accepted it with shaking hands, like a newly-made peeress receiving her tiara.

"My Gawd," she whispered reverently; "ain't it just a dream!"

To be perfectly honest, it seemed to me more in the nature of a nightmare, but wild horses wouldn't have dragged any such hostile criticism out of me.

"I think it will suit you very nicely, Gertie," I said. "It's got just that dash of colour which Edith Terrace wants."

"Yer reely mean it?" she asked eagerly. "Yer reely think I'll look orl right in it? 'Course it do seem a bit funny like with this 'ere frock, but I got a green velveteen wot belonged to Mrs. Oldbury's niece. It won't 'alf go with that."

"It won't indeed," I agreed heartily. Then, looking up from my eggs and bacon, I added: "By the way, Gertie, I've never thanked you for your letter. I had no idea you could, write so well."

"Go on!" said Gertie doubtfully; "you're gettin' at me now."

"No, I'm not," I answered. "It was a very nice letter. It said just what you wanted to say and nothing more. That's the whole art of good letter-writing." Then a sudden idea struck me. "Look here, Gertie," I went on, "will you undertake a little job for me if I explain it to you?"

She nodded. "Oo—rather. I'd do any think for you."

"Well, it's something I may want you to do for me after I've left."

Her face fell. "You ain't goin' away from 'ere—not for good?"

"Not entirely for good," I said. "I hope to do a certain amount of harm to at least one person before I come back." I paused. "It's just possible," I continued, "that after I've gone somebody may come to the house and ask questions about me—how I spent my time while I was here, and that sort of thing. If they should happen to ask you, I want you to tell them that I used to stay in bed most of the day and go to the theatre in the evening. Do you mind telling a lie for me?"

Gertie looked at me in obvious amazement. "I *don't* think," she observed. "Wotjer taike me for—a Sunday-school teacher?"

"No, Gertie," I said gravely; "no girl with your taste in hats could possibly be a Sunday-school teacher." Then pushing away my plate and lighting a cigarette, I added: "I'll leave you a stamped addressed envelope and a telegraph form. You can send me the wire first to say if any one has called, and then write me a line afterwards by post telling me what they were like and what they said."

"I can do that orl right," she answered eagerly. "If they talks to Mrs. Oldbury I'll listen at the keyhole."

I nodded. "It's a practice that the best moralists condemn," I said, "but after all, the recording angel does it." Then getting up from the table, I added: "You might tell Mrs. Oldbury I should like to see her."

When that good lady arrived I acquainted her with the fact that I intended to leave her house in about two hours' time. Any resentment which she might have felt over this slightly abrupt departure was promptly smoothed away by my offer to take on the rooms for at least another fortnight. I did this partly with the object of leaving a pleasant impression behind me, and partly because I had a vague idea that it might come in handy to have some sort of headquarters in London where I was known and recognized as Mr. James Nicholson.

Having settled up this piece of business I sat down and wrote to McMurtrie. It was a task which required a certain amount of care and delicacy, but after two trial essays I succeeded in turning out the following letter, which seemed to me about to meet the situation.

"DEAR DR. McMURTRIE:

"As you have probably heard, I received your letter yesterday, and I am making arrangements to go down to Tilbury tomorrow by the 11.45.

"Of course in a way I am sorry to leave London—it's extraordinary what a capacity for pleasure a prolonged residence in the country gives one—but at the same time I quite agree with you that business must come first.

"I shall start work directly I get down, and if all the things I asked for in my list have been provided, I don't think it will be long before I have some satisfactory news for you. Unless I see you or hear from you before then I will write to the Hotel Russell directly there is anything definite to communicate.

"Meanwhile please give my kind regards to your amiable friend and colleague, and also remember me to his charming daughter.

"Believe me,

"Yours sincerely,

"JAMES NICHOLSON."

With its combined touch of seriousness and flippancy, this appeared to me exactly the sort of letter that McMurtrie would expect me to write. I couldn't resist putting in the bit about his "amiable" friend, for the recollection of Savaroff's manner towards me still rankled gently in my memory. Besides I had a notion it would rather amuse McMurtrie, whose more artistic mind must have been frequently distressed by his colleague's blustering surliness.

I could think of nothing else which required my immediate attention, so going into my bedroom I proceeded to pack up my belongings. I put in everything I possessed with the exception of Savaroff's discarded garments, for although I was keeping on the rooms I had no very robust faith in my prospects of ever returning to them. Then, ringing the bell, I despatched Gertrude to fetch me a taxi, while I settled up my bill with Mrs. Oldbury.

"An' seem' you've taken on the rooms, sir," observed that lady, "I 'opes it's to be a case of 'say orrivar an' not good-bye.'"

"I hope it is, Mrs. Oldbury," I replied. "I shall come back if I possibly can, but one never knows what may happen in life."

She shook her head sombrely. "Ah, you're right there, sir. An' curious enough that's the very identical remark my late 'usband was ser fond o' makin'. I remember 'is sayin' it to me the very night before 'e was knocked dcwn by a bus. Knocked down in Westminister 'e was, and runned over the body by both 'ind wheels. 'E never got over it—not as you might say reely got over it. If ever 'e ate cheese after that it always give 'im a pain in 'is stomick."

An apropos remark about "come wheel come woe" flashed into my mind, but before I could frame it in properly sympathetic language, a taxi drew up at the door with Gertie 'Uggins installed in state alongside the driver.

Both she and Mrs. Oldbury stood on the step, and waved farewell to me as I drove down the street. I was quite sorry to leave them. I felt that they both liked me in their respective ways, and my present list of amiably disposed acquaintances was so small that I objected to curtailing it by the most humble member.

All the way to Tilbury I occupied myself with the hackneyed but engrossing pursuit of pondering over my affairs. Apart from my own private interest in the matter, which after all was a fairly poignant one, the mysterious adventure in which I was involved filled me with a profound curiosity. Latimer's dramatic re-entry on to the scene had thrown an even more sinister complexion over the whole business than it boasted before, and, like a man struggling with a jig-saw problem, I tried vainly to fit together the various pieces into some sort of possible solution.

I was still engaged in this interesting occupation when the train ran into Tilbury station. Without waiting for a porter I collected my various belongings, and stepped out on to the platform.

McMurtrie had told me in his letter that he would arrange for some one to meet me; and looking round I caught sight of a burly red-faced gentleman in a tight jacket and a battered straw hat, sullenly eyeing the various passengers who had alighted. I walked straight up to him.

"Are you waiting for me—Mr. James Nicholson?" I asked.

He looked me up and down in a kind of familiar fashion that distinctly failed to appeal to me.

"That's right," he said. Then as a sort of afterthought he added, "I gotter trap outside."

"Have you?" I said. "I've got a couple of bags inside, so you'd better come and catch hold of one of them."

His unpleasantly red face grew even redder, and for a moment he seemed to meditate some spirited answer. Then apparently he thought better of it, and slouching after me up the platform, possessed himself of the larger and heavier of my two bags, which I had carefully left for him.

The trap proved to be a ramshackle affair with an ill-kept but powerful-looking horse between the shafts. I climbed up, and as I took my seat I observed to my companion that I wished first of all to call at the post-office.

"I dunno nothin' 'bout that," he grunted, flicking his whip. "My orders was to drive you to Warren's Copse."

"I don't care in the least what your orders were," I answered. "You can either go to the post-office or else you can go to the Devil. There are plenty of other traps in Tilbury."

He was evidently unused to this crisp style of dialogue, for after glaring at me for a moment in a sort of apoplectic amazement he jerked his horse round and proceeded slowly down the street.

"'Ave it yer own way," he muttered.

"I intend to," I said cheerfully.

We pulled up at the post-office, a large red-brick building in the main street, and leaving my disgruntled friend sitting in the trap, I jumped out and pushed open the swing door. Except for an intelligent-looking clerk behind the counter the place was empty.

"Good-morning," I said. "I wonder if you could help me out of a slight difficulty about my letters?"

"What sort of a difficulty?" he inquired civilly.

"Well, for the next week or two," I said, "I shall be living in a little hut on the marshes about two miles to the east from here, and quite close to the sea-wall. I am making a few chemical experiments in connection with photography" (a most useful lie this), "and I've told my friends to write or send telegrams here—to the post-office. I wondered, if anything should come for me, whether you had a special messenger or any one who could bring it over. I would be delighted to pay him his proper fee and give him something extra for his trouble. My name is Nicholson—Mr. James Nicholson."

The man hesitated for a moment. "I don't think there will be any difficulty about that—not if you leave written instructions. I shall have to ask the postmaster when he comes in, but I'm pretty certain it will be all right."

I thanked him, and after writing out exactly what I wanted done, I returned to my friend in the trap, who, to judge from his expression, did not appear to have benefited appreciably from my little lesson in patience and politeness. Under the circumstances I decided to extend it.

"I am going across the street to get some things I want," I observed. "You can wait here."

He made an unpleasant sound in his throat, which I think he intended for an ironical laugh. "Wot you want's a bus," he remarked; "a bus an' a bell an' a ruddy conductor."

I came quite close and looked up into his face, smiling. "What you want," I said quietly, "is a damned good thrashing, and if I have any more of your insolence I'll pull you down out of the trap and give you one."

I think something in my voice must have told him I was speaking the literal truth, for although his mouth opened convulsively it closed again without any audible response.

I strolled serenely across the road to where I saw an "Off-Licence." I had acted in an indiscreet fashion, but whatever happened I was determined to put up with no further rudeness from anybody. I had had all the discourtesy I required during my three years in Princetown.

My purchases at the Off-Licence consisted of three bottles of whisky and two more of some rather obscure brand of champagne. It was possible, of course, that McMurtrie's ideas of catering included such luxuries, but there seemed no reason for running any unnecessary risk. As a prospective host it was clearly my duty to take every reasonable precaution.

Armed with my spoils I returned to the trap, and stored them away carefully beneath the seat. Then I climbed up alongside the driver.

"Now you can go to Warren's Copse," I said; and without making any reply the tomato-faced gentleman jerked round his horse's head, and back we went up the street.

I can't say it was exactly an hilarious drive. I felt cheerful enough myself, but my companion maintained a depressed and lowering silence, broken only by an occasional inward grunt, or a muttered curse at the horse. It struck me as curious and not a little sinister that McMurtrie should be employing such an uncouth ruffian, but I supposed that he had some sound reason for his choice. I couldn't imagine McMurtrie doing anything without a fairly sound reason.

Within about ten minutes of leaving the town, we came out on to the main road that bounded the landward side of the marshes. I caught sight of my future home looking very small and desolate against the long stretch of sea-wall, and far in the distance I could just discern the mast of the *Betty* still tapering up above the bank of the creek. It was comforting to know that so far at all events Mr. Gow had neither sunk her nor pawned her.

Warren's Copse proved to be the small clump of trees that I had noticed on the previous day, and my driver pulled up there and jerked the butt of his whip in the direction of the hut.

"There y'are," he said. "We can't get no nearer than this."

There was a good distance to walk across the marsh, and for a moment I wondered whether to insist upon his getting out and carrying one of my bags, I decided, however, that I had had quite enough of the surly brute's company, so jumping down, I took out my belongings, and told him that he was at liberty to depart.

He drove off without a word, but he had not gone more than about thirty yards when he suddenly turned in his seat and called out a parting observation.

"I ain't afraid o' you—you—'ulkin' bully!" he shouted; "an' don't you think it neither."

Then, whipping up the horse, he broke into a smart canter, and disappeared round a bend in the road.

When I had done laughing, I shoved a bottle into each side pocket, and stowed away the other three in the emptier of my two bags. The latter were no light weight to lug along, and by the time I had covered the half-mile of marsh that separated me from the hut I had come to the conclusion that the profession of a railway porter was one that I should never adopt as a private hobby.

As soon as I unlocked the door, I saw that I had not been far wrong in my guess about a caretaker on the previous afternoon. Some one, at all events, had been there in the interval, for the pile of cooking and eating utensils were now arranged on a rough shelf at the back, while the box which I had noticed had been unpacked and its contents set out on the kitchen table.

I glanced over them with some interest. There were packets of tea and sugar, several loaves of bread, and a number of gaily-coloured tins, containing such luxuries as corned beef, condensed milk, tongue, potted meat, and golden syrup. Except for the tea, however, there seemed to be a regrettable dearth of liquid refreshments, and I mentally thanked Providence for my happy inspiration with regard to the Off-Licence.

I pottered about a bit, unpacking my own belongings, and putting things straight generally. As I seemed likely to be spending some time in the place, I thought I might as well make everything as comfortable and tidy as possible to start with; and, thanks to my combined experience of small boats and prison cells, I flatter myself I made rather a good job of it.

By the time I had finished I was feeling distinctly hungry. I opened one of the tongues, and with the additional aid of bread and whisky made a simple but satisfying lunch. Then I sat down on the bed and treated myself to a pipe before going across to the shed to start work. Smoking in business hours is one of those agreeable luxuries which an inventor of high explosives finds it healthier to deny himself.

I could see no sign of any one about when I went outside. Except for a few gulls, which were wheeling backwards and forwards over the sea-wall, I seemed to have the whole stretch of marsh and saltings entirely to myself. Some people, I suppose, would have found the prospect a depressing one, but I was very far from sharing any such opinion. I like marsh scenery, and for the present at all events I was fully able to appreciate the charms which sages of all times are reported to have discovered in solitude.

I shall never forget the feeling of satisfaction with which I closed the door of the shed behind me and looked round its clean, well-lighted interior. A careful examination soon showed me that McMurtrie's share in the work had been done as thoroughly and conscientiously as I had imagined from my brief inspection on the previous day. Everything I had asked for was lying there in readiness, and, much as I disliked and mistrusted the doctor, it was not without a genuine sensation of gratitude that I hung up my coat and proceeded to set to work.

Briefly speaking, my new discovery was an improvement on the famous C. powder, invented by Lemartre. It was derived from the aromatic series of nitrates (which that great scientist always insisted to be the correct basis for stable and powerful explosives), but it owed its enormously increased force to a fresh constituent, the introduction of which was entirely my own idea. I had been working at it for about nine months before my arrest, and after several disappointing failures I had just succeeded in achieving what I believed to be my object, when my experiments had been so unkindly interrupted.

Still, all that remained now was comparatively clear sailing. I had merely to follow out my former process, and I had taken care to order the various ingredients in as fully prepared a state as possible for immediate use. I had also taken care to include one or two other articles, which as a matter of fact had nothing on earth to do with the business in hand. It was just as well, I felt, to obscure matters a trifle, in case any inquiring mind might attempt to investigate my secret.

For hour after hour I worked on, sorting out my various chemicals, and preparing such methods of treatment as were necessary in each case. I was so interested in my task that I paid no attention at all to the time, until with something of a shock I suddenly realized that the light was beginning to fail. Looking at my watch I found that it was nearly half-past seven.

There was still a certain amount to do before I could knock off, so, stopping for a moment to mix myself a well-earned whisky-and-water, I switched on the two electric head-lights which McMurtrie had provided as a means of illumination. With the aid of these I continued my labours for perhaps another hour and a half, at the end of which time I began to feel that a little rest and refreshment would be an agreeable variation in the programme.

After making sure that everything was safe, I turned out the lights, and locking up the door, walked back to the hut. I was just entering, when it suddenly struck me that instead of dining in solitary state off tongue and bread, I might just as well stroll over to the *Betty* and take my evening repast in the engaging company of Mr. Gow.

No sooner had this excellent idea entered my head than I decided to put it into practice. The moon was out, and there appeared to be enough light to see my way by the old route along the river shore, so, walking down to the sea-wall, I climbed over, and set off in the direction of the creek.

It was tricky sort of work, with fine possibilities of spraining one's ankle about it, but by dint of "going delicately," like Agag, I managed to reach the end of my journey without disaster. As I rounded the bend I saw the *Betty* lying out in mid-stream, bathed in a most becoming flood of moonlight. A closer observation showed me the head and shoulders of Mr. Gow protruding from the fo'c's'le hatch.

He responded to my hail by scrambling up on deck and lowering himself into the dinghy, which with a few vigorous jerks he brought to the shore.

"I've come to have supper with you, Mr. Gow," I observed. "Have you got anything to eat?"

He touched his cap and nodded. "I says to meself it must be you, sir, d'rectly I heard you comin' round the crick. There ain't much comp'ny 'bout here at night-time."

"Nor in the daytime either," I added, pushing the boat off from the bank.

"And that's a fact, sir," he remarked, settling down to the oars. "There was one gent round here this morning askin' his way, but except for him we bin remarkable quiet."

"What sort of a gent?" I demanded with interest.

"Smallish, 'e was, sir, an' very civil spoken. Wanted to get to Tilbury."

"Did he ask who the boat belonged to, by any chance?"

Mr. Gow reflected for a moment. "Now you come to mention it, sir, I b'lieve 'e did. Not as I should have told 'im anything, even if I'd known. I don't hold with answerin' questions."

"You're quite right, Mr. Gow," I observed, catching hold of the stern of the *Betty*. "It's a habit that gets people into a lot of trouble—especially in the Law Courts."

We clambered on board, and while my companion made the dinghy fast, I went down into the cabin, and proceeded to rout out the lockers in search of provisions. I discovered a slab of pressed beef, and some rather stale bread and cheese, which I set out on the table, wondering to myself, as I did so, whether the inquisitive stranger of the morning was in any way connected with my affairs. It couldn't have been Latimer, for that gentleman was very far from being "smallish," a remark which applied equally well to our mutual friend with the scar. I was still pondering over the question when I heard Mr. Gow drop down into the fo'c's'le, and summoned him through the connecting door to come and join the feast.

He accepted my invitation with some embarrassment, as became a "paid hand," but a bottle of Bass soon put him at his ease. We began by discussing various nautical topics, such as the relative merits of a centre-board or a keel for small boats, and whether whisky or beer was really the better drink when one was tired and wet through. It was not until we had finished our meal and were sitting outside enjoying our pipes that I broached the question that was at the back of my mind.

"Look here, Gow," I said abruptly, "were you speaking seriously when you suggested that launch ran you down on purpose?"

His face darkened, and then a curious look of slow cunning stole into it.

"Mebbe they did, and mebbe they didn't," he answered. "Anyway, I reckon they wouldn't have bin altogether sorry to see me at the bottom o' the river."

"But why?" I persisted. "What on earth have you been doing to them?"

Mr. Gow was silent for a moment. "'Tis like this, sir," he said at last. "Bein' about the river all times o' the day an' night, I see things as other people misses—things as per'aps it ain't too healthy to see."

"Well, what have you seen our pals doing?" I inquired.

"I don't say I seen 'em doin' nothin'—nothin' against the law, so to speak." He looked round cautiously. "All the same, sir," he added, lowering his voice, "it's my belief as they ain't livin' up there on Sheppey for no good purpose. Artists they calls 'emselves, but to my way o' thinking they're a sight more interested in forts an' ships an' suchlike than they are in pickchers and paintin'."

I looked at him steadily for a moment. There was no doubt that the man was in earnest.

"You think they're spies?" I said quietly.

He nodded his head. "That's it, sir. Spies—that's what they are; a couple o' dirty Dutch spies—damn 'em."

"Why don't you tell the police or the naval people?" I asked.

He laughed grimly. "They'd pay a lot of heed to the likes o' me, wouldn't they? You can lay them two fellers have got it all squared up fine and proper. Come to look into it, an' you'd find they was artists right enough; no, there wouldn't be no doubt about that. As like as not I'd get two years 'ard for perjurin' and blackmail."

To a certain extent I was in a position to sympathize with this point of view.

"Well, we must keep an eye on them ourselves," I said, "that's all. We can't have German spies running up and down the Thames as if they owned the blessed place." I got up and knocked out my pipe. "The first thing to do," I added, "is to summons them for sinking your boat. If they *are* spies, they'll pay up without a murmur, especially if they really tried to do it on purpose."

Mr. Gow nodded his head again, with a kind of vicious obstinacy. "They done it a-purpose all right," he repeated. "They seen me watching of 'em, and they knows that dead men tell no tales."

There scarcely seemed to me to be enough evidence for the certainty with which he cherished this opinion; but the mere possibility of its being a fact was sufficiently disturbing. Goodness knows, I didn't want to mix myself up in any further troubles, and yet, if these men were really German spies, and, in addition to that, sufficiently desperate to attempt a cold-blooded murder in order to cover up their traces, I had apparently let myself in for it with a vengeance.

Of course, if I liked, I could abandon Mr. Gow to pursue his claim without any assistance; but that was a solution which somehow or other failed to appeal to me. In a sense he had become my retainer; and we

Lyndons are not given to deserting our retainers under any circumstances. At least, I shouldn't exactly have liked to face my father in another world with this particular weakness against my record.

Altogether it was in a far from serene state of mind that I climbed down into the dinghy, and allowed Mr. Gow to row me back to the bank.

"Will you be over tomorrow, sir?" he asked, as he stood up in the boat ready to push off.

"I don't think so, I shall be rather busy the next two or three days." Then I paused a moment. "Keep your eyes open generally, Mr. Gow," I added; "and if any more gentlemen who have lost their way to Tilbury come and ask you the name of the *Betty's* owner, tell them she belongs to the Bishop of London."

He touched his cap quite gravely. "Yessir," he said. "Good-night, sir."

"Good-night, Mr. Gow," I replied, and scrambling up the bank, I set off on my return journey.

CHAPTER XVIII
A NEW CLUE TO AN OLD CRIME

It was exactly half-past ten on Tuesday morning when I sat down on the rough wooden bench in my workshop with a little gasp of relief and exhaustion. Before me, on the lead slab, was a small pile of dark brown powder, which an innocent stranger would in all probability have taken for finely ground coffee. It was not coffee, however; it was the fruit of four days and nights of about the most unremitting toil that any human being has ever accomplished. Unless I was wrong—utterly and hopelessly wrong—I had enough of the new explosive in front of me to blow this particular bit of marsh and salting into the middle of next week.

I leaned forward, and picking up a fistful, allowed it to trickle slowly through my fingers. The stuff was quite safe to handle; that was one of its beauties. I could have put a lighted match to it or thrown it on the fire without the faintest risk; the only possible method of releasing its appalling power being the explosion of a few grains of gunpowder or dynamite in its immediate vicinity. I had no intention of allowing that interesting event to occur until I had made certain necessary preparations.

I was still contemplating my handiwork with a sort of fatigued pride, when a sudden sound outside attracted my attention. Getting up and looking through the shed window, I discovered a telegraph-boy standing by the hut, apparently engaged in hunting for the bell.

"All right, sonny," I called out. "Bring it along here."

I walked to the door, and the next minute I was being handed an envelope addressed to me at the Tilbury Post-Office in Joyce's handwriting.

"It came the last post yesterday," explained the lad. "We couldn't let you have it until this morning because there wasn't any one to send."

"Well, sit down a moment, Charles," I said; "and I'll just see if there's any answer."

He seated himself on the bench, staring round at everything with obvious interest. With a pleasant feeling of anticipation I slit open the envelope and pulled out its contents.

"CHELSEA,

"*Monday.*

"DEAREST JAMES,

"It looks rather nice written—doesn't it! I am coming down tomorrow by the train which gets into Tilbury at 2.15. I shall walk across to the *Betty* and sit there peacefully till you turn up. Whatever stage the work is at, don't be later than 7.30. I shall have supper ready by then—and it will be a supper worth eating. My poor darling, you must be simply starved. I've lots to tell you, James, but it will keep till tomorrow.

"With all my love,

"JOYCE."

I read this through (it was so like Joyce I could almost fancy I heard her speaking), and then I turned to the telegraph-boy, who was still occupied in taking stock of his surroundings.

"There's no answer, thank you, Charles," I said. "How much do I owe you?"

He pulled himself together abruptly. "It will be two shillings, the post-office fee, sir."

"Well, there it is," I said; "and there's another shilling for yourself."

He jumped up and pocketed the coins with an expression of gratitude. Then he paused irresolutely. "Beg pardon, sir," he observed, "but ain't you a gentleman who makes things?"

I laughed. "We most of us do that, Charles," I said, "if they're only mistakes."

He looked round the shed with an expression of slight awe. "Can you make fireworks?" he asked.

I glanced instinctively at the little heap of powder. "Of a kind," I admitted modestly. "Why?"

He gave an envious sigh. "I only wondered if it was hard, sir. I'd rather be able to make fireworks than do anything."

"It's not very hard," I said consolingly. "You go on bringing my letters and telegrams for me like a good boy directly they arrive, and before I leave here I'll show you how to do it. Only you mustn't talk about it to anybody, or I shall have everyone asking me the same thing."

His face brightened, and stammering out his thanks and his determination to keep the bargain a profound secret, he reluctantly took his departure. I felt that in future, whatever happened, I was pretty certain to get anything which turned up for me at the post-office without undue delay.

For the next half-hour or so I amused myself by constructing a kind of amateur magazine outside the hut in which to store my precious powder. It was safe enough in a way above ground, as I have already mentioned, but with inquisitive strangers like Mr. Latimer prowling around, I certainly didn't mean to leave a grain of it about while I was absent from the shed. I packed it all away in a waterproof iron box, which I had specially ordered for the purpose, and buried it in the hole that I had dug outside. Then I covered the latter over with a couple of pieces of turf, and carefully removed all traces of my handiwork.

It was not until I had finished this little job that I suddenly realized how tired I was. For the last four days I had scarcely stirred outside the shed, and I don't suppose I had averaged more than three hours' sleep a night the whole time. The excitement and interest of my work had kept me going, and now that it was over I found that I was almost dropping with fatigue.

I locked up the place, and walking across to the hut, opened myself one of the bottles of champagne which I had so thoughtfully purchased at the Off-Licence. It was not exactly a vintage wine, but I was in no mood to be over-critical, and I drank off a couple of glasses with the utmost appreciation. Then I lay down on the bed, and in less than five minutes I was sleeping like a log.

I woke up at exactly half-past four. However tired I am, a few hours' sleep always puts me right again, and by the time I had had a wash and changed into a clean shirt, I felt as fresh as a daisy.

I decided to walk straight over to the *Betty*. I knew that by this time Joyce would be on board, and as there was nothing else to be done in the shed, I thought I might just as well join her now as later. I had been too busy to miss any one very much the last four days, but now that the strain was over I felt curiously hungry to see her again. Besides, I was longing to hear what news she had brought about Tommy and George.

With a view to contributing some modest item towards the supper programme, I shoved the other bottle of champagne into my pocket, and then lighting a cigar, locked up the place, and set off for the creek by my usual route. The tide was very high, and on several occasions I had to scramble up and make my way along the sea-wall in full view of the marsh and the roadway. Fortunately, however, there seemed, as usual, to be no one about, and I reached the mouth of the creek without much fear of having been watched or followed.

The *Betty* was there all right, but I could see no sign of any one on board. I walked up the creek until I was exactly opposite where she was lying, and then putting my hands to my lips I gave her a gentle hail.

In an instant Joyce's head appeared out of the cabin, and the next moment she was on deck waving me a joyous welcome with the frying-pan.

"Oh, it's you!" she cried. "How lovely! Half a second, and I'll come over and fetch you."

"Where's Mr. Gow?" I called out.

"He's gone home. I sent him off for a holiday. There's no one on board but me."

She scrambled aft, and unshipping the dinghy, came sculling towards me across the intervening water. She was wearing a white jersey, and with her arms bare and her hair shining in the sunlight, she made a picture that only a blind man would have failed to find inspiring.

She brought up right against the bank where I was standing, and leaning over, caught hold of the grass.

"Jump," she said. "I'll hang on."

I jumped, and the next moment I was beside her in the boat, and we were hugging each other as cheerfully and naturally as two children.

"You dear, to come so soon!" she said. "I wasn't expecting you for ages."

I kissed her again, and then, picking up the oars, pushed off from the bank. "Joyce," I said, "I've done it! I've made enough of the blessed stuff to blow up half Tilbury."

She clapped her hands joyfully. "How splendid! I knew you would. Have you tried it?"

I shook my head. "Not yet," I said. "We'll do it early tomorrow morning, before any one's about." Then, digging in my scull to avoid a desolate-looking beacon, I added anxiously: "What about Tommy? Is he coming?"

Joyce nodded. "He'll be down tomorrow. I've got a letter for you from him. He saw Mr. Latimer last night."

"Did he!" said I. "Things are moving with a vengeance. What about the gentle George?"

Joyce laughed softly. "Oh," she said; "I've such lots to tell you, I hardly know where to start."

I ran the boat alongside the *Betty*, and we both climbed on board.

"Suppose we start by having some tea," I suggested. "I'm dying for a cup."

"You poor dear," said Joyce. "Of course you shall have one. You can read what Tommy says while I'm getting it ready."

She fetched the letter out of the cabin, and sitting in the well I proceeded to decipher the three foolscap pages of hieroglyphics which Tommy is pleased to describe as his handwriting. As far as I could make out they ran as follows:

"MY DEAR NEIL,

"I suppose I oughtn't to begin like that, in case somebody else got hold of the letter. It doesn't matter really, however, because Joyce is bringing it down, and you can tear the damn thing up as soon as you've read it.

"Well, I've seen Latimer. I wrote to him directly I got back, reminded him who I was, and told him I wanted to have a chat with him about some very special private business. He asked me to come round to his rooms in Jermyn Street last night at ten o'clock, and I was there till pretty near midnight.

"I thought I was bound to find out something, but good Lord, Neil, it came off in a way I'd never dared hope for. Practically speaking, I've got to the bottom of the whole business—at least so far as Latimer's concerned. You see he either had to explain or else tell me to go to the devil, and as he thought I was a perfectly safe sort of chap to be honest with, he decided to make a clean breast of it.

"To start with, it's very much what we suspected. Latimer *is* a Secret Service man, and that's how he comes to be mixed up in the job. It seems that some little while ago the Admiralty or one of the other Government departments got it into their heads that there were a number of Germans over in England spying out the land in view of a possible row over this Servian business. Latimer was told off amongst others to look into the matter. He had been sniffing around for some weeks without much luck, when more or less by chance he dropped across the track of those two very identical beauties who ran down Gow's boat in the Thames last Friday.

"Somehow or other they must have got wind of the fact that he was after them, and they evidently made up their minds to get rid of him. They seem to have set about it rather neatly. The man with the scar, who is either one of them or else in with them, introduced himself to Latimer as a member of the French Secret Service. He pretended that he had some special information about the case in hand, and although Latimer was a bit suspicious, he agreed to dine at Parelli's and hear what the fellow had to say.

"Well, you know the rest of that little incident. If it hadn't been for you there's not the faintest doubt that Latimer would have copped it all right, and I can tell you he's by way of being rather particularly grateful. I was specially instructed to send you a message to that effect next time I was writing.

"What the connection is between your crowd and these Germans I can't exactly make out. Of course if you're right in your idea about the chap with the scar spying on you in London it's perfectly obvious they're working together in some way. At the same time I'm quite sure that Latimer knows nothing about it. The reason he came down to look at the hut on Friday was because a report about it had been sent to him by one of his men—he has two fellows working under him—and he thought it might have something to do with the Germans. He described the way you had caught him quite frankly, and told me how he'd had to invent a lie about the Surveyor in order to get out of it.

"Exactly what he means to do next I don't know. He has got some plan on, and I've a notion he wants me to help him—at least he sounded me pretty plainly last night as to whether I'd be game to lend him a hand. I need hardly tell you I jumped at the idea. It seems to me our only possible chance of finding out anything. I am to see him or hear from him tomorrow, and directly I know what's in the wind I'll either write to you or come and look you up.

"Joyce will tell you all about George and McMurtrie. If they aren't both up to some kind of particularly dirty mischief I'll eat my whole wardrobe. We must talk it over thoroughly when we meet.

"I'm longing to see you again, and hear all about the work and what's been going on down there.

"So long, old son,

"Yours as ever,

"TOMMY."

I was just making out the last words, when Joyce emerged from the cabin, carrying some tea on a tray.

"Here you are, Neil," she said. "I have cut you only two slices of bread and butter, because I don't want you to spoil your supper. There's cold pheasant and peas and new potatoes."

I pulled out the bottle of champagne from my pocket. "If they're as new as this wine," I observed, "they ought to be delicious."

Joyce accepted my contribution, and after reading the label, placed it carefully on the floor of the well. "Sarcon et fils," she repeated. "I always thought they made vinegar."

"Perhaps they do," I replied. "We shall know when we drink it."

Joyce laughed, and sitting down beside me, poured me out a cup of tea. "You've read Tommy's letter," she said. "What do you think about it?"

I took a long drink. "From the little I've seen of Mr. Bruce Latimer," I said, "I should put him down as being one of the most accomplished liars in England." I paused. "At the same time," I added, "I think he's a fine fellow. I like his face."

Joyce nodded her head. "But you don't believe his story?"

I shrugged my shoulders. "It may be true," I said. "Tommy seems to think so anyhow. If it is, things are a bit simpler than I imagined—that's all."

"And if it isn't?" said Joyce.

"Ah!" said I, "if it isn't—"

I left the sentence unfinished, and helped myself to a second bit of bread and butter.

There was a short silence.

"Tell me about George, Joyce," I went on. "What are these particular dark doings that Tommy's hinting about?"

Joyce leaned forward with her chin on her hands, her blue eyes fixed on mine.

"Neil," she said slowly, "I've found out something at last—something I thought I was never going to. I know who the man was in Marks's rooms on the day that he was murdered."

I was so surprised that I gulped down a mouthful of nearly boiling tea.

"I wish you'd break these things more gently, Joyce," I said. "Who was it?"

"It was Dr. McMurtrie."

I put down the teacup and stared at her in the blankest amazement.

"Dr. McMurtrie!" I repeated incredulously.

She nodded. "Listen, and I'll tell you exactly how it all happened. I dined with George, as you know, at the Savoy on Friday, and we went into the whole business of my going away with him. He has got that twelve thousand pounds, Neil; there's no doubt about it. He showed me the entry in his pass-book and the acknowledgment from the bank, and he even offered to write me a cheque for a couple of hundred right away, to buy clothes with for the trip."

"From what I remember of George," I said, "he must be desperately in love with you."

Joyce gave a little shiver of disgust. "Of course I let him think I was giving way. I wanted to find out where the money had come from, but try as I would, I couldn't get him to tell me. That makes me feel so certain there's something wrong about it. In the end I arranged to dine with him again tomorrow night, when I said I'd give him my final answer. On Saturday morning, however, I changed my mind, and wrote him a note to say I'd come Thursday instead. I didn't mean to tie myself to be back tomorrow, in case you wanted me here."

She paused.

"I had to go up Victoria Street, so I thought I'd leave the letter at his office. I'd just got there, and I was standing outside the door opening my bag, when a man came down the steps. I looked up as he passed, and—oh Neil!—it was all I could do to stop myself from screaming. I knew him at once; I knew his cold wicked face just as well as if it had been only three days instead of three years. It was the man I'd seen in Marks's rooms on the afternoon of the murder."

She stopped again, and took a deep breath.

"I was horribly excited, and yet at the same time I felt quite cool. I let him get about ten yards away down the street, and then I started off after him. He walked as far as the Stores. Then he called an empty taxi that was coming past, and I heard him tell the driver to go to the Hotel Russell. I thought about how you'd followed the man with the scar, and I made up my mind I'd do the same thing. I had to wait for several seconds before another taxi came by, but directly it did I jumped in and told the man to drive me to the corner of Russell Square.

"I got there just as the other taxi was drawing up in front of the hotel. A porter came forward and opened the door, and I saw the man get out and go up the steps. I waited for one moment, and then I walked along to the entrance myself. The porter was still standing there, so I went straight up to him and asked him quite simply what the name of the gentleman was who had just gone inside. He sort of hesitated, and then he said to me: 'That gentleman, Miss?—that's Dr. McMurtrie.'"

Once more she paused, and, pushing away the tray, I lit myself a cigar. "It's lucky you've had some practice in surprises," I observed.

Joyce nodded. "Of course I was absolutely flabbergasted, but I don't think I showed anything. I sort of rummaged in my bag for a minute till I'd recovered; then I gave the man half a crown and asked him if he knew how long Dr. McMurtrie was staying. I think he was in doubt as to whether I was a female detective or a lady reporter; anyhow he took the money and said he was very sorry he didn't know, but that if I wanted an interview at any time he had no doubt it might be arranged. I thanked him, and said it didn't matter for the moment, and there I thought it best to leave things. You see I knew that whether McMurtrie stayed on at the Russell or not you were bound to see him again, and there was nothing to be gained by asking questions which the porter would probably repeat to him. It would only have helped to put him on his guard—wouldn't it?"

"My dear Joyce," I said, "I think you did splendidly. Sherlock Holmes couldn't have done better." I got up and walked to the end of the cockpit. "But good Lord!" I added, "this does complicate matters. You're absolutely certain it was McMurtrie you saw at Marks's flat?"

"Absolutely," repeated Joyce with emphasis. "I should remember his face if I lived to be a hundred."

I clenched my fists in a sudden spasm of anger. "There's some damned villainy underneath all this, Joyce," I said. "If McMurtrie was there that afternoon the odds are that he knows who committed the murder."

"He did it himself," said Joyce calmly. "I'm as sure of it as I am that I'm sitting here."

"But why?" I demanded—"why? Who on earth *was* Marks? Nobody in Chelsea seemed to know anything about him, and nothing came out at the trial. Why should any one have wanted to kill him except me?"

Joyce shook her head. "I don't know," she said stubbornly; "but I'm quite certain it was McMurtrie. I feel it inside me."

"And in any case," I continued, "what the devil is he doing messing about with George? I'm the only connecting-link between them, and he can't possibly mean to betray me—at all events, until he's got the secret of the powder. He knows George would give me up tomorrow."

Joyce made a gesture of perplexity. "I know," she said. "It's an absolute mystery to me too. I've been puzzling and puzzling over it till my head aches, and I can't see any sort of explanation at all."

"The only thing that's quite plain," I said, "is the fact that McMurtrie and Savaroff have been lying to me from the start. They are no more powder-merchants than you are. They want to get hold of my invention for some reason—to make money out of it, I suppose—and then they're prepared to clear out and leave me to George and the police. At least, that's what it's beginning to look like."

"Well, anyhow," said Joyce, "you're not tied to them any longer by your promise."

"No," I said; "it takes two to keep a bargain. Besides," I added rather bitterly, "I can afford the privilege of breaking my word. It's only what you'd expect from a convict."

Joyce got up, and coming to where I was sitting, slipped her arm through mine and softly stroked my hand. "Don't, Neil," she said. "I hate you to say anything that isn't fine and generous. It's like hearing music out of tune."

I drew her to me, and half closing her eyes, she laid her cheek against mine. We remained silent for a moment or two, and then, giving her a little hug, I sat up and took hold of her hands.

"Look here, Joyce," I said, "we won't just bother about anything for the rest of the day. We'll be cheerful and jolly and foolish, like we were on Friday. God knows how all this infernal tangle is going to pan out, but we may as well snatch one evening's happiness out of it while we've got the chance."

Joyce kissed me, and then jumping lightly from the seat, pulled me up with her. "We will," she said. "After all, we've got a boat and a lovely evening and a cold pheasant and a bottle of champagne—what more can any one want?"

"Well," I said, "it may sound greedy, but as a matter of fact I want some of those peas and new potatoes you were talking about just now."

She let go my hands, and opening one of the lockers, took out a large basin with a couple of bags in it. "There you are," she laughed. "You can skin them and shell them while I wash up the tea-things and lay the table. It's a man's duty to do the dangerous work."

Joyce had always had the gift of scattering a kind of infectious gaiety around her, and that night she seemed to be in her most bewitching and delightful mood. I think she made up her mind to try and wipe out from my memory for the time being all thoughts of the somewhat harassed state of existence in which it had pleased Providence to land me. If so, she succeeded admirably.

We cooked the supper between us. I boiled the peas and potatoes, and then, when we had done the first course, Joyce got up and made a brilliantly successful French omelette out of some fresh eggs which she had brought down for that inspired purpose.

It was very charming in the little low-ceilinged cabin, with the lamp swinging overhead and no sound outside but the soft lapping of the tide upon the sides of the boat. We lay and talked for some time after we had finished, while I smoked a cigar, and Joyce, stretched out luxuriously on the other bunk, indulged in a couple of cigarettes.

"We won't wash up," I said. "I'll just shove everything through into the fo'c's'le, and we'll leave them there for Mr. Gow. A certain amount of exercise will be good for him after his holiday."

"Do," said Joyce sleepily. "And then come and sit over here, Neil. I want to stroke your hair."

I cleared away the things, and shutting up the table, which worked on a hinge, spread out my own cushions on the floor alongside of Joyce's bunk. The latter was just low enough to let me rest my head comfortably on her shoulder.

How long we lay like that I really don't know. My whole body and mind were steeped in a strange, delightful sense of peace and contentment, and I began to realize, I think for the first time, how utterly necessary and dear to me Joyce had become. I slid my arm underneath her—she lay close up against me, her hair, which she had loosened from its fastenings, half covering us both in its soft beauty.

The lamp flickered and died down, but we didn't trouble to relight it. Outside the night grew darker and darker, and through the open hatch we could just see a solitary star shining down on us from between two banks of cloud. Cool and sweet, a faint breeze drifted in from the silent marshes.

Then, quite suddenly, it seemed to me, a strange madness and music filled the night for both of us. I only knew that Joyce was in my arms and that we were kissing each other with fierce, unheeding passion. There were tears on her cheeks—little sweet, salt tears of love and happiness that felt all wet against my lips.

It was only a moment—just one brief moment of unutterable beauty— and then I remembered. With a groan I half raised myself in the darkness.

"I must go, Joyce," I whispered. "I can't stay here. I daren't."

She slipped her soft bare arms round my neck, and drew my face down to hers.

"Don't go," she whispered back. "Not if you don't want to. What does it matter? I am all yours, Neil, anyway."

For a moment I felt her warm fragrant breath upon my face, and her heart beating quickly against mine. Then, with an effort—a big effort—I tore myself away.

"Joyce dear," I said, "it would only make things worse. Oh, my dear sweet Joyce, I want you like the night wants the dawn, but we can't cheat life. Suppose we fail—suppose there's only death or prison in front of me. It will be hard enough now, but if—"

I broke off, and with a little sob Joyce sat up and felt for my hand.

"You're right, darling," she said; "but oh, my dear, my dear!" She lifted up my hand and passed it softly backwards and forwards across her eyes. Then, with a little laugh that had tears close behind it, she added: "Do you know, my Neil, I'm conceited enough to think you're rather wonderful."

I bent down and kissed her with infinite tenderness.

"I am, Joyce," I said. "Exactly how wonderful you'll never know."

Then I lifted her up in my arms, and we went out of the cabin into the cool darkness of the night.

"I'll row myself ashore," I said, "and leave the dinghy on the beach. I shall be back about four o'clock, if that's not too early for you. We ought to get our explosion over before there's any one about."

Joyce nodded. "I don't mind how early you come. The sooner the better."

"Try and get some sleep," I added; "you'll be tired out tomorrow if you don't."

"I'll try," said Joyce simply; "but I don't think I shall. I'm not even sure I want to."

I kissed her once more, and slipping down into the dinghy, pulled off for the shore. Everything around was dark and silent—the faint splash of my oars alone breaking the utter stillness. Landing at my usual spot, more by luck than judgment, I tugged the boat up out of reach of the tide, and then, turning round, waved good-night to the *Betty*.

It was too dark to see anything, but I think Joyce sent me back my message.

CHAPTER XIX
LAUNCHING A NEW INVENTION

The eastern sky was just flushing into light when I got back to the creek at four o'clock. It was a beautiful morning—cool and still—with the sweet freshness of early dawn in the air, and the promise of a long unclouded day of spring sunshine.

I tugged the dinghy down to the water, and pushed off for the *Betty*, which looked strangely small and unreal lying there in the dim, mysterious twilight. The sound I made as I drew near must have reached Joyce's ears. She was up on deck in a moment, fully dressed, and with her hair twisted into a long bronze plait that hung down some way below her waist. She looked as fresh and fair as the dawn itself.

"Beautifully punctual," she called out over the side. "I knew you would be, so I started getting breakfast."

I caught hold of the gunwale and scrambled on board.

"It's like living at the Savoy," I said. "Breakfast was a luxury that had never entered my head."

"Well, it's going to now," she returned, "unless you're in too great a hurry to start. It's all ready in the cabin."

"We can spare ten minutes certainly," I said. "Experiments should always be made on a full body."

I tied up the dinghy and followed her inside, where the table was decorated with bread and butter and the remnants of the cold pheasant, while a kettle hissed away cheerfully on the Primus.

"I don't believe you've been to bed at all, Joyce," I said. "And yet you look as if you'd just slipped out of Paradise by accident."

She laughed, and putting her hand in my side-pocket, took out my handkerchief to lift off the kettle with.

"I didn't want to sleep," she said. "I was too happy, and too miserable. It's the widest-awake mixture I ever tried." Then, picking up the teapot, she added curiously: "Where's the powder? I expected to see you arrive with a large keg over your shoulder."

I sat down at the table and produced a couple of glass flasks, tightly corked.

"Here you are," I said. "This is ordinary gunpowder, and this other one's my stuff. It looks harmless enough, doesn't it?"

Joyce took both flasks and examined them with interest. "You've not brought very much of it," she said. "I was hoping we were going to have a really big blow-up."

"It will be big enough," I returned consolingly, "unless I've made a mistake."

"Where are you going to do it?" she asked.

"Somewhere at the back of Canvey Island," I said. "There's no one to wake up there except the sea-gulls, and we can be out of sight round the corner before it explodes. I've got about twenty feet of fuse, which will give us at least a quarter of an hour to get away in."

"What fun!" exclaimed Joyce. "I feel just like an anarchist or something; and it's lovely to know that one's launching a new invention. We ought to have kept that bottle of champagne to christen it with."

"Yes," I said regretfully; "it was the real christening brand too."

There was a short silence. "I've thought of a name for it," cried Joyce suddenly. "The powder, I mean. We'll call it Lyndonite. It sounds like something that goes off with a bang, doesn't it?"

I laughed. "It would probably suggest that to the prison authorities," I said. "Anyhow, Lyndonite it shall be."

We finished breakfast, and going up on deck I proceeded to haul in the anchor, while Joyce stowed away the crockery and provisions below. For once in a way the engine started without much difficulty, and as the tide was running out fast it didn't take us very long to reach the mouth of the creek.

Once outside, I set a course down stream as close to the northern shore as I dared go. Except for a rusty-looking steam tramp we had the whole river to ourselves, not even a solitary barge breaking the long stretch of grey water. One by one the old landmarks—Mucking Lighthouse, the Thames Cattle Wharf, and Hole Haven—were left behind, and at last the entrance to the creek that runs round behind Canvey Island came into sight.

One would never accuse it of being a cheerful, bustling sort of place at the best of times, but at five o'clock in the morning it seemed the very picture of uninhabited desolation. A better locality in which to enjoy a little quiet practice with new explosives it would be difficult to imagine.

I navigated the *Betty* in rather gingerly, for it was over three years since I had visited the spot. Joyce kept on sounding diligently with the lead either side of the boat, and at last we brought up in about one and a half fathom, just comfortably out of sight of the main stream.

"This will do nicely," I said. "We'll turn her round first, and then I'll row into the bank and fix things up under that tree over there. We can be back in the river before anything happens."

"Can't we stop and watch?" asked Joyce. "I should love to see it go off."

I shook my head. "Unless I've made a mistake," I said, "it will be much healthier round the corner. We'll come back and see what's happened afterwards."

By the aid of some delicate manoeuvring I brought the *Betty* round, and then getting into the dinghy pulled myself ashore.

It was quite unnecessary for my experiment to make any complicated preparations. All I had to do was to dig a hole in the bank with a trowel that I had brought for the purpose, empty my stuff into that, and tip in the gunpowder on top. When I had finished I covered the whole thing over with earth, leaving a clear passage for the fuse, and then lighting the end of the latter, jumped back into the boat and pulled off rapidly for the *Betty*.

We didn't waste any time dawdling about. Joyce seized the painter as I climbed on board, and hurrying to the tiller I started off down the creek as fast as we could go, taking very particular pains not to run aground.

We had reached the mouth, and I was swinging her round into the main river, when a sudden rumbling roar disturbed the peacefulness of the dawn. Joyce, who was staring out over the stern, gave a little startled cry, and glancing hastily back I was just in time to see a disintegrated-looking tree soaring gaily up into the air in the midst of a huge column of dust and smoke. The next moment a rain of falling fragments of earth and wood came splashing down into the water—a few stray pieces actually reaching the *Betty*, which rocked vigorously as a miniature tidal wave swept after us up the creek.

I put down my helm and brought her round so as to face the stricken field.

"We seem to have done it, Joyce," I observed with some contentment.

She gave a little gasping sort of laugh. "It was splendid!" she said. "But, oh, Neil, what appalling stuff it must be! It's blown up half Canvey Island!"

"Never mind," I said cheerfully. "There are plenty of other islands left. Let's get into the dinghy and see what the damage really amounts to. I fancy it's fairly useful."

We anchored the *Betty*, and then pulled up the creek towards the scene of the explosion, where a gaping aperture in the bank was plainly visible. As we drew near I saw that it extended, roughly speaking, in a half-circle of perhaps twenty yards diameter. The whole of this, which had previously been a solid bank of grass and earth, was now nothing but a muddy pool. Of the unfortunate tree which had marked the site there was not a vestige remaining.

I regarded it all from the boat with the complacent pride of a successful inventor. "It's even better than I expected, Joyce," I said. "If one can do this with three-quarters of a pound, just fancy the effect of a couple of hundredweight. It would shift half London."

Joyce nodded. "They'll be more anxious than ever to get hold of it, when they know," she said. "What are you going to do? Write and tell McMurtrie that you've succeeded?"

"I haven't quite decided," I answered. "I shall wait till tomorrow or the next day, anyhow. I want to hear what Sonia has got to say first." Then, backing away the boat, I added: "We'd better get out of this as soon as we can. It's just possible some one may have heard the explosion and come pushing along to find out what's the matter. People are so horribly inquisitive."

Joyce laughed. "It would be rather awkward, wouldn't it? We couldn't very well say it was an earthquake. It looks too neat and tidy."

Fortunately for us, if there was any one in the neighbourhood who had heard the noise, they were either too lazy or too incurious to investigate the cause. We got back on board the *Betty* and took her out into the main stream without seeing a sign of any one except ourselves. The hull of the steam tramp was just visible in the far distance, but except for that the river was still pleasantly deserted.

"What shall we do now, Joyce?" I asked. "It seems to me that this is an occasion which distinctly requires celebrating."

Joyce thought for a moment. "Let's go for a long sail," she suggested, "and then put in at Southend and have asparagus for lunch."

I looked at her with affectionate approval. "You always have beautiful ideas," I said. Then a sudden inspiration seized me. "I've got it!" I cried. "What do you say to running down to Sheppey and paying a call on our German pals?"

Joyce's blue eyes sparkled. "It would be lovely," she said, with a deep breath; "but dare we risk it?"

"There's no risk," I rejoined. "When I said 'pay a call,' I didn't mean it quite literally. My idea was to cruise along the coast and just find out exactly where their precious bungalow is, and what they do with that launch of theirs when they're not swamping inquisitive boatmen. It's the sort of information that might turn out useful."

Joyce nodded. "We'll go," she said briefly. "What about the tide?"

"Oh, the tide doesn't matter," I replied. "It will be dead out by the time we get to Southend; but we only draw about three foot six, and we can cut across through the Jenkin Swatch. There's water enough off Sheppey to float a battleship."

It was the work of a few minutes to pull in the anchor and haul up the sails, which filled immediately to a slight breeze that had just sprung up from the west. Leaving a still peaceful, if somewhat mutilated, Canvey Island behind us, we started off down the river, gliding along with an agreeable smoothness that fitted in very nicely with my state of mind.

Indeed I don't think I had ever felt anything so nearly approaching complete serenity since my escape from Dartmoor. It is true that the tangle in which I was involved, appeared more threatening and complicated than ever, but one gets so used to sitting on a powder mine that the situation was gradually ceasing to distress me.

At all events I had made my explosive, and that was one great step towards a solution of some sort. If McMurtrie was prepared to play the game with me I should in a few days be in what the newspapers call "a position of comparative affluence," while if his intentions were less straightforward I should at least have some definite idea as to where I was. Sonia's promised disclosures were a guarantee of that.

But apart from these considerations the mere fact of having Joyce sitting beside me in the boat while we bowled along cheerfully through the water was quite enough in itself to account for my new-found happiness. One realizes some things in life with curious abruptness, and I knew now how deeply and passionately I loved her. I suppose I had always done so really, but she had been little more than a child in the old Chelsea days, and the sort of brotherly tenderness and pride I had had for her must have blinded me to the truth.

Anyhow it was out now; out beyond any question of doubt or argument. She was as necessary and dear to me as the stars are to the night, and it seemed ridiculously impossible to contemplate any sort of existence without her. Not that I wasted much energy attempting the feat; the present was sufficiently charming to occupy my entire time.

We passed Leigh and Southend, the former with its fleet of fishing-smacks and the latter with its long unlovely pier, and then nosed our way delicately into the Jenkin Swatch, that convenient ditch which runs right across the mouth of the Thames. The sun was now high in the sky, and one could see signs of activity on the various barges that were hanging about the neighbourhood waiting for the tide.

I pointed away past the Nore Lightship towards a bit of rising ground on the low-lying Sheppey coast.

"That's about where our pals are hanging out," I said. "There's a little deep-water creek there, which Tommy and I used to use sometimes, and according to Mr. Gow their bungalow is close by."

Joyce peered out under her hand across the intervening water. "It's a nice situation," she observed, "for artists."

I laughed. "Yes," I said. "They are so close to Sheerness and Shoeburyness, and other places of beauty. I expect they've done quite a lot of quiet sketching."

We reached the end of the Swatch, and leaving Queenborough, with its grim collection of battleships and coal hulks, to starboard, we stood out to sea along the coastline. It was a fairly long sail to the place which I had pointed out to Joyce, but with a light breeze behind her the *Betty* danced along so gaily that we covered the distance in a surprisingly short time.

As we drew near, Joyce got out Tommy's field-glasses from the cabin, and kneeling up on the seat in the well, focused them carefully on the spot.

"There's the entrance to the creek all right," she said, "but I don't see any sign of a bungalow anywhere." She moved the glasses slowly from side to side. "Oh, yes," she exclaimed suddenly, "I've got it now—right up on the cliff there, away to the left. One can only just see the roof, though, and it seems some way from the creek."

She resigned the glasses to me, and took over the tiller, while I had a turn at examining the coast.

I soon made out the roof of the bungalow, which, as Joyce had said, was the only part visible. It stood in a very lonely position, high up on a piece of rising ground, and half hidden from the sea by what seemed like a thick privet hedge. To judge by the smoke which I could just discern rising from its solitary chimney, it looked as if the occupants were addicted to the excellent habit of early rising.

There was no other sign of them to be seen, however, and if the launch was lying anywhere about, it was at all events invisible from the sea. I refreshed my memory with a long, careful scrutiny of the entrance to the creek, and then handing the glasses back to Joyce I again assumed control of the boat.

"Well," I observed, "we haven't wasted the morning. We know where their bungalow door is, anyway."

Joyce nodded. "It may come in very handy," she said, "in case you ever want to pay them a surprise call."

Exactly how soon that contingency was going to occur we neither of us guessed or imagined!

We reached the Nore Lightship, and waving a courteous greeting to a patient-looking gentleman who was spitting over the side, commenced our long beat back in the direction of Southend. It was slow work, for the tide was only just beginning to turn, and the wind, such as there was of it, was dead in our faces. However, I don't think either Joyce or I found the time hang heavily on our hands. If one can't be happy with the sun and the sea and the person one loves best in the world, it seems to me that one must be unreasonably difficult to please.

We fetched up off Southend Pier at just about eleven o'clock. A hoarse-voiced person in a blue jersey, who was leaning over the end, pointed us out some moorings that we were at liberty to pick up, and then watched us critically while I stowed away the sails and locked up everything in the boat which it was possible to steal. I had been to Southend before in the old days.

These simple precautions concluded, Joyce and I got in the dinghy and rowed to the steps. We were met by the gentleman in blue, who considerately offered to keep his eye on the boat for us while I "and the lady" enjoyed what he called "a run round the town." I accepted his proposal, and having agreed with his statement that it was "a nice morning for a sail," set off with Joyce along the mile of pier that separated us from the shore.

I don't know that our adventures for the next two or three hours call for any detailed description. We wandered leisurely and cheerfully through the town, buying each other one or two trifles in the way of presents, and then adjourned for lunch to a large and rather dazzling hotel that dominated the sea front. It was a new effort on the part of Southend since my time, but, as Joyce said, it "looked the sort of place where one was likely to get asparagus."

Its appearance did not belie it. At a corner table in the window, looking out over the sea, we disposed of what the waiter described as "two double portions" of that agreeable vegetable, together with an excellent steak and a bottle of sound if slightly too sweet burgundy. Then over a couple of cigarettes we discussed our immediate plans.

"I think I'd better catch the three-thirty back," said Joyce. "I've got one or two things I want to do before I meet George, and in any case you mustn't stay here too long or you'll miss the tide."

"That doesn't really matter," I said. "Only I suppose I ought to get back just in case Tommy has turned up. I can't leave him sitting on a mud-flat all night."

Joyce laughed. "He'd probably be a little peevish in the morning. Men are so unreasonable."

I leaned across the table and took her hand. "When are you coming down again?" I asked. "Tomorrow?"

Joyce thought for a moment. "Tomorrow or the next day. It all depends if I see a chance of getting anything more out of George. I'll write to you or send you a wire, dear, anyhow."

I nodded. "All right," I said; "and look here, Joyce; you may as well come straight to the hut next time. It's not the least likely there'll be any one there except me, and if there was you could easily pretend you wanted to ask the way to Tilbury. You see, if Gow wasn't about, you would have to pull the dinghy all the way down the bank before you got on board the *Betty*, and that's a nice, muddy, shin-scraping sort of job at the best of times."

"Very well," said Joyce. Then squeezing my hand a little tighter she added: "And my own Neil, you *will* be careful, won't you? I always seem to be asking you that, but, oh my dear, if you knew how horribly frightened I am of anything happening to you. It will be worse than ever now, after last night. I don't seem to feel it when I'm actually with you—I suppose I'm too happy—but when I'm away from you it's just like some ghastly horrible sword hanging over our heads all the time. Neil darling, as soon as you get this money from McMurtrie—if you do get it—can't we just give up the whole thing and go away and be happy together?"

I lifted her hand and pressed the inside of it against my lips.

"Joyce," I said, "think what it means. It's just funking life—just giving it up because the odds seem too heavy against us. I shouldn't have minded killing Marks in the least. I should be rather proud of it. If I had, we would go away together tomorrow, and I should never worry my head as to what any one in the world was saying or thinking about me." I paused. "But I didn't kill him," I added slowly, "and that just makes all the difference."

Joyce's blue eyes were very near tears, but they looked back steadily and bravely into mine.

"Yes, yes," she said. "I didn't really mean it, Neil. I was just weak for the moment—that's all. Right down in my heart I want everything for you; I could never be contented with less. I want the whole world to know how they've wronged you; I want you to be famous and powerful and splendid, and I want the people who've abused you to come and smirk and grovel to you, and say that they knew all the time that you were innocent." She stopped and took a deep breath. "And they shall, Neil. I'm as certain of it as if I saw it happening. I seem to know inside me that we're on the very point of finding out the truth."

I don't think my worst enemy would accuse me of being superstitious, but there was a ring of conviction in Joyce's voice which somehow or other affected me curiously.

"I believe you're right," I said. "I've got something of that sort of feeling too. Perhaps it's infectious." Then, letting go her hand, to spare the feelings of the waiter who had just come into the room, I sat back in my chair and ordered the bill.

We didn't talk much on our way to the station. I think we were both feeling rather depressed at the prospect of doing without each other for at least twenty-four hours, and in any case the trams and motors and jostling crowd of holiday-makers who filled the main street would have rendered any connected conversation rather a difficult art.

A good many people favoured Joyce with glances of admiration, especially a spruce-looking young constable who officially held up the traffic to allow us to cross the road. He paid no attention at all to me, but I consoled myself with the reflection that he was missing an excellent chance of promotion.

At the station I put Joyce into a first-class carriage, kissed her affectionately under the disapproving eye of an old lady in the opposite corner, and then stood on the platform until the train steamed slowly out of the station.

I turned away at last, feeling quite unpleasantly alone. It's no good worrying about what can't be altered, however, so, lighting a cigar, I strolled back philosophically to the hotel, where I treated myself to the luxury of a hot bath before rejoining the boat.

It must have been pretty nearly half-past four by the time I reached the pier-head. My friend with the hoarse voice and the blue jersey was still hanging around, looking rather thirsty and exhausted after his strenuous day's work of watching over the dinghy. I gave him half a crown for his trouble, and followed by his benediction pulled off for the *Betty*.

The wind had gone round a bit to the south, and as the tide was still coming in I decided to sail up to the creek in preference to using the engine. The confounded throb of the latter always got on my nerves, and apart from that I felt that the mere fact of having to handle the sails would keep my mind lightly but healthily occupied. Unless I was mistaken, a little light healthy occupation was exactly what my mind needed.

As occasionally happens on exceptionally fine days in late spring, the perfect clearness of the afternoon was gradually beginning to give place to a sort of fine haze. It was not thick enough, however, to bother me in any way, and under a jib and mainsail the *Betty* swished along at such a satisfactory pace that I was in sight of Gravesend Reach before either the light or the tide had time to fail me.

I thought I knew the entrance to the creek well enough by now to run her in under sail, though it was a job that required a certain amount of cautious handling. Anyhow I decided to risk it, and, heading for the shore, steered her up the narrow channel, which I had been careful to take the bearings of at low water.

I was so engrossed in this feat of navigation that I took no notice of anything else, until a voice from the bank abruptly attracted my attention. I looked up with a start, nearly running myself aground, and there on the bank I saw a gesticulating figure, which I immediately recognized as that of Tommy. I shouted a greeting back, and swinging the *Betty* round, brought up in almost the identical place where we had anchored on the previous night.

Tommy, who had hurried down to the edge of the water, gave me a second hail.

"Buck up, old son!" he called out. "There's something doing."

A suggestion of haste from Tommy argued a crisis of such urgency that I didn't waste any time asking questions. I just threw over the anchor, and tumbling into the dinghy sculled ashore as quickly as I could.

"Sorry I kept you waiting, Tommy," I said, as he jumped into the boat. "Been here long?"

"About three hours," he returned. "I was beginning to wonder if you were dead."

I shook my head. "I'm not fit to die yet," I replied. "What's the matter?"

He looked at his watch. "Well, the chief matter is the time. Do you think I can get to Sheppey by half-past nine?"

I paused in my rowing. "Sheppey!" I repeated. "Why damn it, Tommy, I've just come back from Sheppey."

It was Tommy's turn to look surprised. "The devil you have!" he exclaimed. "What took you there?"

"To be exact," I said, "it was the *Betty*"; and then in as few words as possible I proceeded to acquaint him with the morning's doings. I was just finishing as we came alongside.

"Well, that's fine about the powder," he said, scrambling on board. "Where's Gow?"

"Joyce sent him off for a holiday," I answered, "and he hasn't come back yet." Then hitching up the dinghy I added curiously: "What's up, Tommy? Let's have it."

"It's Latimer," he said. "I told you I was expecting to hear from him. He sent me a message round early this morning, and I've promised him I'll be in the creek under the German's bungalow by half-past nine. I must get there somehow."

"Oh, we'll get there all right," I returned cheerfully, "What's the game?"

"I think he's having a squint round," said Tommy. "Anyhow I know he's there on his own and depending on me to pick him up."

"But what made him ask you?" I demanded.

"He knew I had a boat, and I fancy he's working this particular racket without any official help. As far as I can make out, he wants to be quite certain what these fellows are up to before he strikes. You don't get much sympathy in the Secret Service if you happen to make a mistake."

"Well, it's no good wasting time talking," I said. "If we want to be there by half-past nine we must push off at once."

"But what about you?" exclaimed Tommy. "You can't come! He's seen you, you know, at the hut."

"What does it matter?" I objected. "If he didn't recognize me as the chap who sent him the note at Parelli's, we can easily fake up some explanation. Tell him I'm a new member of the Athenians, and that you happened to run across me and brought me down to help work the boat. There's no reason one shouldn't be a yachtsman and a photographer too."

I spoke lightly, but as a matter of fact I was some way from trusting Tommy's judgment implicitly with regard to Latimer's straightforwardness about the restaurant incident, and also about his visit to the hut. All the same, I was quite determined to go to Sheppey. Things had come to a point now when there was nothing to be gained by over-caution. Either Latimer had recognized me or else he hadn't. In the first event, he knew already that Tommy had been trying to deceive him, and that the mythical artist person was none other than myself. If that were so, I felt it was best to take the bull by the horns, and try to find out exactly what part he suspected me of playing. I had at least saved his life, and although we live in an ungrateful world, he seemed bound to be more or less prejudiced in my favour.

Apart from these considerations, Tommy would certainly want some help in working the *Betty*. He knew his job well enough, but with a haze on the river and the twilight drawing in rapidly, the mouth of the Thames is no place for single-handed sailing—especially when you're in a hurry.

Tommy evidently recognized this, for he raised no further objections.

"Very well," he said, with a rather reckless laugh. "We're gambling a bit, but that's the fault of the cards. Up with the anchor, Neil, and let's get a move on her."

I hauled in the chain, and then jumped up to attend to the sails, which I had just let down loosely on deck, in my hurry to put off in the dinghy. After a couple of unsuccessful efforts and two or three very successful oaths, Tommy persuaded the engine to start, and we throbbed off slowly down the creek—now quite a respectable estuary of tidal water.

I sat back in the well with a laugh. "I never expected a second trip tonight," I said. "I'm beginning to feel rather like the captain of a penny steamer."

Tommy, who was combining the important duties of steering and lighting a pipe, looked up from his labours.

"The Lyndon-Morrison Line!" he observed. "Tilbury to Sheppey twice daily. Passengers are requested not to speak to the man at the wheel."

"I think, Tommy," I said, "that we must make an exception in the case of Mr. Latimer."

CHAPTER XX
APPROACHING A SOLUTION

A Chinese proverb informs us that "there are three hundred and forty-six subjects for elegant conversation," but during the trip down I think that Tommy and I confined ourselves almost exclusively to two. One was Mr. Bruce Latimer, and the other was Joyce's amazing discovery about McMurtrie and Marks.

Concerning the latter Tommy was just as astonished and baffled as I was.

"I'm blessed if I know what to think about it, Neil," he admitted. "If it was any one else but Joyce, I should say she'd made a mistake. What on earth could McMurtrie have had to do with that Jew beast?"

"Joyce seems to think he had quite a lot to do with him," I said.

Tommy nodded. "I know. She's made up her mind he did the job all right; but, hang it all, one doesn't go and murder people without any conceivable reason."

"I can conceive plenty of excellent reasons for murdering Marks," I said impartially. "I should hardly think they would have appealed to McMurtrie, though. The chief thing that makes me suspicious about him is the fact of his knowing George and hiding it from me all this time. I suppose that was how he got hold of his information about the powder. George was almost the only person who knew of it."

"I always thought the whole business was a devilish odd one," growled Tommy; "but the more one finds out about it the queerer it seems to get. These people of yours—McMurtrie and Savaroff—are weird enough customers on their own, but when it comes to their being mixed up with both George *and* Marks ..." he paused. "It will turn out next that Latimer's in it too," he added half-mockingly.

"I shouldn't wonder," I said. "I can't swallow everything he told you, Tommy. It leaves too much unexplained. You see, I'm pretty certain that the chap who tried to do him in is one of McMurtrie's crowd, and in that case—"

"In that case," interrupted Tommy, with a short laugh, "we ought to have rather an interesting evening. Seems to me, Neil, we're what you might call burning our boats this journey."

The old compunction I had felt at first against dragging Tommy and Joyce into my affairs suddenly came back to me with renewed force.

"I'm a selfish brute, Thomas," I said ruefully. "I think the best thing I could do really would be to drop overboard. The Lord knows what trouble I shall land you in before I've finished."

"You'll land me into the trouble of telling you not to talk rot in a minute," he returned. Then, standing up and peering out ahead over the long dim expanse of water, dotted here and there with patches of blurred light, he added cheerfully: "You take her over now, Neil, We're right at the end of the Yantlet, and after this morning you ought to know the rest of the way better than I do."

He resigned the tiller to me, and pulling out his watch, held it up to the binnacle lamp.

"Close on a quarter to nine," he said. "We shall just do it nicely if the engine doesn't stop."

"I hope so," I said. "I should hate to keep a Government official waiting."

We crossed the broad entrance into Queenborough Harbour, where the dim bulk of a couple of battleships loomed up vaguely through the haze. It was a strange, exhilarating sensation, throbbing along in the semi-darkness, with all sorts of unknown possibilities waiting for us ahead. More than ever I felt what Joyce had described in the morning—a sort of curious inward conviction that we were at last on the point of finding out the truth.

"We'd better slacken down a bit when we get near," said Tommy. "Latimer specially told me to bring her in as quietly as I could."

I nodded. "Right you are," I said. "I wasn't going to hurry, anyhow. It's a tricky place, and I don't want to smash up any more islands. One a day is quite enough."

I slowed down the engine to about four knots an hour, and at this dignified pace we proceeded along the coast, keeping a watchful eye for the entrance to the creek. At last a vague outline of rising ground showed us that we were in the right neighbourhood, and bringing the *Betty* round, I headed her in very delicately towards the shore. It was distressingly dark, from a helmsman's point of view, but Tommy, who had gone up into the bows, handed me back instructions, and by dint of infinite care we succeeded in making the opening with surprising accuracy.

The creek was quite small, with a steep bank one side perhaps fifteen feet high, and what looked like a stretch of mud or saltings on the other. Its natural beauties, however, if it had any, were rather obscured by the darkness.

"What shall we do now, Tommy?" I asked in a subdued voice. "Turn her round?"

He came back to the well. "Yes," he said, "turn her round, and then I'll cut out the engine and throttle her down. She'll make a certain amount of row, but we can't help that. I daren't stop her; or she might never start again."

We carried out our manoeuvre successfully, and then dropped over the anchor to keep us in position. I seated myself on the roof of the cabin, and pulling out a pipe, commenced to fill it.

"I wonder how long the interval is," I said. "I suppose spying is a sort of job you can't fix an exact time-limit to."

Tommy looked at his watch again. "It's just on a quarter to ten now. He told me not to wait after half-past."

I stuffed down the baccy with my thumb, and felt in my pocket for a match.

"It seems to me—" I began.

The interesting remark I was about to make was never uttered. From the high ground away to the left came the sudden crack of a revolver shot that rang out with startling viciousness on the night air. It was followed almost instantly by a second.

Tommy and I leaped up together, inspired simultaneously by the same idea. Being half way there, however, I easily reached the painter first.

"All right," I cried, "I'll pick him up. You haul in and have her ready to start."

I don't know exactly what the record is for getting off in a dinghy in the dark, but I think I hold it with something to spare. I was away from the ship and sculling furiously for the shore in about the same time that it has taken to write this particular sentence.

I pulled straight for the direction in which I had heard the shots. It was the steepest part of the cliff, but under the circumstances it seemed the most likely spot at which my services would be required. People are apt to take a short cut when revolver bullets are chasing about the neighbourhood.

I stopped rowing a few yards from the shore, and swinging the boat round, stared up through the gloom. There was just light enough to make out the top of the cliff, which appeared to be covered by a thick growth of gorse several feet in height. I backed away a stroke or two, and as I did so, there came a sudden snapping, rustling sound from up above, and the next instant the figure of a man broke through the bushes.

He peered down eagerly at the water.

"That you, Morrison?" he called out in a low, distinct voice, which I recognized at once.

"Yes," I answered briefly. It struck me as being no time for elaborate explanations.

Mr. Latimer was evidently of the same opinion. Without any further remark, he stepped forward to the edge of the cliff, and jumping well out into the air, came down with a beautiful splash about a dozen yards from the boat.

He rose to the surface at once, and I was alongside of him a moment later.

"It's all right," I said, as he clutched hold of the stern. "Morrison's in the *Betty*; I'm lending him a hand."

I caught his arm to help him in, and as I did so he gave a little sharp exclamation of pain.

"Hullo!" I said, shifting my grip. "What's the matter?"

With an effort he hoisted himself up into the boat.

"Nothing much, thanks," he answered in that curious composed voice of his. "I think one of our friends made a luckier shot than he deserved to. It's only my left arm, though."

I seized the sculls, and began to pull off quickly for the *Betty*.

"We'll look at it in a second," I said. "Are they after you?"

He laughed. "Yes, some little way after. I took the precaution of starting in the other direction and then doubling back. It worked excellently."

He spoke in the same rather amused drawl as he had done at the hut, and there was no hint of hurry or excitement in his manner. I could just see, however, that he was dressed in rough, common-looking clothes, and that he was no longer wearing an eye-glass. If he had had a cap, he had evidently parted with it during his dive into the sea.

A few strokes brought us to the *Betty*, where Tommy was leaning over the side ready to receive us.

"All right?" he inquired coolly, as we scrambled on board.

"Nothing serious," replied Latimer. "Thanks to you and—and this gentleman."

"They've winged him, Tommy," I said. "Can you take her out while I have a squint at the damage?"

Tommy's answer was to thrust in the clutch of the engine, and with an abrupt jerk we started off down the creek. As we did so there came a sudden hail from the shore.

"Boat ahoy! What boat's that?"

It was a deep, rather dictatorial sort of voice, with the faintest possible touch of a foreign accent about it.

Latimer replied at once in a cheerful, good-natured bawl, amazingly different from his ordinary tone:

"Private launch, *Vanity*, Southend; and who the hell are you?"

Whether the vigour of the reply upset our questioner or not, I can't say. Anyhow he returned no answer, and leaving him to think what he pleased, we continued our way out into the main stream.

"Come into the cabin and let's have a look at you," I said to Latimer. "You must get those wet things off, anyhow."

He followed me inside, where I took down the small hanging lamp and placed it on the table. Then very carefully I helped him strip off his coat, bringing to light a grey flannel shirt, the left sleeve of which was soaked in blood.

I took out my knife, and ripped it up from the cuff to the shoulder. The wound was about a couple of inches above the elbow, a small clean puncture right through from side to side. It was bleeding a bit, but one could see at a glance that the bullet had just missed the bone.

"You're lucky," I said. "Another quarter of an inch, and that arm would have been precious little use to you for the next two months. Does it hurt much?"

He shook his head. "Not the least," he replied carelessly. "I hardly knew I was hit until you grabbed hold of me."

I tied my handkerchief round as tightly as possible just above the place, and then going to the locker hauled out our spare fancy costume which had previously done duty for Mr. Gow.

"You get these on first," I said, "and then I'll fix you up properly."

I thrust my head out through the cabin door to see how things were going, and found that we were already clear of the creek and heading back towards Queenborough. Tommy, who was sitting at the tiller puffing away peacefully at a pipe, removed the latter article from his mouth.

"Where are we going to, my pretty maid?" he inquired.

"I don't know," I said; "I'll ask the passenger as soon as I've finished doctoring him."

I returned to the cabin, where Mr. Latimer, who had stripped off his wet garments, was attempting to dry himself with a dishcloth. I managed to find him a towel, and then, as soon as he had struggled into a pair of flannel trousers and a vest, I set about the job of tying up his arm. An old shirt of Tommy's served me as a bandage, and although I don't profess to be an expert, I knew enough about first aid to make a fairly serviceable job of it. Anyhow Mr. Latimer expressed himself as being completely satisfied.

"You'd better have a drink now," I said. "That's part of the treatment."

I mixed him a stiff peg, which he consumed without protest; and then, after he had inserted himself carefully into a jersey and coat, we both went outside.

"Hullo!" exclaimed Tommy genially. "How do you feel now?"

Our visitor sat down on one of the side seats in the cockpit, and contemplated us both with his pleasant smile.

"I feel extremely obliged to you, Morrison," he said. "You have a way of keeping your engagements that I find most satisfactory."

Tommy laughed. "I had a bit of luck," he returned. "If I hadn't picked up our pal here I doubt if I should have got down in time after all. By the way, there's no need to introduce you. You've met each other before at the hut, haven't you?"

Latimer, who was just lighting a cigar which I had offered him, paused for a moment in the operation.

"Yes," he said quietly. "We have met each other before. But I should rather like to be introduced, all the same."

Something in his manner struck me as being a trifle odd, but if Tommy noticed it he certainly didn't betray the fact.

"Well, you shall be," he answered cheerfully. "This is Mr. James Nicholson."

Latimer finished lighting his cigar, blew out the match, and dropped it carefully over the side.

"Indeed," he said. "It only shows how extremely inaccurate one's reasoning powers can be."

There was a short but rather pregnant pause. Then Tommy leaned forward.

"What do you mean?" he asked, in that peculiarly gentle voice which he keeps for the most unhealthy occasions.

Latimer's face remained beautifully impassive. "I was under the mistaken impression," he answered slowly, "that I owed my life to Mr. Neil Lyndon."

For perhaps three seconds none of us spoke; then I broke the silence with a short laugh.

"We are up against it, Thomas," I observed.

Tommy looked backwards and forwards from one to the other of us.

"What shall we do?" he said quietly. "Throw him in the river?"

"It would be rather extravagant," I objected, "after we've just pulled him out."

Latimer smiled. "I am not sure I don't deserve it. I have lied to you, Morrison, all through in the most disgraceful manner." Then he paused. "Still it *would* be extravagant," he added. "I think I can convince you of that before we get to Queenborough."

Tommy throttled down the engine to about its lowest running point.

"Look here, Latimer," he said. "We're not going to Queenborough, or anywhere else, until we've got the truth out of you. You understand that, of course. You've put yourself in our power deliberately, and you must have some reason. One doesn't cut one's throat for fun."

He spoke in his usual pleasant fashion, but there was a grim seriousness behind it which no one could pretend to misunderstand. Latimer, at all events, made no attempt to. He merely nodded his head approvingly.

"You're quite right," he said. "I had made up my mind you should hear some of the truth tonight in any case; that was the chief reason why I asked you to come and pick me up. When I saw you had brought Mr. Lyndon with you, I determined to tell you everything. It's the simplest and best way, after all."

He stopped for a moment, and we all three sat there in silence, while the *Betty* slowly throbbed her way forward, splashing off the black water from either bow. Then Latimer began to speak again quite quietly.

"I *am* in the Secret Service," he said; "but you can forget the rest of what I told you the other night, Morrison. I am after bigger game than a couple of German spies—though they come into it right enough. I am on the track of three friends of Mr. Lyndon's, who just now are as badly wanted in Whitehall as they probably are in hell."

I leaned back with a certain curious thrill of satisfaction.

"I thought so," I said softly.

He glanced at me with his keen blue eyes, and the light of the lamp shining on his face showed up its square dogged lines of strength and purpose. It was a fine face—the face of a man without weakness and without fear.

"It's nearly twelve months ago now," he continued, "that we first began to realize at headquarters that there was something queer going on. There's always a certain amount of spying in every country—the sort of quiet, semi-official kind that doesn't do any one a ha'porth of practical harm. Now and then, of course, somebody gets dropped on, and there's a fuss in the papers, but nobody really bothers much about it. This was different, however. Two or three times things happened that did matter very much indeed. They were the sort of things that showed us pretty plainly we were up against something entirely new—some kind of organized affair that had nothing on earth to do with the usual casual spying.

"Well, I made up my mind to get to the bottom of it. Casement, who is nominally the head of our department, gave me an absolutely free hand, and I set to work in my own way quite independently of the police. It was six months before I got hold of a clue. Then some designs—some valuable battleship designs—disappeared from Devonport Dockyard. It was a queer case, but there were one or two things about it which made me pretty sure it was the work of the same gang, and that for the time, at all events, they were somewhere in the neighbourhood.

"I needn't bother you now with all the details of how I actually ran them to earth. It wasn't an easy job. They weren't the sort of people who left any spare bits of evidence lying around, and by the time I found out where they were living it was just too late." He turned to me. "Otherwise, Mr. Lyndon, I think we might possibly have had the pleasure of meeting earlier."

A sudden forgotten recollection of my first interview with McMurtrie flashed vividly into my mind.

"By Jove!" I exclaimed. "What a fool I am! I knew I'd heard your name somewhere before."

Latimer nodded. "Yes," he said. "I daresay I had begun to arouse a certain amount of interest in the household by the time you arrived." He paused. "By the way, I am still quite in the dark as to how you actually got in with them. Had they managed to send you a message into the prison?"

"No," I said. "I'm equally in the dark as to how you've found out who I am, but you seem to know so much already, you may as well have the truth. It was chance; just pure chance and a bicycle. I hadn't the remotest notion who lived in the house. I was trying to steal some food."

Latimer nodded again. "It was a chance that a man like McMurtrie wasn't likely to waste. I don't know yet how you're paying him for his help, but I should imagine it's a fairly stiff price. However, we'll come back to that afterwards.

"I was just too late, as I told you, to interrupt your pleasant little house-party. I managed to find out, however, that some of you had gone to London, and I followed at once. It was then, I think, that the doctor decided it was time to take the gloves off.

"So far, although I'd been on their heels for weeks, I hadn't set eyes on any of the gang personally. All the same, I had a pretty good idea of what McMurtrie and Savaroff were like to look at, and I fancy they probably guessed as much. Anyhow, as you know, it was the third member of the brotherhood—a gentleman who, I believe, calls himself Hoffman—who was entrusted with the job of putting me out of the way."

A faint mocking smile flickered for a moment round his lips.

"That was where the doctor made his first slip. It never pays to underestimate your enemy. Hoffman certainly had a good story, and he told it well, but after thirteen years in the Secret Service I shouldn't trust the Archbishop of Canterbury till I'd proved his credentials. I agreed to dine at Parelli's, but I took the precaution of having two of my own men there as well—one in the restaurant and one outside in the street. I had given them instructions that, whatever happened, they were to keep Hoffman shadowed till further orders.

"Well, you know how things turned out almost as well as I do. I was vastly obliged to you for sending me that note, but as a matter of fact I hadn't the least intention of drinking the wine. Indeed, I turned away purposely to give Hoffman the chance to doctor it. What did beat me altogether was who you were. I naturally couldn't place you at all. I saw that you recognized one of us when you came in, and that you were watching our table pretty attentively in the glass. I had a horrible suspicion for a moment that you were a Scotland Yard man, and were going to bungle the whole business by arresting Hoffman. That was why I sent you my card; I knew if you were at the Yard you'd recognize my name."

"I severed my connection with the police some time ago," I said drily. "What happened after dinner? I've been longing to know ever since."

"I got rid of Hoffman at the door, and from the time he left the restaurant my men never lost him again. They shadowed him to his lodgings—he was living in a side street near Victoria—and for the next two days I got a detailed report of everything he did. It was quite interesting reading. Amongst other things it included paying a morning visit to the hut you're living in at present, Mr. Lyndon, and going on from there to spend the afternoon calling on some friends at Sheppey."

I laughed gently, and turned to Tommy. "Amazingly simple," I said, "when you know how it's done."

Tommy nodded. "I've got all that part, but I'm still utterly at sea about how he dropped on to you."

"That was simpler still," answered Latimer. "One of my men told me that the hut was empty for the time, so I came down to have a look at it." He turned to me. "Of course I recognized you at once as the obliging stranger of the restaurant. That didn't put me much farther on the road, but when Morrison rolled up with his delightfully ingenious yarn, he gave me just the clue I was looking for. I knew his story was all a lie because I'd seen you since. Well, a man like Morrison doesn't butt into this sort of business without a particularly good reason, and it didn't take me very long to guess what his reason was. You see I remembered him chiefly in connection with your trial. I knew he was your greatest friend; I knew you had escaped from Dartmoor and disappeared somewhere in the neighbourhood of McMurtrie's place, and putting two and two together there was only one conclusion I could possibly come to."

"My appearance must have taken a little getting over," I suggested.

Latimer shrugged his shoulders. "Apart from your features you exactly fitted the bill, and I had learned enough about McMurtrie's past performances not to let that worry me. What I couldn't make out was why he should have run the risk of helping you. Of course you might have offered him a large sum of money—if you had it put away somewhere—but in that case there seemed no reason why you should be hanging about in a hut on the Thames marshes."

"Why didn't you tell the police?" asked Tommy.

"The police!" Latimer's voice was full of pleasant irony. "My dear Morrison, we don't drag the police into this sort of business; our great object is to keep them out of it. Mr. Lyndon's affairs had nothing to do with me officially apart from his being mixed up with McMurtrie. Besides, my private sympathies were entirely with him. Not only had he tried to save my life at Parelli's, but ever since the trial I have always been under the impression he was fully entitled to slaughter Mr.—Mr.—whatever the scoundrel's name was."

I acknowledged the remark with a slight bow. "Thank you," I said. "As a matter of sober fact I didn't kill him, but I shouldn't be the least sorry for it if I had."

Latimer looked at me for a moment straight in the eyes.

"We've treated you beautifully as a nation," he said slowly. "It's an impertinence on my part to expect you to help us."

I laughed. "Go on," I said. "Let's get it straightened out anyhow."

"Well, the straightening out must be largely done by you. As far as I'm concerned the rest of the story can be told very quickly. For various reasons I got to the conclusion that in some way or other the two gentlemen on Sheppey had a good deal to do with the matter. My men had been making a few inquiries about them, and from what we'd learned I was strongly inclined to think they were a couple of German naval officers over here on leave. If that was so, the fact that they were in communication with Hoffman made it pretty plain where McMurtrie was finding his market. My men had told me they were generally away on the mainland in the evening, and I made up my mind I'd have a look at the place the first chance I got. I asked Morrison to come down and pick me up in his boat for two reasons— partly because I wanted to keep in touch with you both, and partly because I thought it might come in handy to have a second line of retreat."

"It *was* rather convenient, as things turned out," interposed Tommy.

"Very," admitted Latimer drily. "They got back to the garden just as I had opened one of the windows, and shot at me from behind the hedge. If it hadn't been for the light they must have picked me off."

He stopped, and standing up in the well, looked round. By this time we were again just off the entrance to Queenborough, and the thick haze that had obscured everything earlier in the evening was rapidly thinning away. A watery moon showed up the various warships at anchor—dim grey formless shapes, marked by blurred lights.

"What do you say?" he asked, turning to Tommy. "Shall we run in here and pick up some moorings? Before we go any further I want to hear Lyndon's part of the story, and then we all three shall know exactly where we are. After that you can throw me in the sea, or—or—well, I think there are several possible alternatives."

"We'll find out anyhow," said Tommy.

He turned the *Betty* towards the shore, and we worked our way carefully into the harbour. We ran on past the anchored vessels, until we were right opposite the Queenborough jetty, where we discovered some unoccupied moorings which we promptly adopted. It was a snug berth, and a fairly isolated one—a rakish-looking little gunboat being our nearest neighbour.

In this pleasant atmosphere of law and order I proceeded to narrate as briefly and quickly as possible the main facts about my escape and its results. I felt that we had gone too far now to keep anything back. Latimer had boldly placed his own cards face upwards on the table, and short of sending him to the fishes, there seemed to be nothing else to do except to follow his example. As he himself had said, we should then at least know exactly how we stood with regard to each other.

He listened to me for the most part in silence, but the few interruptions that he did make showed the almost fierce attention with which he was following my story. I don't think his eyes ever left my face from the first word to the last.

When I had finished he sat on for perhaps a minute without speaking. Then very deliberately he leaned across and held out his hand.

We exchanged grips, and for once in my life I found a man whose fingers seemed as strong as my own.

"I don't know whether that makes you an accessory after the fact," I said. "I believe it's about eighteen months for being civil to an escaped convict."

He let go my hand, and getting up from his seat leaned back against the door of the cabin facing us both.

"You may be an escaped convict, Mr. Lyndon," he said slowly, "but if you choose I believe you can do more for England than any man alive."

There was a short pause.

"It seems to me," interrupted Tommy, "that England is a little bit in Neil's debt already."

"That doesn't matter," I observed generously. "Let's hear what Mr. Latimer has got to say." I turned to him. "Who are McMurtrie and Savaroff?" I asked, "and what the devil's the meaning of it all?"

"The meaning is plain enough to a certain point," he answered. "I haven't the least doubt that they intend to sell the secret of your powder to Germany, just as they've sold their other information. If I knew for certain it was only that, I should act, and act at once."

He stopped.

"Well?" I said.

"I believe there's something more behind it—something we've got to find out before we strike. For the last two months Germany has taken a tone towards us diplomatically that can only have one explanation. They mean to get their way or fight, and if it comes to a fight they're under the impression they're going to beat us."

"And you really believe McMurtrie and Savaroff are responsible for their optimism?" I asked a little incredulously.

Latimer nodded. "Dr. McMurtrie," he said in his quiet drawl, "is the most dangerous man in Europe. He is partly English and partly Russian by birth. At one time he used to be court physician at St. Petersburg. Savaroff is a German Pole—his real name is Vassiloff. Between them they were largely responsible for the early disasters in the Japanese war."

For a moment no one spoke. Then Tommy leaned forward. "I say, Latimer," he exclaimed, "is this serious history?"

"The Russian Government," replied Latimer, "are most certainly under that impression."

"But if they know about it," I objected, "how is it that McMurtrie and Savaroff aren't in Siberia? I've never heard that the Russians are particularly tender-hearted where traitors are concerned."

Latimer indulged in that peculiarly dry smile of his. "If the Government had got hold of them I think their destination would have been a much warmer one than Siberia. As it was they disappeared just in time. There was a gang of them—four or five at the least—and all men of position and influence. They must have made an enormous amount of money out of the Japs. In the end one of them rounded on the others—at least that's what appears to have happened. Anyhow McMurtrie and Savaroff skipped, and skipped in such a hurry that they seem to have left most of their savings behind them. I suppose that's what made them start business again in England."

"You're absolutely sure they're the same pair?" asked Tommy.

"Absolutely. I've got their full description from the Russian police. It tallies in every way—even to Savaroff's daughter. There *is* a girl with them, I believe?"

"Yes," I said. "There's a girl." Then I paused for a moment. "Look here, Latimer," I went on. "What is it you want me to do? I'll help you in any way I can. When I made my bargain with McMurtrie I hadn't a notion what his real game was. I don't in the least want to buy my freedom by selling England to Germany. The only thing I flatly and utterly refuse to do is to serve out the rest of my sentence. If it's bound to come out who I am, you must give me your word I shall have a reasonable warning. I don't much mind dying—especially if I can arrange for ten minutes with George first—but quite candidly I'd see England wiped off the map before I'd go back to Dartmoor."

Latimer made a slight gesture with his hands. "You've saved my life, once at all events," he said. "It may seem a trifle to you, but it's a matter of quite considerable importance to me. I don't think you need worry about going back to Dartmoor—not as long as the Secret Service is in existence."

"Well, what is it you want me to do?" I asked again.

He was silent for a moment or two, as though arranging his ideas. Then he began to speak very slowly and deliberately.

"I want you to go on as if nothing had happened. Write to McMurtrie the first thing tomorrow morning and tell him that you've made the powder. He is sure to come down to the hut at once. You can show him that it's genuine, but on no account let him have any of it to take away. Tell him that you will only hand over the secret on receipt of a written agreement, and make him see that you're absolutely serious. Meanwhile let me know everything that happens as soon as you possibly can. Telegraph to me at 145 Jermyn Street. You can send in the messages to Tilbury by the man who's looking after your boat. Use some quick simple cypher—suppose we say the alphabet backwards, Z for A and so on. Have you got plenty of money?"

I nodded. "I should like to have some sort of notion what you're going to do," I said. "It would be much more inspiriting than working in the dark."

"It depends entirely on the next two days. I shall go back to London tonight and find out if either of my men has got hold of any fresh information. Then I shall put the whole thing in front of Casement. If he agrees with me I shall wait till the last possible moment before striking. We've enough evidence about the Devonport case to arrest McMurtrie and Savaroff straight away, but I feel it would be madness while there's a chance of getting to the bottom of this business. Perhaps you understand now why I've risked everything tonight. We're playing for high stakes, Mr. Lyndon, and you—" he paused—"well, I'm inclined to think that you've the ace of trumps."

I stood up and faced him. "I hope so," I said. "I'm rather tired of being taken for the Knave."

"Isn't there a job for me?" asked Tommy pathetically. "I'm open for anything, especially if it wants a bit of physical violence."

"There will probably be a demand for that a little later on," said Latimer in his quiet drawl. "At present I want you to come back with me to London. I shall find plenty for you to do there, Morrison. The fewer people that are mixed up in this affair the better." He turned to me. "You can take the boat back to Tilbury alone if we go ashore here?"

I nodded, and he once more held out his hand.

"We shall meet again soon," he said—"very soon I think. Have you ever read Longfellow?"

It was such a surprising question that I couldn't help smiling.

"Not recently," I said. "I haven't been in the mood for poetry the last two or three years."

He held my hand and his blue eyes looked steadily into mine.

"Ah," he said. "I don't want to be too optimistic, but there's a verse in Longfellow which I think you might like." He paused again. "It has something to do with the Mills of God," he added slowly.

CHAPTER XXI
SONIA'S SUDDEN VISIT

One's feelings are queer things. Personally I never have the least notion how a particular situation will affect me until I happen to find myself in it.

I should have thought, for instance, that Latimer's revelations would have left me in a state of vast excitement, but as a matter of fact I don't think I ever felt cooler in my life. I believe every other emotion was swallowed up in the relief of finding out something definite at last.

I know anyhow that that was my chief sensation as I rowed the dinghy towards the wet slimy causeway, lit by its solitary lamp. There was a boat train to town in the early hours of the morning which Latimer had suggested that he and Tommy should catch, and it certainly seemed a safer plan than coming back to Tilbury with me.

When I had parted from them, under the sleepy eye of a depressed-looking night watchman, I returned to the *Betty* and proceeded to let go my moorings. I then ran up the sails, and gliding gently past the warships and a big incoming steamer, floated out into the broad peaceful darkness of the Thames estuary. I was in no hurry, and now that the mist had cleared away it was a perfect night for drifting comfortably up river with the tide.

The dawn was just beginning to break by the time I reached my old anchorage in the creek. In spite of my long and slightly strenuous day, I didn't feel particularly tired, so after stowing away the sails and tidying up things generally, I sat down in the cabin and began to compose my letter to McMurtrie.

I started off by telling him that I had completed my invention some days earlier than I expected to, and then gave him a brief but dramatic description of the success which had attended my first experiment. I am afraid I was a trifle inaccurate with regard to details, but the precise truth is a luxury that very few of us can afford to indulge in. I certainly couldn't. When I had finished I addressed the envelope to the Hotel Russell, and then, turning into one of the bunks, soon dropped off into a well-deserved sleep.

I don't know whether it was Nature that aroused me, or whether it was Mr. Gow. Anyway I woke up with the distinct impression that somebody was hailing the boat, and thrusting my head up through the hatch I discovered my faithful retainer standing on the bank.

He greeted me with a slightly apologetic air when I put off to fetch him.

"Good-mornin', sir. I hope I done right stoppin' ashore, sir. The young lady told me I wouldn't be wanted not till this mornin'."

"The young lady was quite correct," I said. "You weren't." Then as we pushed off for the *Betty* I added: "But I'm glad you've come back in good time today. I want you to go in and post a letter for me at Tilbury as soon as we've had some breakfast. You might get a newspaper for me at the same time."

"Talkin' o' noos, sir," observed Mr. Gow with sudden interest, "'ave you heard tell about the back o' Canvey Island bein' blown up yesterday mornin'?"

"Blown up!" I repeated as we ran alongside. "Who on earth did that?"

Mr. Gow shook his head as he clambered on board after me. "No one don't seem to know," he remarked. "'Twere done arly in the mornin', they reckon. There's some as says 'tis the suffrinjettes, but to my way o' thinkin' sir; it's more like to have somethin' to do with them blarsted Dutchmen as sunk my boat."

"By Jove!" I exclaimed, "I wonder if it had. They seem to be mischievous devils."

Mr. Gow nodded emphatically. "They are, sir, and that's a fact. 'Tis time somebody took a quiet look round that house o' theirs, some day when they ain't there."

How very nearly this desirable object had been achieved on the previous evening I thought it unnecessary to mention, but I was hugely relieved to learn that so far there was no suspicion as to who was really responsible for the damage to the creek. Apart from the inconvenience which it would have entailed, to be arrested for blowing up a bit of mud in a Thames backwater would have been a sad come-down for a convicted murderer!

As soon as he had provided me with some breakfast, Mr. Gow departed for Tilbury with my letter to McMurtrie in his pocket. He was away for a couple of hours, returning with a copy of the *Daily Mail* and the information that there were no letters for me at the post-office.

I handed him over the *Betty*, with instructions not to desert her until he was relieved by either Tommy or Joyce or me, and then set off for the hut by my usual route. It was less than thirty hours since I had left it, but so many interesting things had happened in the interval it seemed more like three weeks.

For any one entangled in such a variety of perils as I appeared to be, I spent a surprisingly peaceful day. Not a soul came near the place, and except for reading the *Mail* and indulging in a certain amount of hard thinking, I enjoyed the luxury of doing absolutely nothing. After the exertion and excitements of the previous twenty-four hours, this lull was exactly what I needed. It gave me time to take stock of my position in the light of Latimer's amazing revelations—a process which on the whole I found fairly satisfactory. If the likelihood of proving my innocence still seemed a trifle remote, I had at least penetrated some of the mystery which surrounded Dr. McMurtrie and his friends, and more and more it was becoming obvious to me that the two problems were closely connected. Anyhow I turned into bed in an optimistic mood, and with the stimulating feeling that in all probability I had a pleasantly eventful day in front of me.

It certainly opened in the most promising fashion. I woke up at eight, and was making a light breakfast off a tin of sardines and some incredibly stale bread, when through the little window that looked out towards the Tilbury road I suddenly spotted my youthful friend from the post-office approaching across the marsh. I opened the door, and he came up with a respectful grin of recognition.

"Letter for you, sir," he observed, "come this morning, sir."

He handed me an envelope addressed in Joyce's writing, and stood by while I read it, thoughtfully scratching his head with the peak of his cap. It was only a short note, but beautifully characteristic of Joyce.

"MY OWN NEIL,—

"I'm coming down to see you tomorrow afternoon. I've got several things to tell you, but the chief reason is because I want to kiss you and be kissed by you. Everything else seems rather unimportant compared with that.

"JOYCE."

"Any answer, sir?" inquired the boy, when he saw I had finished reading.

"Yes, Charles," I said; "there is an answer, but I'm afraid I can't send it by post. Wait a minute, though," I added, as he began to put on his cap, "I want you to send off a wire for me if you will. It will take a minute or two to write."

I went into the hut, and hastily scribbled a telegram to Latimer, telling him that I had written to McMurtrie, but that otherwise there was nothing to report. I copied this out carefully in the simple cypher we had agreed on, and handed it to the boy, together with five shillings.

"You can keep the change," I said, "and buy fireworks with it. I've been too busy to make any yet."

He gurgled out some expressions of gratitude and took his departure, while I renewed my attack upon the sardines and bread.

Fortified by this simple cheer, I devoted the remainder of the morning to tidying up my shed. I felt that I was living in such uncertain times that it would be just as well to remove all possible traces of the work I had been engaged on, and by midday the place looked almost as tidy as when I had first entered it.

I then treated myself to a cigar and began to keep a look-out for Joyce. She had not said in her letter what time she would arrive, but I knew that there were a couple of trains early in the afternoon, and I remembered that I had told her to come straight to the hut.

It must have been getting on for two when I suddenly caught sight of a motor car with a solitary occupant coming quickly along the Tilbury road. It pulled up as it reached the straggling plantation opposite the hut, and a minute later a girl appeared from between the trees, and started to walk towards me across the marsh.

I was a little surprised, for I didn't know that Joyce included motor driving amongst her other accomplishments, and she had certainly never mentioned to me that there was any chance of her coming down in a car. Then, a moment later, the truth suddenly hit me with paralysing abruptness. It was not Joyce at all; it was Sonia.

I don't know why the discovery should have given me such a shock, for in a way I had been expecting her to turn up any time. Still a shock it undoubtedly did give me, and for a second or so I stood there staring stupidly at her like a man who has suddenly lost the use of his limbs. Then, pulling myself together, I turned away from the window and strode to the door.

She came up to me swiftly and eagerly, moving with that strange lissom grace that always reminded me of some untamed animal. Her hurried walk across the marsh had brought a faint tinge of colour into the usual ivory clearness of her skin, and her dark eyes were alive with excitement.

I held out my hands to welcome her. "I was beginning to think you'd forgotten the address, Sonia," I said.

With that curious little deep laugh of hers she pulled my arms round her, and for several seconds we remained standing in this friendly if a trifle informal attitude. Then, perceiving no reasonable alternative, I bent down and kissed her.

"Ah!" she whispered. "At last! At last!"

Deserted as the marsh was, it seemed rather public for this type of dialogue, so drawing her inside the hut I closed the door.

She looked round at everything with rapid, eager interest. "I have heard all about the powder," she said. "It's quite true, isn't it? You have done what you hoped to do?"

I nodded. "I've blown up about twenty yards of Canvey Island with a few ounces of it," I said. "That seems good enough for a start."

She laughed again with a sort of fierce satisfaction. "You have done something more than that. You have given me just the power I needed to help you." She came up and with a quick impulsive gesture laid her two hands on my arm. "Neil, Neil, my lover! In a few hours from now you can have everything you want in the world. Everything, Neil—money, freedom, love—" She broke off, panting slightly with her own vehemence, and then drawing my face down to hers, kissed me again on the lips.

I suppose I ought to have felt rather ashamed of myself, but I think I was too interested in what she was going to say to worry much about anything else.

"Tell me, Sonia," I said. "What am I to do? Can I trust your father and McMurtrie?"

She let go my arm, and stepping back sat down on the edge of the small table which I had been using as a writing-desk.

"Trust them!" she repeated half scornfully. "Yes, you can trust them if you want to go on being cheated and robbed. Can't you see—can't you guess the way they have been lying to you?"

"Of course I can," I said coolly; "but when one's between the Devil and Dartmoor, I prefer the Devil every time. I don't enjoy being cheated, but it's much more pleasant than being starved or flogged."

She leaned forward, holding the edge of the table with her hands. "There's no need for either. As I've told you, in a few hours from now we can be away from England with money enough to last us for our lives. Do you know what your invention is worth? Do you know what use they mean to make of it?"

"I imagine they hope to sell it," I answered. "It wouldn't be difficult to find a customer."

"Difficult!" She lowered her voice to a quick eager whisper. "They have got a customer. The best customer in Europe. A customer that will pay anything in the world for such a secret as yours."

I gazed at her with a carefully assumed expression of amazement and dawning intelligence.

"Good Lord, Sonia!" I said slowly; "do you mean—?"

She made an impatient movement with her hands. "Listen! I am going to tell you everything. What's the good of you and I beating about the bush?" She paused. "We are spies," she said quite simply, "professional spies. Of course it sounds absurd and impossible to you—an Englishman—but all the same it's the truth. You don't know what sort of man Dr. McMurtrie is."

"I appear to be learning," I observed.

"He has been a friend of my father's for years. They were in Russia together at one time—and then Paris, Vienna—oh, everywhere. It has always been the same; in each country they have found out things that other Governments have been willing to pay for. At least, the doctor has. The rest of us, my father, myself, Hoffman"—she shrugged her shoulders—"we are his puppets, his tools. Everything we have done has been planned and arranged by him."

There was a short silence.

"How long have you been here?" I asked. "What brought you to England?"

"We have been here just over three years," she answered slowly. "There was a man in London that Dr. McMurtrie and my father wanted to find. Eight years ago he betrayed them in St. Petersburg."

A sudden idea—so wild as to be almost incredible—flashed into my mind.

I moistened my lips. "Who was he?" I asked steadily.

She shook her head. "I don't know his name. I only know that he is dead. I think Dr. McMurtrie would kill any one who betrayed him—if he could."

I crossed the room and sat down on the edge of the bed. I felt strangely excited.

"And after that," I said quietly, "I suppose the doctor thought he might as well stop here and do a little business?"

"I think it was suggested to him from Berlin. He had sent them all sorts of information when we were in Paris, and, of course, as things are now, they were still more anxious to get hold of anything about the English army or navy." She paused. "What they specially wanted were the plans of the Lyndon-Marwood torpedo."

"Yes," I said. "I dare say they did. A lot of people have wanted them, but unfortunately they're not for sale."

Sonia laughed softly. "The exact price we paid for them," she said, "was twelve thousand pounds."

I sat up with a jerk. This time my surprise was utterly genuine.

"You bought them!" I said incredulously. "Bought them from some one in the Admiralty?"

Again Sonia shook her head. "Don't you remember what you read in the *Daily Mail* about the robbery at your offices in Victoria Street?"

I stared at her for a second, and then suddenly the real truth dawned on me.

"So George sold them to you?" I said.

She nodded. "Ever since you went to prison the business has been going to pieces. He wanted money badly—very badly indeed. Dr. McMurtrie found this out. He found out too that there was a copy of the plans in the office, and—well, you can guess the rest. The burglary, of course, was arranged between them. It was meant to cover your cousin in case the Government found out that the Germans had got hold of the plans."

"And have they found out?" I asked.

Again Sonia shrugged her shoulders. "I can't say. The doctor and my father never tell me anything that they can keep to themselves. Most of what I know I have picked up from listening to them and putting things together in my own head afterwards. I am useful to them, and to a certain point they trust me; but only so far. They know I hate them both."

She made the statement with a detached bitterness that spoke volumes for its sincerity.

I felt too that she was telling me the truth about George. A man who could lie as he did at the trial was quite capable of betraying his country or anything else. Still, the infernal impudence and treachery of his selling my beautiful torpedo to the Germans filled me with a furious anger such as I had not felt since I crouched, dripping and hunted, in the Walkham woods.

I looked up at Sonia, who was leaning forward and watching me with those curious half-sullen, half-passionate eyes of hers.

"Why did George tell those lies about me at the trial?" I asked.

"I don't know for certain; I think he wanted to get rid of you, so that he could steal your invention. Of course he saw how valuable it was. You had told him about the notes, and I think he felt that if you were safely out of the way he would be able to make use of them himself."

"He must have been painfully disappointed," I said. "They were all jotted down in a private cypher. No one else could possibly have understood them."

She nodded. "I know. He offered to sell them to us. He suggested that the Germans might be willing to pay a good sum down for them on the chance of being able to make them out."

Angry as I was, I couldn't help laughing. It was so exactly like George to try and make the best of a bad speculation.

"I can hardly see the doctor doing business on those lines," I said.

"It was too late in any case," she answered calmly. "Just after he made the offer you escaped from prison." There was another pause. "And what were you all doing down in that God-forsaken part of the world?" I demanded.

The question was a little superfluous as far as I was concerned, but I felt that Sonia would be expecting it.

"Oh, we weren't there for pleasure," she said curtly. "We wanted to be near Devonport, and at the same time we wanted a place that was quite quiet and out-of-the-way. Hoffman found the house for us, and we took it furnished for six months."

"It was an extraordinary stroke of luck," I said, "that I should have come blundering in as I did."

Sonia laughed venomously. "It was the sort of thing that would happen to the doctor. The Devil looks after his friends."

"As a matter of fact," I objected, "I was thinking more of myself."

Sonia took no notice of my interruption. "Why, it meant everything to him," she went on eagerly. "It practically gave him the power to dictate his own terms to the Germans. You see, he knew something about their plans. He knew—at least he could guess—that the moment war was declared they meant to make a surprise attack on all the big dockyards—just like the Japs did at Port Arthur. Well, think of the difference an explosive as powerful as yours would make! Why, it would put England absolutely at their mercy. They could blow up Portsmouth, Sheerness, and Devonport before any one really knew that the war had started."

She spoke rapidly, almost feverishly, leaning forward and gripping the edge of the table, till the skin showed white on her knuckles. I think I was equally excited, but I tried not to show it.

"Yes," I said; "it sounds a promising notion."

"Promising!" she echoed. "Well, it was promising enough for the Germans to offer us anything we wanted the moment we could give them the secret. Now perhaps you can understand why we were so hospitable and obliging to you."

"And you believe McMurtrie never meant to keep his word to me?" I asked.

She laughed again scornfully. "If you knew him as well as I do, you wouldn't need to ask that. He would simply have disappeared with the money and left you to rot or starve."

I took out my case, and having given Sonia a cigarette, lit one myself.

"It's an unpleasant choice," I said, "but I gather there's a possible alternative."

She lighted her own cigarette and threw away the match. Her dark eyes were alight with excitement.

"Listen," she said. "All the Germans want is the secret. Do you suppose they care in the least whom they get it from? You have only got to prove to them that you can do what you say, and they will pay you the money just as readily as they would the doctor."

There was a magnificent simplicity about the idea that for a moment almost took my breath away.

"How could I get in touch with them?" I asked.

She leaned forward again, and lowered her voice almost to a whisper.

"I can take you now—now right away—to the two men who are in charge of the whole business. I know that they have an absolutely free hand to make the best terms they can."

"Who are they?" I demanded, with an eagerness I made no attempt to hide.

"Their names are Seeker and von Brünig, and they're living in a small bungalow on Sheppey. They are supposed to be artists. As a matter of fact, von Brünig is a captain in the Germany Navy. I don't know who the other man is; I think he has been sent over specially about the powder."

Her statement fitted in so exactly with what I had already found out from Latimer and Gow, that I hadn't the remotest doubt she was telling me the literal truth. Of its importance—its vital importance to England—there could be no question. I felt my heart beating quickly with excitement, but the obvious necessity for fixing on some scheme of immediate action kept my brain cool and clear. The first thing was to gain a moment or two to think in.

"You realize what all this means, Sonia?" I said. "You're quite prepared to throw over your father and McMurtrie? You know how the doctor deals with people who betray him—when he gets the chance?"

"I am not afraid of them," she answered defiantly. "They are nothing to me; I hate them both—and Hoffman too. It's you I want. You are the only man I ever have wanted." She paused, and I saw her breast rising and falling rapidly with the stress of her emotion. "We will go away together—somewhere the other side of the world—America, Buenos Ayres—oh, what does it matter where?—there are plenty of places! What does anything matter so long as we love each other!"

She half rose to her feet, but I jumped up first.

"One moment, Sonia," I said. "Let me think."

Thrusting my hands in my pockets, I strode across the room, and pulling up in front of the little window, stared out across the marsh. As I did so, I felt as if some one had suddenly placed a large handful of crushed ice inside my waistcoat. About two hundred yards away, strolling cheerfully and unconcernedly towards the hut, was the charming but painfully inopportune figure of Joyce.

It was a most unpleasant second. In my excitement at listening to Sonia's revelations, I had clean forgotten for the time that Joyce was coming, and now it was too late for the recollection to be of much practical use. Except for an earthquake, or the sudden arrival of the end of the world, nothing could stop her from reaching the hut in another five minutes.

I stood quite still, racking my brains as to what was the best thing to do. It was no use trying to signal to her from the window, for Sonia would be certain to see me; while if I made some excuse for going outside, Joyce would probably call out to me before I had time to warn her. My only hope seemed to lie in the chance of her hearing us talking as she came up to the door, in which case she would know at once that there was some one there and go straight on to the *Betty*.

I had just reached this conclusion when a queer sound behind me made me spin round as if I had been struck. Sonia, who had risen to her feet, was standing and facing me; her whole attitude suggestive of a highly-annoyed tigress. I don't think I have ever seen such a malevolent expression on any human being's face in my life. For an instance we stood staring at each other without speaking, and then quite suddenly I realized what was the matter.

Clutched tight in her right hand was a letter—a letter which I recognized immediately as the one I had received from Joyce that morning. Like a fool I must have left it lying on the desk, and while I was looking out of the window she had evidently picked it up and read it.

I hadn't much time, however, for self-reproaches.

"So, you have been lying to me all through," she broke out bitterly. "This girl is your mistress; and all the time you have simply been using me to help yourself. Oh, I see it all now. I see why you were so anxious to come to London. While I have been working and scheming for you, you and she ..." Her voice failed from very fury, and tearing the letter in pieces, she flung them on the ground at my feet.

I suppose I attempted some sort of reply, for she broke out again more savagely than ever.

"She *is* your mistress! Do you dare to deny it, with that letter staring me in the face? Coming down to 'kiss you and be kissed by you,' is she? Well, she's used to that, at all events!" Her voice choked again, and with her hands clenched she made a quick step forward in my direction.

Then quite suddenly I saw her whole expression change. The anger in her eyes gave place to a gleam of recognition, and the next moment her lips parted in a peculiarly malicious smile. She was looking past me through the open window.

"Ah!" she said. "So that's why you were standing there! You didn't expect me to be here when she arrived, did you?" With a mocking laugh she turned to the doorway. "Never mind," she added viciously: "you will be able to introduce us."

Even if I had tried to prevent her it would have been too late. With a swift movement she flung back the door, and stepped forward across the threshold.

Joyce was standing about fifteen yards away, facing the hut. She had evidently just heard the sound of Sonia's voice, and had pulled up abruptly, as I expected she would. Directly the door opened, she turned as if to continue her walk.

Sonia laughed again. "Please don't go away," she said.

There was a moment's pause, and then I too advanced to the door. I saw that there was nothing else for it except the truth.

"Joyce," I said, "this is Sonia. She has just read your letter, which I left lying on the desk."

It must have been a bewildering situation even to such a quick-witted person as Joyce, but all the same one would never have guessed the fact from her manner. For perhaps a second she stood still, looking from one to the other of us; then, with that sudden engaging smile of hers, she came forward and held out her hand to Sonia.

"I am so glad to meet you," she said simply. "Neil has told me how good you have been to him."

Sonia remained quite motionless. She had drawn herself up to her full height, and she stared at Joyce with a cool hatred she made no attempt to conceal.

"Yes," she said; "I have no doubt he told you that. He will have a lot more to tell you as soon as I've gone. You will have plenty to talk about when you're not kissing." With a low, cruel little laugh she stepped forward. "Make the most of him while you've got him," she added. "It won't be for long."

As the last word left her lips, she suddenly raised the glove she was holding in her hand, and struck Joyce fiercely across the face.

In one stride I was up with them—God knows what I meant to do—but, thrusting out her arm, Joyce motioned me back.

"It's all right, Neil dear," she said. "I should have done exactly the same."

For a moment we all three remained just as we were, and then without a word Sonia turned on her heel and walked off rapidly in the direction of the Tilbury road.

CHAPTER XXII
THE POLICE TAKE ACTION

"What have we done, Neil?"

Joyce put the question with a calmness that was truly delightful.

"It seems to me," I said, "that we've torn it badly." Then, with a last look at Sonia's retreating figure, I added: "Come inside, and I'll try to explain."

We entered the hut, where the floor was still strewn with the fragments of Joyce's letter. She seated herself on the edge of the bed and waited patiently while I took a couple of turns up and down the room.

"Joyce," I said, "I deserve kicking. I'm not sure I haven't messed up the whole business."

"Tell me," she said quietly. "I know about Latimer already; I saw Tommy at the flat this morning."

"Well, that simplifies things," I said; and without wasting any further time in self-reproaches, I plunged straight into the story of Sonia's surprise visit and its abrupt and spirited ending.

"How I could have been such an ass I don't know," I finished ruefully. "I must have put the letter down on the table after I'd done reading it, and there I suppose it was sitting the whole time."

Joyce, who had listened to me without interrupting, nodded her head. "It was just one of those things that had got to happen," she said philosophically. "It's no good worrying now. The thing is, what are we to do about it?"

I thought for a moment.

"We must let Latimer know at once," I said. "I'll write out what Sonia told me—just the main facts, and you must take the letter straight up to London, and find him as soon as you can. I shall stop here, as he asked me to."

Joyce's face looked a little troubled.

"What do you think Sonia will do?" she asked.

"Goodness knows!" I said. "She seemed to have some particularly unpleasant intention at the back of her mind; but I don't quite see what it is."

"She won't care what she does," said Joyce. "I know exactly how she feels. Suppose she were to go to the police?"

"She could hardly do that," I objected. "She'd be incriminating herself."

"But suppose she does," persisted Joyce. "Suppose they come and arrest you here; Latimer won't be able to help you then."

"I can't go back now, Joyce," I said seriously. "I can't get out of it just because it might be dangerous to me. After all, it's England they're scheming against."

"And what if it is?" she returned indignantly. "A nice way England's treated you!"

I came over to the bed and took her hands in mine.

"Come, Joyce," I said, "you don't really mean that. I want encouraging, not depressing. All my natural instincts are to look after myself and let England go to the devil."

Half laughing and half crying, she jumped up and threw her arms round me.

"No, no, no," she said. "I want you to do the right thing always; but oh, Neil, I'm so frightened of losing you. I just can't do without you now."

"Well," I said, "I'm hanged if I can do without you, so we're in the same boat."

I kissed her twice, and then, sitting down at the table, made a brief summary of what I had learned from Sonia. Latimer so far knew nothing of my relations with the latter, so I was compelled to explain how badly I had behaved in order to account for her visit. I then gave him a short description of the painful way in which the interview had terminated, and added the information that I was waiting on at the hut in the expectation of a visit from McMurtrie.

"You can explain things more fully to him, Joyce," I said. "It's no good trying to keep anything back now; we've gone too far. The great thing is to get that letter to him as soon as you possibly can. Tommy will probably know where he is."

She nodded. "I shall find him all right." She slipped the envelope inside her dress, and glanced at the watch she was wearing on her wrist. "There are several things I wanted to tell you," she added, "but they none of them matter for the moment. If I go at once, I can just catch the three-thirty."

"I'll come as far as the road with you," I said. "I daren't leave the hut for long, in case McMurtrie turns up."

We went outside and had a good look round. Sonia had long since disappeared, and the place wore its usual aspect of utter desolation. I took the precaution of locking the door, however, and then at a sharp pace we set off together across the marsh.

"Tell me about George," I said. "How are you getting on with the elopement plan?"

Joyce smiled. "I think George is growing a little impatient. He wants to get away as soon as possible."

"Yes," I said; "I have no doubt the Mediterranean sounds attractive to him. There's a pretty stiff penalty attached to selling Government secrets if you happen to be found out. Besides, I expect he's still worrying a lot about me."

Joyce nodded. "He told me last night that I was the only thing that was keeping him in London. You see I can't quite make up my mind whether I love him well enough to come away."

"That's unfortunate for George," I said. "Latimer will probably act at once as soon as he gets that letter, and directly he does I mean to go straight to Cheyne Walk, unless I'm dead or in prison."

Joyce took my arm. "Neil," she said, "whatever happens you mustn't be arrested. If you think there's any chance of it you must go on board the *Betty* and take her somewhere down the river. You can let me know at the flat where you are. Promise me you will, Neil. You see if the police once got hold of you, even Latimer mightn't be able to do anything."

For a moment I hesitated. So far I had told Joyce nothing of the wild suspicion about Marks's identity which Sonia's revelations had put into my head. I didn't want to rouse hopes in her which might turn out quite baseless. Besides, even if I were really on the right track, and Marks was the man who had betrayed the gang in St. Petersburg, it was quite another thing to prove that they were responsible for splitting his skull. I had nothing to support the idea beyond Joyce's bare word that she had seen McMurtrie in the flat on the afternoon of the murder. Sonia's testimony might have been useful, but after today I could hardly picture her in the witness-box giving evidence on my behalf.

On the whole, therefore, I thought it best for the present to keep the matter to myself. I promised, however, that in the event of my observing anything in the nature of a policeman stealthily approaching the hut I would at once seek sanctuary on the *Betty*—an assurance which might have sounded worthless to some people, but certainly seemed to comfort Joyce.

Anyhow she said good-bye to me with her usual cheerfulness and pluck, and we parted after a last affectionate kiss in full view of the open marsh. Then I returned to the hut suffering from that novel and highly unpleasant sense of loneliness that Joyce's departures had begun to awake in me.

I don't think there is anything much more trying to one's nerves than having to sit and wait for some critical event which may happen at any moment. I have had a good deal of practice at waiting in my life, but I never remember the hours dragging so desperately slowly as they did the remainder of that afternoon.

A dozen times I went over what Latimer and Sonia had told me, putting together their different stories in my mind and trying to think if there was any point I had overlooked. I could see none. The mere way in which they had corroborated each other was enough to make me feel sure that they were both speaking the truth. Besides, everything that had happened from the moment I had crept in through the kitchen window at McMurtrie's house pointed to the same conclusion.

I may appear stupid not to have seen through the doctor earlier, but after all a gang of professional spies is hardly the sort of thing one expects to run up against in a Devonshire village. A few years ago, indeed, I should have laughed at the idea of their existence anywhere outside the pages of a shilling shocker, but my three years in Dartmoor had led me to take a rather more generous view of what life can throw up in the way of scoundrels.

Whether they had killed Marks or not, I had little doubt now that they were wholly responsible for the attempt to murder Latimer. Though I had good evidence that when it came to the point the two gentlemen on Sheppey didn't stick at trifles, I could hardly fancy a couple of German Naval officers deliberately countenancing such methods. If they had, they certainly deserved the worst fate that even Mr. Gow could wish them.

Somehow or other my private interest in the affair seemed to have been temporarily forced into the background. I felt I was probably doing the best thing I could for myself in throwing in my lot with Latimer, but in any case his enthusiasm had got hold of me, and at all risks I was determined to stick to my side of the bargain. I knew that in her heart Joyce would have hated me to do otherwise.

My chief danger, as she had instantly seen, was the chance of Sonia betraying me to the police. The latter, who knew nothing of the part I was playing as a sort of unpaid bottle-washer to the Secret Service, would at once jump at the chance of arresting an escaped convict—especially such a well-advertised one as myself. However improbable Sonia's story might sound, they would at least be certain to take the trouble to investigate it.

On the other hand, of course Sonia might not go to the police at all, and even if she did, it was quite possible that Latimer would strike first and so give me the chance of clearing out.

Anyhow, forewarned as I was, I felt it would be an uncommonly bright policeman who succeeded in arresting me. In the day-time, so long as I kept a good look out, anything like a surprise attack was impossible, and after that night I made up my mind that I would sleep on the *Betty*. The only thing was, I should most certainly have to deprive myself of the luxury of a skipper. Useful as he was at taking letters into Tilbury, it would be decidedly embarrassing to have him on board if I happened to arrive in a hurry on the beach with two perspiring detectives in hot pursuit.

At six o'clock, as there was still no sign of a visitor, I decided to walk over to the *Betty* and tell Mr. Gow that he could treat himself to another holiday. It would only take me about half an hour, and in case McMurtrie turned up while I was away I could leave a message on the door to the effect that I should be back before seven.

I did this, pinning it up carefully with a drawing-tack and then after making sure that everything was secure I started off for the creek.

I found Mr. Gow in his usual restful attitude, his head and shoulders sticking up out of the fo'c's'le hatch, and a large pipe protruding from his mouth. With the instincts of a true retainer he promptly removed the latter as soon as he heard my hail, and hoisting himself up on deck put off in the dinghy.

"I'm not coming aboard," I said. "I only walked over to tell you that you can have a couple of days ashore. We shan't be using the boat till Saturday or Sunday."

He thanked me and touched his cap (I could see he was beginning to think it was rather a soft job he had stumbled into), and then, with the air of some one breaking unpleasant tidings, he added: "Do you happen to know, sir, as we're clean out o' petrol?"

I didn't happen to know it, but under the circumstances it was information I was glad to acquire.

"Can you get me some—soon?" I asked.

He nodded. "I'll bring along a couple o' cans in the mornin', sir, and leave 'em aboard."

"Any news?" I asked.

"Well, sir, I seed the Dutchmen's launch goin' down this arternoon—travellin' proper they was too, same as when they swamped me. I suppose you ain't bin able to do nothin' about that matter not yet, sir?"

"I'm looking into it, Mr. Gow," I said. "I have a friend helping me, and between us I think we shall be able to get some satisfaction out of them. I shall probably have more to tell you on Saturday."

With this answer he seemed quite content. "Well, I'll just run back aboard and get my bag, sir," he observed. "I reckon I'd better pull the dinghy up on top o' the bank when I done with her. If any o' them Tilbury folk should 'appen to come along they won't see 'er then—not among the long grass."

It was a sensible suggestion on the face of it, but in view of the fact that I might find it necessary to embark rather abruptly, I couldn't afford to risk any unnecessary delays.

"Don't bother about that tonight, Gow," I said. "Just drag her above high-water mark. It's quite possible I may be using her in the morning."

Having thus provided for my retreat in the case of an emergency, I returned to the hut by the usual route along the sea-front. I took the precaution of putting up my head and inspecting the place carefully before climbing over the sea-wall, but I might as well have saved myself the trouble. The marsh was quite deserted, and when I reached the hut I found my little notice still pinned to the door, and no trace of any one having paid me a visit in my absence.

I remained in the same state of splendid isolation for the rest of the evening. There was no difficulty about keeping watch, for as soon as the sun went down a large obliging moon appeared in the sky, lighting up the marsh and the Tilbury road almost as clearly as if it were day-time. I could have seen a rabbit a hundred yards off, let alone anything as big and obvious as a Scotland Yard detective.

At about one in the morning I turned in for a couple of hours' rest. I felt that if Sonia had gone straight to the authorities they would have acted before this, while if she was sleeping on her wrath there was no reason I shouldn't do the same. I had given up any expectation of McMurtrie until the next morning.

I woke at half-past three, and resumed my vigil in the pure cool twilight of early dawn. I watched the sun rise over the river, and gradually climb up into a sky of pale blue and lemon that gave promise of another radiantly fine day. There was scarcely a breath of wind stirring, and everything was so deliciously quiet and peaceful that it almost seemed as if the events of the last three years were merely the memory of some particularly vivid nightmare.

"Almost," I say, for as a matter of fact I was never for a moment under any such pleasant delusion. If I had been, I should have had an early awakening, for at eight o'clock, just as I was thinking of routing out something in the nature of breakfast, I saw a little black dot advancing along the Tilbury road, which soon resolved itself into the figure of my faithful Charles.

He struck off across the marsh and came up to the hut, where I was standing at the door waiting for him.

"Two telegrams and a letter for you, sir," he said, producing them from his bag. "They came this morning, sir."

With an assumption of leisurely indifference that I was very far from feeling, I took them out of his hand. The letter was addressed in McMurtrie's writing, but I put it aside for a moment in favour of the two wires. The first was from Joyce.

"Saw L. late yesterday evening. He will act today. Agrees with my suggestion about the *Betty* if necessary. J."

I thrust it into my pocket and opened the other.

"A copper come last nite and ask for you. He see Misses O."

For an instant I stared at this cryptic message in bewilderment; then suddenly the recollection of my final instructions to Gertie 'Uggins rushed into my mind.

So Sonia *had* gone to the police, or had at least contrived to send them a message which served the same purpose. Their visit to Edith Terrace was probably explained by the fact that she had given them both addresses so as better to establish the truth of her story. Anyhow the murder was out, and with a new and not unpleasant thrill of excitement I crushed up Gertie's wire in my hand and tore open McMurtrie's letter.

"DEAR MR. NICHOLSON,

"I have been away on business and have only just received your letter, otherwise I should have come to see you this afternoon. In the first place allow me to congratulate you most heartily on your success, of which personally I was never in any doubt.

"For the moment I have left the Hotel Russell, and am staying with some friends in Sheppey. I shall run up the river in their launch early tomorrow morning, as I believe there is a small creek close to the hut where we can put in.

"Please have a specimen of the powder ready, and if it is possible I should like you to arrange for an actual demonstration, as I shall have a friend with me who is already considerably interested in our little company, and would be prepared to put up further capital if convinced of the merits of your invention.

"You can expect us about high water, between half-past nine and ten.

"Your sincere friend,

"L.J. McMURTRIE."

As I read the signature McMurtrie's smiling mask-like face seemed suddenly to rise up in front of me, and all my old instincts of distrust and repulsion came to keep it company. So he was at the bungalow, and in little over an hour he would be here—he and the mysterious friend who was "already considerably interested in our little company." I smiled grimly at the phrase; it was so characteristic of the doctor; though when he wrote it he could little have guessed how thoroughly I should be able to appreciate it.

He was also equally ignorant of the complications introduced into the affair by Sonia. Unless I had been altogether misled by Gertie's message, it was probable that the police were even now on their way to arrest me, just as McMurtrie's launch was most likely setting out from the little creek under the bungalow. There seemed every prospect of my having a busy and interesting morning.

At this point in my reflections I looked up, and found Charles eyeing me with an air of respectful patience. I took some money out of my pocket, and selecting a ten-shilling piece placed it in his grubby but not unwilling palm.

"You are a most useful boy, Charles," I said, "and you can keep the change as usual."

He pocketed the coin with a gratified stammer.

"You ain't 'ad time to make no fireworks yourself, sir?" he hazarded, after a short pause.

"Not yet," I replied; "but it looks as if I should today."

He brightened up still further at the news, and observing that he hoped there would be some letters to bring the next morning departed on his return journey.

I went back into the hut and shut the door. Now that matters were so rapidly approaching a climax, I felt curiously cheerful and light-hearted. I suppose it was a reaction from the strain and hard work of the previous week, but anyhow the thought that in all probability the police were hard on my track didn't seem to worry me in the least. The only point was whether they would reach the hut before McMurtrie did. I hoped not, for I was looking forward to an interview with the doctor, but it certainly seemed as well to take every precaution.

I started by unearthing the box of powder from outside, and filling up my flask from it. Then, when I had covered it over again, I collected all the papers which I had not burned on the previous day, and stored them away in my inside pockets. Finally I opened a tinned tongue, and aided by the dry remains of my last loaf, made a healthy if not very exciting breakfast. I never believe in conducting violent exertions on an empty tummy.

All this time, I need hardly say, I was keeping an uncommonly sharp look-out over the marsh. The most likely way in which any one who didn't wish to be seen would attempt to approach the hut was along the Tilbury road, and it was towards the last clump of trees, behind which Sonia had left her car the previous day, that I directed my chief attention.

Three-quarters of an hour passed, and I was just beginning to think that McMurtrie would be the winner after all, when I suddenly caught sight of something dark slinking across the exposed part of the road beyond the plantation. Standing very still, I watched carefully from the window. I have excellent eyesight, and I soon made out that there were three separate figures all stooping low and moving with extreme caution towards the shelter of the trees.

A sudden and irresistible desire to laugh seized hold of me; there was something so intensely funny about the strategic pains they were taking, when all the while they might just as well have advanced boldly across the open marsh. Still it was hardly the time to linger over the comic side of the affair, so retiring from the window, I threw a last quick glance round the hut to make quite sure that I had left nothing I wanted behind. Then walking to the door I opened it and stepped quietly outside.

I decided that it was impossible to reach the sea-wall without being seen, so I made no attempt to do so. I just set off in the direction of the creek, strolling along in the easy, unhurried fashion of a man taking a morning constitutional.

I had not gone more than ten yards, when from the corner of my eye I saw three figures break simultaneously out of the plantation. They no longer made any pretence about their purpose. One of them cut straight down towards the hut, a second came running directly after me, while the third started off as rapidly as possible along the road, so as to head me off if I attempted to escape inland.

Any further strategy on my part appeared to be out of place. I grasped the position in one hurried glance, and then, buttoning my coat and ramming down my cap, openly and frankly took to my heels. I heard the gentlemen behind shout out something which sounded like a request that I should stop, but I was too occupied to pay much attention. The marsh was infested with small drains, and one had to keep one's eyes glued on the ground immediately ahead to avoid coming an unholy purler. That was the only thing I was afraid of, as I was in excellent condition, and I have always been a very fair runner.

When I had covered about a couple of hundred yards I looked back over my shoulder. I expected to find that I had widened the gap, but to my dismay I discovered that my immediate pursuer had distinctly gained on me. I could just see that he was a tall, active-looking fellow in a policeman's uniform, with a long raking stride that was carrying him over the ground in the most unpleasant fashion. Unless he fell over a drain and broke his silly neck it seemed highly probable that he would arrive at the creek almost as soon as I did.

As I ran I prayed fervently in my heart that Mr. Gow had followed my instructions and left the dinghy within easy reach of the water. Otherwise I was in a tight place, for though I could swim to the *Betty* all right, it would be impossible to take her out of the creek in a dead calm and with no petrol aboard for the engine. I should be compelled to stand at bay until a breeze got up, repelling boarders with the boat-hook!

Just before I reached the sea-wall I looked round a second time. My pursuer was now only about thirty yards distant, but it was evident that his efforts had begun to tell on him. He again shouted out some breathless advice to the effect that it would be "best" for me to surrender, but without waiting to argue the point I scrambled up the bank and cast a hurried, anxious glance round for the dinghy.

Any doubts I might have had about Mr. Gow's trustworthiness were instantly dispelled. The boat was lying on the mud only a few yards out of reach of the tide. With a gasp of thankfulness I leaped on to the saltings, and clearing the distance in about three strides, clutched hold of the gunwale and began to drag it towards the water.

Just as I reached that desirable element the figure of my pursuer appeared above the bank. I gave a last savage wrench, but my foot slipped in the treacherous mud, and I as nearly as possible stumbled to my knees. That final tug, however, had done the trick. The boat was floating, and with a wild effort I scrambled in, and seizing an oar, shoved off furiously from the shore.

I was only just in time. Jumping from the sea-wall, the policeman fairly hurled himself across the intervening space, and without a moment's hesitation plunged into the creek after me. I shortened my oar, and as he made a grab for the stern I suddenly lunged forward with all the force I could command. The blade took him fair and square in the wind, and with a loud observation that sounded like "Ouch!" he sat down abruptly in the water. Before he could recover himself I was ten yards from the shore, sculling vigorously for the centre of the stream.

I made no attempt to reach the *Betty*. There was still a dead calm, and by going on board I should merely have been shutting myself up in a prison from which there was no escape. My best plan seemed to be to make for the open river, when I might either pick up McMurtrie and his launch, or else row across to the opposite shore.

I accordingly headed for the mouth of the creek, while my pursuer, who by this time had sufficiently recovered to stagger to his feet, waded dismally back to the shore. Here he was joined by his two companions, who had evidently been following the chase with praiseworthy determination.

For a moment I saw them all three consulting together, and then my friend the policeman started hastily throwing off his clothes with the apparent intention of swimming across the river, while the other two came running along the bank after me. They were both in plain clothes, but the unmistakable stamp of a Scotland Yard detective was clearly imprinted on each of them.

They soon caught me up, and hurrying on ahead reached the mouth of the creek, while I was still some twenty yards short of it. I was just wondering what on earth they hoped to do, when, looking over my shoulder, I saw one of them scramble up the sea-wall, and begin to shout and wave his arms as if he had suddenly gone mad.

A few savage pulls brought me up level, and then turning in my seat I discovered the cause of his excitement. Some way out in the stream was a small coast-guard cutter with three men on board, two of whom were at the oars. They had evidently grasped that there was something serious the matter, for they had brought their boat round and were already heading in towards the shore.

My position began to look a trifle unhealthy. I was out of practice for sculling, and if the coast-guards chose to interfere it was obviously only a question of a few minutes before they would succeed in rowing me down. For a moment I had some idea of going ashore on the opposite bank, and again trusting to my heels. Then I saw that my friend the policeman, who could apparently swim as well as he could run, was already half way across the creek, and would be on my track long before I could get the necessary start. On the whole it seemed best to stick to the water, so digging in my sculls I pulled out into the main stream.

As I rounded the sea-wall I could hear the man who was standing on top bawling out my name to the coast-guards, and hurling them frantic injunctions to cut me off. I cast one swift glance up and down the river, and as I did so I nearly gave a shout of excitement. A couple of hundred yards away, but coming up at a tremendous pace, was a large white petrol launch, which I recognized immediately as the one that had swamped Mr. Gow.

Whether the coast-guards saw her too I really can't say. I doubt if they did, for by this time they had evidently realized who I was, and their whole attention was fixed on preventing my escape. They were rowing towards me with tremendous energy, the officer in charge half standing up in the stern and encouraging them to still fiercer efforts.

Putting every ounce I could into my stroke, I set off down stream. It was just a question as to whether I could clear them, and I doubt if any winner of the Diamond Sculls could have shoved that dinghy along much faster than I did for the next few seconds. Nearer and nearer we drew to each other, and for one instant I thought that I had done the trick. Then from the corner of my eye I saw the cutter fairly leap forward through the water, and the next moment, with a jolt that almost flung me out of the seat, she bumped alongside.

Dropping his oar, one of the men leaned over and grabbed hold of my gunwale.

"No go, Mister," he observed breathlessly. "You got to come along with us."

The words had hardly left his lips when with a wild shout the officer in charge leaped to his feet.

"Look out, there!" he yelled. "Port, you fools! Port your helm!"

I swung round, and got a momentary glimpse of a sharp white prow with a great fan of water curling away each side of it, and then, before I could move, there came a jarring, grinding crash, mixed with a fierce volley of shouts and oaths.

CHAPTER XXIII
IN THE NICK OF TIME

My impressions of what happened next are a trifle involved. Something hit me violently in the side, almost knocking me silly, while at the same moment the boat seemed to disappear from beneath me, and I was flying head first into the water. I struck out instinctively as I fell, and came to the surface almost at once. I just remember a blurred vision of floating wreckage, with something white rising up in front of me. Then a rope came hurtling through the air, and caught me full in the face. I clutched at it wildly, and the next thing I knew I was being dragged violently through the water and hauled in over the side of the launch.

It was all over so quickly that for a moment I scarcely realized what had happened. I just lay where I was, gasping for breath, and spitting out a large mouthful of the Thames which I had unintentionally appropriated. Above the throbbing of the engine and the swish of the screw I could still hear a confused medley of shouts and curses.

With an effort I sat up and looked about me. We had already changed our course, and were swinging round in a half-circle, preparatory to heading back down stream. The smashed remains of the two boats were bobbing about behind us, and in the midst of them I could make out the figures of the coast-guards, clinging affectionately to various bits of wreckage.

Besides myself, there were three other men in the launch. Dr. McMurtrie was sitting on the seat just opposite, pouring out the contents of a flask into a small metal cup. Against the cabin door leaned Savaroff, eyeing me with his usual expression of hostile mistrust. The third passenger was the man with the auburn beard, whom I had seen in the launch on the day I picked up Mr. Gow. He was busy with the tiller, and for the moment was paying scant attention to any of us.

McMurtrie got up with the cup in his hand and came across to where I was sitting.

"Drink this," he said.

"This," proved to be some excellent old brandy, which I tossed off with no little gratitude. It was exactly what I wanted to pull me together.

"Are you hurt?" he asked.

I felt myself carefully before replying. "I'm all right now," I said. "I got rather a crack in the ribs, but I don't think anything's gone."

"We seem to have arrived just in time to prevent your arrest," he said quietly. "Perhaps you will be good enough to explain what has happened? At present we are rather in the dark."

He spoke with his usual suavity, but there was a veiled menace in his voice which it was impossible to overlook. Savaroff scowled at me more truculently than ever. It was obvious that both of them were entirely ignorant of Sonia's part in the affair, and suspected me of some extraordinary bit of clumsiness. I prepared myself for some heavy lying.

"I know precious little more about it than you do," I said coolly. "I was getting things ready for you this morning, when I happened to look out of the window, and saw three men crawling towards the hut on their hands and knees. As one of them was wearing a policeman's uniform, I thought I had better cut and run. Well, I cut and ran. I made for the creek because I thought you might be there. You weren't; but there was a dinghy on the shore, which I suppose belonged to a small yacht that was anchored out in the channel. Anyhow, I took the liberty of borrowing it. I meant to row out into the river, and try to pick you up before they could get hold of a boat and follow me. If it hadn't been for these infernal coast-guards, I'd have managed it all right. I don't think they really had anything to do with the business, but they just happened to be passing, and of course when the police shouted to them they cut in at once." I paused. "And that's the whole story," I finished, "as far as I know anything about it."

They had all three listened to me with eager attention. Even the man with the auburn beard had kept on looking away from his steering to favour me with quick glances out of his hard blue eyes. I think I came through the combined scrutiny with some credit.

McMurtrie was the first to break the ensuing silence.

"Have you any idea how you have betrayed yourself? You can speak quite freely. Our friend Mr. von Brünig knows the position."

I thought it best to take the offensive. "I haven't betrayed myself," I said angrily. "Somebody must have done it for me. I've not left the hut since I came down except for an occasional breath of air."

"But earlier—when you were in London?" he persisted.

I shook my head. "I have been down here a week. You don't imagine the police would have waited as long as that."

I knew I was putting them in a difficulty, for by this time they must be all aware that Latimer was still on their track, and it was obviously conceivable that my attempted arrest might be due in some way to my connection with them; anyhow I saw that even Savaroff was beginning to regard me a shade less suspiciously.

"Have you brought any of the powder with you?" asked McMurtrie.

It struck me instantly that if I said yes, I should be putting myself absolutely in their power.

"I hadn't time to get any," I answered regretfully. "I had buried it outside the hut, and they came on me so suddenly there was no chance of digging it up. Now I have once done it, however, I can make some more very quickly."

It was the flattest lie I have ever told; but I managed to get it off with surprising ease. It is astonishing what rapid strides one can make in the art of perjury with a very little practice.

Savaroff gave a grunt of disappointment, and McMurtrie turned to von Brünig, who was frowning thoughtfully, and made some almost inaudible remark in German. The latter answered at some length, but he kept his voice so low that, with my rather sketchy knowledge of that unpleasant language, it was impossible for me to overhear what he was saying. Besides, he evidently didn't intend me to, and I had no wish to spoil the good impression I had apparently made by any appearance of eavesdropping.

It seemed to me that my course lay pretty straight in front of me. Latimer had all the information now he was likely to get, and I knew from Joyce's wire that he intended to act immediately. In addition to this, the running down of the cutter would be known to Scotland Yard as soon as ever the men who had been sent to arrest me could get to a telephone, and the river-police and coast-guards everywhere would be warned to keep a sharp look-out for von Brünig's launch. In an hour or two at the most something was bound to happen, and the way in which I could make myself most useful seemed to be in delaying the break-up and escape of the party as long as possible. If I had to be arrested, I was determined that the others should be roped in as well.

I had just arrived at this point in my meditations when McMurtrie and von Brünig came to an end of their muttered conversation.

The former turned back to me. "You probably understand, Mr. Lyndon, that this unfortunate affair with the police alters our plans entirely. At present I am quite unable to see how they have found you out, unless you have betrayed yourself by some piece of unintentional carelessness. Anyhow, the fact remains that they know where you are, and that very probably they will be able to trace this launch."

Savaroff nodded. "As likely as not we shall have a shot across our bows when we get to Sheerness," he growled.

McMurtrie, as usual, took no notice of his interruption. "There is only one thing to do," he said. "Mr. von Brünig, who, as I have already told you, is interested in our syndicate, has offered to put his country house in Germany at our service. We must cross over to Holland before the police have time to interfere."

"Do you mean now, at once?" I asked, with a sudden inward feeling of dismay.

McMurtrie nodded. "We have to pick up a couple of friends at Sheppey first. After that we can run straight across to The Hague."

The proposal was so obviously sensible that, without arousing his suspicion, I could see no way for the moment of raising any objection. The great thing was to keep the "syndicate" together, and to delay our departure until Latimer had had time to scoop the lot of us. Could anything provide him with a more favourable opportunity than the collection of the whole crowd in that remote bungalow at Sheppey? It was surely there if anywhere he would strike first, and I hoped, very feelingly, that he would not be too long about it. My powers of postponing our voyage to Holland appeared to have a distinct time-limit.

"There seems nothing else to do," I said. "I am sorry to have been the cause of changing all our plans; but the whole thing is as much a mystery to me as it is to you. However the police got on to my track, it wasn't through any carelessness of mine. I am no more anxious to go back to Dartmoor now than I was six weeks ago."

This last observation at least was true; and I can only hope the recording angel jotted it down as a slight set-off against the opposite column.

Savaroff removed his bulky form from in front of the cabin door, and crossing the well, sat down beside the others. They began to talk again in German; but as before I could only catch the merest scraps of their conversation. Once I heard Sonia's name mentioned by McMurtrie, and I just caught Savaroff's muttered reply to the effect that she was all right where she was, and could follow us to Germany later. As far as I could judge, they none of them had the remotest suspicion that she was in any way connected with the crisis.

All this while we had been throbbing along down stream at a terrific pace, keeping well to the centre of the river, and giving such small vessels as we passed a reasonably wide berth. If there was any trouble coming to us it seemed most likely to materialize in the neighbourhood of Southend or Sheerness, which were the two places to which the police would be almost certain to send a description of the launch as soon as they could get to a telephone. As we reached the first danger-zone, I noticed von Brünig beginning to cast rather anxious glances towards the shore. No one seemed to pay any attention to us, however, and without slackening speed, we swept out into the broad highway of the Thames estuary.

There were several torpedo-boats lying off Sheerness, but these also remained utterly indifferent to our presence. Apparently the police had been too occupied in rescuing their coast-guard allies from a watery grave to reach a telephone in time, and we passed along down the coast unsuspected and unchallenged.

Whatever von Brünig's weak points might be, he could certainly steer a motor-boat to perfection. He turned into the little creek under the bungalow at a pace which I certainly wouldn't have cared to attempt even in my wildest mood, and brought up in almost the identical spot where we had anchored the *Betty* on the historic night of Latimer's rescue.

We had a small collapsible Berthon boat on board, just big enough to hold four at a pinch. I watched Savaroff getting it ready, wondering grimly whether there was any chance of their leaving me on the launch with only one member of the party as a companion. It would have suited me excellently, though it might have been a little inconvenient for my prospective guardian.

McMurtrie, however, promptly shattered this agreeable possibility by inviting me to take a seat in the boat. I think he believed I had told him the truth, but he evidently had no intention of letting me out of his sight again until I had actually handed him over the secret of the powder.

We landed at the foot of a little winding path, and dragged our boat out of the water on to a narrow strip of shingle. Then we set off up the cliff at a rapid pace, with von Brünig leading the way and Savaroff bringing up the rear.

The bungalow was situated about a couple of hundred yards from the summit, almost hidden by the high privet hedge which I had noticed from the sea. This hedge ran right round the garden, the only entrance being a small white gate in front of the house. Von Brünig walked up, the path followed by the rest of us, and thrusting his key into the lock pushed open the door.

We found ourselves in a fairly big, low-ceilinged apartment, lighted by a couple of French windows opening on to the side garden. They were partly covered by two long curtains, each drawn half way across. The place was comfortably furnished, and an easel with a half-finished seascape on it bore eloquent witness to the purity of its tenants' motives.

Von Brünig looked round with a sort of impatient surprise.

"Where are the others?" he demanded harshly. "Why have they left the place empty in this way?"

"They must have walked over to the post-office," said McMurtrie. "I know Hoffman wanted to send a telegram. They will be back in a minute, I expect."

Von Brünig frowned. "They ought not to have done so. Seeker at least should have known better. After the other night—" He paused, and crossing the room threw open a door and disappeared into an adjoining apartment.

Without waiting for an invitation, I seated myself on a low couch in the farther corner of the room. I felt quite cool, but I must admit that the situation was beginning to strike me as a little unpromising. Unless Latimer turned up precious soon it seemed highly probable that he would be too late. Considering the importance of getting me safely to Germany, neither von Brünig nor McMurtrie was likely to stay a minute longer than was necessary. I might, of course, refuse to go with them, but in that case the odds were that I should simply be overpowered and taken on board by force. Von Brünig himself looked a pretty tough handful to tackle, while Savaroff was about as powerful as a well-grown bullock. Once I was safe in the former's "country house" they would no doubt reckon on finding some means of bringing me quickly to reason.

With a bag in one hand and a bundle of papers in the other von Brünig came back into the room.

"I shall not wait," he announced curtly. "The risks are too great. Seeker and your friend must follow as best they can."

"They are bound to be here in a minute," objected Savaroff.

Von Brünig turned on him with an angry gleam in his blue eyes. "I shall not wait," he repeated harshly. "The future of Germany is of more importance than their convenience."

McMurtrie stepped forward, serene and imperturbable as ever.

"I think Mr. von Brünig is right, Savaroff," he said. "The police may have recognized the launch, and in that case it would be madness for us not to go while we have the chance. We can leave a note for the others."

If Savaroff had any further objections he kept them to himself. He turned away with a shrug on his broad shoulders, while McMurtrie sat down at the table and hastily wrote a few lines which he showed to von Brünig. The other nodded his head approvingly.

"That will do very well," he said. "It will be safe if any one else should find it. Seeker knows where to come to."

McMurtrie put the note in an envelope which he placed in the centre of the table.

"And now," he said, pushing back his chair, "the sooner we are out of this the better."

I felt that if I was going to interfere the right time had now arrived. Von Brünig's reply to Savaroff had given me just the opening I needed.

"One moment, gentlemen!" I said, getting up from the couch.

They all three turned in obvious surprise at the interruption.

"Well?" rapped out von Brünig, "what is it?"

"I was under the impression," I said, "that this new explosive of mine was to be put on the market as an ordinary commercial enterprise."

McMurtrie rose from his chair and took a step forward.

"You are perfectly right," he said. "Why should you think otherwise?"

"In that case," I replied steadily, "I should like to know what Mr. von Brünig meant by his remark about the 'future of Germany.'"

There was a short pause.

"Ach, Himmel!" broke out von Brünig. "What does it matter? What are we wasting time for? Tell him if he wishes."

"Why, certainly," said McMurtrie, smiling. "There is no mystery about it. I was merely keeping the matter quiet until it was settled." He turned to me. "The German Government have made us a very good offer for your invention, provided of course that it will do what you claim."

"It will do what I claim all right," I said coolly, "but I don't wish to sell it to the German Government."

There was a sort of explosive gasp from von Brünig and Savaroff, and I saw McMurtrie's eyes narrow into two dangerous cat-like slits.

"You don't-wish!" he repeated icily. "May I ask why?"

"Certainly," I said. "With the sole command of an explosive as powerful as mine, Germany would be in a position to smash England in about six weeks."

"And suppose she was," interrupted von Brünig. "What in God's name does it matter to you—an escaped convict?"

His voice rang with impatience and contempt, and I felt my own temper rising.

"It matters just sufficiently," I said, "that I'll see you in hell first."

McMurtrie came slowly up to me, and looked me straight in the eyes. His face was white and terrible—a livid mask of controlled anger.

"You fool," he said almost pityingly. "You incredible fool! Do you imagine that you have any choice in the matter?"

Von Brünig and Savaroff moved up alongside of him, and I stood there confronting the three of them.

"You have heard my choice," I said.

McMurtrie laughed. It was precisely the way in which I should imagine the devil laughs on the rare occasions when he is still amused.

"You are evidently a bad judge of character, Mr. Lyndon," he said. "People who attempt to break faith with me are apt to find it a very unhealthy occupation."

I felt utterly reckless now. I had done my best to delay things, and if neither the police nor the Secret Service was ready to take advantage of it, so much the worse for them—and me.

"I can quite believe you, doctor," I said pleasantly. "I should imagine you were a dangerous ruffian from the intelligent way in which you murdered Marks."

It was a last desperate stroke, but it went home with startling effect.

Savaroff's face flushed purple, and with a fierce oath he gripped the back of a chair and swung it up over his head. The doctor stopped him with a gesture of his hand. As for von Brünig, he stood where he was, staring from one to the other of us in angry bewilderment. He evidently hadn't the remotest notion what I was talking about.

McMurtrie was the first to speak. "Yes," he said, in his coolest, silkiest voice. "I did kill Marks. He was the last person who betrayed me. I rather think you will envy him before I have finished with you, Mr. Lyndon."

"A thousand devils!" cried von Brünig furiously: "what does all this nonsense mean? We may have the police here any moment. Knock him on the head, the fool, and—"

"Stop!"

The single word cut in with startling clearness. We all spun round in the direction of the sound, and there, standing in the window just between the two curtains, was the solitary figure of Mr. Bruce Latimer. He was accompanied by a Mauser pistol which flickered thoughtfully over the four of us.

"Keep still," he drawled—"quite still, please. I shall shoot the first man who moves."

There was a moment of rather trenchant silence. Then von Brünig moistened his lips with his tongue.

"Are you mad, sir?" he began hoarsely. "By what—"

With a lightning-like movement McMurtrie slipped his right hand into his side pocket, and as he did so Latimer instantly levelled his pistol. The two shots rang out simultaneously, but except for a cry and a crash of broken glass I knew nothing of what had happened. In one stride I had flung myself on Savaroff, and just as he drew his revolver I let him have it fair and square on the jaw. Dropping his weapon, he reeled backwards into von Brünig, and the pair of them went to the floor with a thud that shook the building. Almost at the same moment both the door and the window burst violently open, and two men came charging into the room.

The first of the intruders was Tommy Morrison. I recognized him just as I was making an instinctive dive for Savaroff's revolver, under the unpleasant impression that Hoffman and the other German had returned from the post-office. You can imagine the delight with which I scrambled up again, clutching that useful if rather belated weapon in my hand.

One glance round showed me everything there was to see.

Face downwards in a little pool of blood lay the motionless figure of McMurtrie. Savaroff also was still—his huge bulk sprawled in fantastic helplessness across the floor. Only von Brünig had moved; he was sitting up on his hands, staring in a half-dazed fashion down the barrel of Latimer's Mauser.

It was Latimer himself who renewed the conversation.

"Come and fix up these two, Ellis," he said. "I will see to the other."

The man who had burst in with Tommy, a lithe, hard-looking fellow in a blue suit, walked crisply across the room, and pulling out a pair of light hand-cuffs snapped them round von Brünig's wrists. He then performed a similar service for the still unconscious Savaroff.

The next moment Latimer, Tommy, and I were kneeling round the prostrate figure of the doctor. We lifted him up very gently and turned him over on to his back, using a rolled-up rug as a pillow for his head. He had been shot through the right lung and was bleeding at the mouth.

Latimer bent over and made a brief examination of the wound. Then with a slight shake of his head he knelt back.

"I'm afraid there's no hope," he remarked dispassionately. "It's a pity. We might have got some useful information out of him."

There was a short pause, and then quite suddenly the dying man opened his eyes. It may have been fancy, but it seemed to me that for a moment a shadow of the old mocking smile flitted across his face. His lips moved, faintly, as though he were trying to speak. I bent down to listen, but even as I did so there came a fresh rush of blood into his throat, and with a long shudder that strange sinister spirit of his passed over into the darkness. I shall always wonder what it was that he left unsaid.

CHAPTER XXIV
EXONERATED

It was Tommy who pronounced his epitaph. "Well," he observed, "he was a damned scoundrel, but he played a big game anyhow."

Latimer thrust his hand into the dead man's pocket, and drew out a small nickel-plated revolver. One chamber of it was discharged.

"Not a bad shot," he remarked critically. "Fired at me through his coat, and only missed my head by an inch."

He got up and looked round the room at the shattered window and the other traces of the fray, his gaze coming finally to rest on the prostrate figure of Savaroff.

"That was a fine punch of yours, Lyndon," he added. "I hope you haven't broken his neck."

"I don't think so," I said. "Necks like Savaroff's take a lot of breaking." Then, suddenly remembering, I added hastily: "By the way, you know that there are two more of the crowd—Hoffman and a friend of von Brünig's? They might be back any minute."

Latimer shook his head almost pensively. "It's improbable," he said. "I have every reason to believe that at the present moment they are in Queenborough police station."

I saw Tommy grin, but before I could make any inquiries von Brünig had scrambled to his feet. His face looked absolutely ghastly in its mingled rage and disappointment. After a fashion I could scarcely help feeling sorry for him.

"I demand an explanation," he exclaimed hoarsely. "By what right am I arrested?"

Latimer walked up to him, and looked him quietly in the eyes.

"I think you understand very well, *Captain* von Brünig," he said.

There was a pause, and then, with a glance that embraced the four of us, the German walked to the couch and sat down. If looks could kill I think we should all have dropped dead in our tracks.

Providence, however, having fortunately arranged otherwise, we remained as we were, and at that moment there came from outside the unmistakable sound of an approaching car. I saw Latimer open his watch.

"Quick work, Ellis," he remarked, with some satisfaction. "I wasn't expecting them for another ten minutes. Tell them to come straight in." He snapped the case and turned back to me. "Suppose we try and awake our sleeping friend," he added. "He looks rather a heavy weight for lifting about."

Between us we managed to hoist Savaroff up into a chair, while Tommy stepped across the room and fetched a bottle of water which was standing on the sideboard. I have had some practice in my boxing days of dealing with knocked-out men, and although Savaroff was a pretty hard case, a little vigorous massage and one or two good sousings soon produced signs of returning consciousness. Indeed, he had just recovered sufficiently to indulge in a really remarkable oath when the door swung open and Ellis came back into the room, accompanied by two other men. One of them was dressed in ordinary clothes, the other wore the uniform of a police sergeant.

I shall never forget the face of the latter as he surveyed the scene before him.

"Gawd bless us!" he exclaimed. "What's up now, sir? Murder?"

"Not exactly, Sergeant," replied Latimer soothingly. "I shot this man in self-defence. The other two I give into your charge. There is a warrant out for all three of them."

It appeared that the sergeant knew who Latimer was, for he treated him with marked deference.

"Very well, sir," he said. "If 'e's dead, 'e's dead; anyhow, I've orders to take my instructions entirely from you." Then, dragging a note-book out of his pocket, he added with some excitement: "There's another thing, sir, a matter that the Tilbury station have just telephoned through about. It seems"—he consulted his references—"it seems that when they were in that launch of theirs they run down a party o' coast-guards, who'd got hold of Lyndon, the missing convict. Off Tilbury it was. D'you happen to know anything about this, sir?"

Latimer nodded his head. "A certain amount, Sergeant," he said. "You will find the launch in the creek at the bottom of the cliff." He paused. "This is Mr. Neil Lyndon," he added; "I will be responsible for his safe keeping."

I don't know what sort of experiences the Isle of Sheppey usually provides for its police staff, but it was obvious that, professionally speaking, the sergeant was having the day of his life. He stared at me for a moment with the utmost interest, and then, recollecting himself, turned and saluted Latimer.

"Very good, sir," he said; "and what do you want me to do?"

"I want you to stay here for the present with one of my men, while we go to the station. I shall send the car back, and then you will take the two prisoners into Queenborough. My man will remain in charge of the bungalow."

The sergeant saluted again, and Latimer turned to me.

"You and Morrison must come straight to town," he said. "We shall just have time to catch the twelve-three."

It was at this point that Savaroff, who had been regarding us with the half-stupid stare of a man who has newly recovered consciousness, staggered up unsteadily from his chair. His half-numbed brain seemed suddenly to have grasped what was happening.

"Verfluchter Schweinhund!" he shouted, turning on me. "So it was you, then—"

He got no further. However embarrassed the sergeant might be by exceptional events, he was evidently thoroughly at home in his own department.

"'Ere!" he said, stepping forward briskly, "stow that, me man!" And with a sudden energetic thrust in the chest, he sent Savaroff sprawling backwards on the couch almost on top of von Brünig.

"Don't you use none of that language 'ere," he added, standing over them, "or as like as not you'll be sorry for it."

There was a brief pause. "I see, Sergeant," said Latimer gravely, "that I am leaving the case in excellent hands."

He gave a few final instructions to Ellis, who was also staying behind, and then the four of us left the bungalow and walked quietly down the small garden path that led to the road. Just outside the gate stood a powerful five-seated car.

"Start her up, Guthrie," said Latimer; and then turning to us, he added, with a smile: "I want you in front with me, Lyndon. I know Morrison's dying for a yarn with you, but he must wait."

Tommy nodded contentedly. "I can wait," he observed; "it's a habit I've cultivated where Neil's concerned."

We all clambered into the car, and, slipping in his clutch Latimer set off at a rapid pace in the direction of Queenborough. It was not until we had rounded the first corner that he opened the conversation.

"How did you know about Marks?" he asked, in that easy drawling voice of his.

"I didn't know for certain," I said quietly. "It was more or less of a lucky shot."

Then, as he seemed to be waiting for a further explanation, I repeated to him as briefly as possible what Sonia had told me about McMurtrie's reason for visiting London.

"I didn't go into all this in my letter to you," I finished, "because in the first place there was only just time for Joyce to catch the train, and in the second I didn't want to disappoint her in case it should turn out to be all bunkum. You must have been rather amazed when I suddenly sprung it on McMurtrie."

He shook his head, smiling. "Oh no," he said—"hardly amazed." He paused. "You see, I knew about it already," he added placidly.

If there was any amazement to spare at that moment it was certainly mine.

"You knew about it!" I repeated. "You knew that McMurtrie had killed Marks?"

He nodded coolly. "You remember telling me in the boat that your friend Miss—Miss Aylmer, isn't it?—had recognized him as the man she saw at the flat on the day of the murder?"

"Yes," I said.

"Well, if that was so, and you had been wrongly convicted, which I was inclined to believe, the doctor's presence on the scene seemed to require a little looking into. I knew that at that time he had only just arrived in London, so the odds were that he and Marks were old acquaintances. I hunted up the evidence in your trial—I had rather forgotten it—and I found just what I expected. Beyond the fact that Marks was a foreigner and had been living in London for about eight years, no one seemed to know anything about him at all. The police were so confident in their case against you that apparently they hadn't even bothered to make the usual inquiries. If they had taken the trouble to communicate with St. Petersburg, they could have found out all about Mr. Marks without much difficulty. The authorities there have a wonderfully complete system of remembering their old friends."

"But three years afterwards—" I began.

"It makes very little difference, especially as just at present we are on excellent terms with the Russian Secret Service. They took the matter up for me, and last night I got the full particulars I wanted about the man who had given away McMurtrie and his friends in St. Petersburg. There can be no question that he and Marks were the same person."

I took a long—a very long breath.

"There remains," I said, "the Home Office."

"I don't think you need be seriously worried about the Home Office," returned Latimer serenely. "By this time they have a full statement of the case—except, of course, for my direct evidence that I heard the doctor actually bragging of his achievement. I had a long interview with Casement before I left London this morning, and he said he would go round directly after breakfast. He evidently arrived just too late to prevent the order for your arrest."

I nodded. "Sonia must have gone to the police last night," I said; and then in a few words I told him of the telegram I had received from Gertie 'Uggins, and how it had just enabled me to get away.

"I don't know," I finished, "how much my double escape complicates matters. However unjust my sentence was, there's no denying I've committed at least three felonies since. I've broken prison, plugged a warder in the jaw, and shoved an oar into a policeman's tummy. Do you think there's any possible chance of the Home Secretary being able to overlook such enormities?"

Latimer laughed easily. "My dear Lyndon," he said, "in return for what you've done for us, you could decimate the police force if you wanted to." Then, speaking more seriously, he added: "I tell you frankly, there's every chance of a huge European war in the near future, and you can see the different position we should be in if the Germans had got hold of this new powder of yours. Apart from that, the Government owe you every possible sort of reparation for the shameful way you've been treated. If there's any 'overlooking' to be done, it will be on your side, not on theirs."

We were entering the dreary main street of Queenborough as he spoke, and before I could answer he drew up outside the post-office.

"We've just time to send off a telegram," he said. "I want to make sure of seeing Lammersfield and Casement directly we get to town. They will probably be at lunch if I don't wire."

He entered the building, and Tommy took advantage of his brief absence to lean over the back of the seat and grip my hand.

"We've done it, Neil," he said. "Damn it, we've done it!"

"*You've* done it, Tommy," I retorted. "You and Joyce between you."

There was a short pause, and then Tommy gave vent to a deep satisfied chuckle.

"I'm thinking of George," he said simply.

It was such a beautiful thought that for a moment I too maintained a voluptuous silence.

"We must find out whether they're going to prosecute him," I said. "I don't want to clash with the Government, but whatever happens I mean to have my five minutes first. They're welcome to what's left of him."

Tommy nodded sympathetically, and just at that moment Latimer came out of the post-office.

We got to the railway station with about half a minute to spare. The train was fairly crowded, but a word from Latimer to the station-master resulted in our being ushered into an empty "first" which was ceremoniously locked behind us. It was not a "smoker," but with a fine disregard for such trifles Latimer promptly produced his cigar case, and offered us each a delightful-looking Upman. There are certainly some advantages in being on the side of the established order.

Soothed by the fragrant tobacco, and with an exquisite feeling of rest and freedom, I lay back in the corner and listened to Latimer's pleasantly drawling voice, as he described to me how he had accomplished his morning's coup.

It seems that, accompanied by Tommy and his own man Ellis, he had arrived at Queenborough by the early train. Instructions had already been wired through from London that the Sheppey police were to put themselves entirely at his disposal; and having commandeered a car, the three of them, together with our friend the sergeant, set off to the bungalow. They pulled up some little distance away and waited for Guthrie, Latimer's other assistant, who had been keeping an eye on the place during the night. He reported that McMurtrie and Savaroff and von Brünig had just put off in the launch, leaving the other two behind.

"I guessed they had gone to pay you a visit," explained Latimer drily, "and it seemed to me a favourable chance of doing a little calling on our own account."

The net result of that little call had been the bloodless capture of Hoffman and the other German spy, who had been surprised in the prosaic act of swallowing their breakfast.

Having been favoured by fortune so far, Latimer had promptly proceeded to make the best use of his opportunity. It struck him that, whatever might be the result of their visit to me, the other members of the party were pretty sure to come back to the bungalow. The idea of hiding behind the curtain at once suggested itself to him. It was just possible that in this way he might pick up some valuable information before he was discovered, while in any case it would give him the advantage of taking them utterly by surprise.

His first step had been to tie up the prisoners, and pack them off in the car to Queenborough police station with Guthrie and the sergeant as an escort. (I should have loved to have heard his conversation with Hoffman while the former operation was in progress!) He then carefully removed all inside and outside traces of the raid on the bungalow, and picked out a couple of convenient hiding-places in the garden, where Tommy and Ellis could he in ambush until they were wanted. A shot from his revolver or the smashing of the French window was to be the signal for their united entrance on the scene.

"Well, you know the end of the story as well as I do," he finished, nicking off the ash of his cigar. "Things could scarcely have turned out better, except for that unfortunate accident with McMurtrie." He paused. "I wouldn't have shot him for the world," he added regretfully, "but he really left me no choice."

"He would have been hanged anyway," put in Tommy consolingly.

Latimer smiled. "I didn't mean to suggest that it was likely to keep me awake at night. I was only thinking that we might perhaps have got some useful information out of him."

"It seems to me," I said gratefully, "that we did."

Through the interminable suburbs and slums of South-East London we steamed slowly into London Bridge Station and drew up at the platform. There was a taxi waiting almost opposite our carriage, and promptly securing the driver Latimer instructed him to take us "as quickly as possible" to No. 10 Downing Street.

The man carried out his order with almost alarming literalness, but Providence watched over us and we reached the Foreign Office without disaster. Favoured with a respectful salute from the liveried porter on duty, Latimer led the way into the hall.

We followed him down a short narrow passage to another corridor, where he unlocked and opened a door on the left, ushering us into a small room comfortably fitted up as an office.

"This is my own private den," he said; "so no one will disturb you. I will go and see if Casement has come. If so, he is probably upstairs with Lammersfield. I will give them my report, and then no doubt they will want to see you. You won't have to wait very long."

He nodded pleasantly and left the room, closing the door after him. For all his quiet, almost lethargic manner, it was curious what an atmosphere of swiftness and decision he seemed to carry about with him.

I turned to Tommy.

"Where's Joyce?" I asked.

"She's at the flat," he announced. "She said she would wait there until she heard from us. I saw her last night, you know. I was having supper at Hatchett's with Latimer when she turned up with your letter. She'd come on from his rooms."

"There are many women," I said softly, "but there is only one Joyce."

Tommy chuckled. "That's what Latimer thinks. After she left us—I was staying the night with him in Jermyn Street and we'd all three gone back there to talk it over—he said to me in that funny drawling way of his: 'You know, Morrison, that girl will be wasted, even on Lyndon. She ought to be in the Secret Service.'"

I laughed. "I'm grateful to the Secret Service," I said, "but there are limits even to gratitude."

For perhaps three-quarters of an hour we remained undisturbed, while Latimer was presumably presenting his report to the authorities. Every now and then we heard footsteps pass down the corridor, and on one occasion an electric bell went off with a sudden vicious energy that I should never have expected in a Government office. The time passed quickly, for we had plenty to talk about; indeed, our only objection to waiting was the fact that we were both beginning to get infernally hungry, and it seemed likely to be some time yet before we should be able to get anything to eat.

At last there came a discreet knock at the door, and an elderly clean-shaven person with the manners of a retired butler appeared noiselessly upon the threshold. He bowed slightly to us both.

"Lord Lammersfield wishes to see you, gentlemen. If you will be good enough to follow me, I will conduct you to his presence."

We followed him along the corridor and up a rather dingy staircase, when he tapped gently at a door immediately facing us. "Come in," called out a voice, and with another slight inclination of his head our guide turned the handle and ushered us into the room.

It was a solemn-looking sort of apartment furnished chiefly with bookcases, and having a general atmosphere of early Victorian stuffiness. At a big table in the centre two men were sitting. One was Latimer; the other I recognized immediately as Lord Lammersfield.

I had never known him personally in the old days, but I had often seen him walking in the Park, or run across him at such popular rest cures as Kempton and Sandown Park. He had changed very little in the interval; his hair was perhaps a trifle greyer, otherwise he looked just the same debonair picturesque figure that the Opposition caricaturists had loved to flesh their pencils on.

He got up as we entered, regarding us both with a pleasant whimsical smile that put me entirely at my ease at once.

"This is Lyndon," said Latimer, indicating me; "and this is Morrison."

Lord Lammersfield came round the table and shook hands cordially with us both.

"Sit down, gentlemen," he said, "sit down. If half of what Mr. Latimer has told me is true, you must be extremely tired."

We all three laughed, and Tommy promptly took advantage of the invitation to seat himself luxuriously in a big leather arm-chair. I remained standing.

"To be quite truthful," I said, "it's been the most refreshing morning I can ever remember."

Lord Lammersfield looked at me for a moment with the same smile on his lips.

"Yes," he said drily; "I suppose there is a certain stimulus in saving England before breakfast. Most of my own work in that line is accomplished in the afternoon." Then, with a sudden slight change in his manner, he took a step forward and again held out his hand.

"Mr. Lyndon," he said, "as a member of the Government, and one who is therefore more or less responsible for the law's asinine blunders, I am absolutely ashamed to look you in the face. I wonder if you add generosity to your other unusual gifts."

For the second time we exchanged grips. "I have common gratitude at all events, Lord Lammersfield," I said. "I know that you have tried to help me while I was in prison, and—"

He held up his other hand with a gesture of half-ironical protest. "Ah!" he exclaimed, "I am afraid that any poor efforts of mine in that direction were due to the most flagrant compulsion." He paused. "Whatever else you are unlucky in, Mr. Lyndon," he added smilingly, "you can at least be congratulated on your friends."

Then he turned to Latimer. "I think it would be as well if I explained the position before Casement and Frinton arrive."

Latimer expressed his agreement, and motioning me to a chair, Lord Lammersfield again seated himself at the table. His manner, though still quite friendly and unstilted, had suddenly become serious.

"For the moment, Mr. Lyndon," he said, "the Prime Minister is out of London. We have communicated with him, and we expect him back tonight. In his absence it falls to me to thank you most unreservedly both on behalf of the Government and the nation for what you have done. It would be difficult to overrate its importance."

I began to feel a trifle embarrassed.

"I really don't want any thanks," I said. "I just drifted into it; and anyway one doesn't sell one's country, even if one is an escaped convict."

Lord Lammersfield laughed drily. "There are many men," he said, "in your position who would have found it an extraordinarily attractive prospect. I am not at all sure I shouldn't have myself." He paused. "We can't give you those three years of your life back," he went on, "but fortunately we can make some sort of amends in other ways. I have no doubt that the moment the Prime Minister is fully acquainted with the circumstances he will arrange for what we humorously call a 'free pardon'; that is to say, the Law will very graciously forgive you for having been unjustly sent to prison. As for the rest—" he shrugged his shoulders—"well, I don't imagine you will be precisely the loser for not having sold your secret to the Wilhelmstrasse. Our own War Office are quite prepared to deal in any original methods of scattering death that happen to be on the market just at present."

There was a brief pause.

"And are we free now?" inquired Tommy, with a rather pathetic glance at the clock.

"You should be very shortly," returned Lammersfield. "Mr. Casement has gone across to the Home Office to explain the latest developments to Sir George Frinton. We are expecting them both here at any moment."

"Sir George Frinton?" I echoed. "Why, I thought Mr. McCurdy was at the Home Office."

Lammersfield smiled tolerantly: "You have been busy, Mr. Lyndon, and some of the more important facts of modern history have possibly escaped you. McCurdy resigned from the Government nearly three months ago."

"But Sir George Frinton!" I exclaimed. "Why, I know the old boy; I have a standing invitation to go and look him up." And then, without waiting for any questions, I described to them in a few words how the Home Secretary and I had travelled together from Exeter to London, and the favourable impression I had apparently made.

Both Lammersfield and Latimer were vastly amused—the former lying back in his chair and laughing softly to himself in undisguised merriment.

"How perfectly delightful!" he observed. "Poor old Frinton has his merits, but—"

The libel he was about to utter on his distinguished colleague was suddenly cut short by a knock at the door; and, in answer to his summons, the butler-looking person entered and announced that Sir George Frinton and Mr. Casement were waiting for an audience.

"Show them up at once," said his lordship gravely; and then turning to Latimer as the man left the room he added, with a reflective smile: "I should never have believed that the Foreign Office could be so entertaining."

CHAPTER XXV
A LITTLE FAMILY PARTY

The moment that Sir George Frinton reached the threshold, one could see that he was seriously perturbed. He entered the room in an energetic, fussy sort of manner, and came bustling across to Lord Lammersfield, who had risen from the table to meet him. He was followed by a grey-haired, middle-aged man, who strolled in quietly, looked across at Latimer, and then threw a sharp penetrating glance at Tommy and me.

It was Lammersfield who spoke first. "I was sorry to bother you, Frinton," he said pleasantly, "but the matter has so much to do with your department I thought you ought to be present."

Sir George waved away the apology. "You were perfectly right, Lord Lammersfield—perfectly right. I should have come over in any case. It is an astounding story. I have been amazed—positively amazed—at Mr. Casement's revelations. Can it be possible there is no mistake?"

"Absolutely none," answered Latimer calmly. "Our people have moved with the utmost discretion, and we have the entire evidence in our hands." He turned to Casement. "You have acquainted Sir George with the whole of this morning's events?"

The quiet man nodded. "Everything," he observed, in rather fatigued voice.

"I understand," said the Home Secretary, "that this man Lyndon is actually here."

With a graceful gesture Lord Lammersfield indicated where I was standing.

"Let me introduce you to each other," he said. "Mr. Neil Lyndon—Sir George Frinton."

I bowed respectfully, and when I raised my head again I saw that the Home Secretary was contemplating me with a puzzled stare.

"You—your face seems strangely familiar to me," he observed.

"You evidently have a good memory, Sir George," I replied. "I had the honour and pleasure of travelling up from Exeter to London with you about a fortnight ago."

A sudden light came into his face, and adjusting his spectacles he stared at me harder than ever.

"God bless my soul!" he exclaimed. "Of course, I remember now." He paused. "And do you mean to tell me that you—an escaped convict—were actually aware that you were travelling with the Home Secretary?"

I saw no reason for dimming the glory of the incident.

"You were kind enough to give me one of your cards," I reminded him.

"Why, yes, to be sure; so I did—so I did." Again he paused and gazed at me with a sort of incredulous amazement. "You must have nerves of steel, sir. Most men in such a situation would have been paralysed with terror."

The idea of Sir George paralysing anybody with terror struck me as so delightful that I almost burst out laughing, but by a great effort I just managed to restrain myself.

"As an escaped convict," I said, "one becomes used to rather desperate situations."

Lammersfield, the corner of whose mouth was twitching suspiciously, broke into the conversation.

"It was a remarkable coincidence," he said, "but you see how it confirms Casement's story if any further confirmation were needed."

Sir George nodded. "Yes, yes," he said. "I suppose there can be no doubt about it. The proofs of it all seem beyond question." He turned to me. "Taking everything into consideration, Mr. Lyndon, you appear to have acted in a most creditable and patriotic manner. I understand that the moment you discovered the nature of the plot in which you were involved you placed yourself entirely at the disposal of the Secret Service. That is right, Mr. Latimer, is it not?"

Latimer stepped forward. "If Mr. Lyndon had chosen to do it, sir," he said, "he could have sold his invention to Germany and escaped with the money. At that time he had no proof to offer that he had been wrongly convicted. Rather than betray his country, however, he was prepared to return to prison and serve out his sentence."

As an accurate description of my attitude in the matter it certainly left something to be desired, but it seemed to have a highly satisfactory effect upon Sir George. He took a step towards me, and gravely and rather pompously shook me by the hand.

"Sir," he said, "permit me to congratulate you both on your conduct and on the dramatic establishment of your innocence. It will be my pleasant duty as Home Secretary to see that every possible reparation is made to you for the great injustice that you have suffered."

Lammersfield, who had gone back to his seat at the table, again interrupted.

"You agree with me, don't you, Frinton, that, pending any steps you and the Prime Minister choose to take in the matter, Mr. Lyndon may consider himself a free man?"

Sir George seemed a trifle embarrassed. "Well—er—to a certain extent, most decidedly. I have informed Scotland Yard that he has voluntarily surrendered himself to the Secret Service, so there will be no further attempt to carry out the arrest. I—I presume that Mr. Casement and Mr. Latimer will be officially responsible for him?"

The former gave a reassuring nod. "Certainly, Sir George," he observed.

"I am entirely in your hands, sir," I put in. "There are one or two little things I wanted to do, but if you prefer that I should consider myself under arrest—"

"No, no, Mr. Lyndon," he interrupted; "there is no necessity for that— no necessity at all. Strictly speaking, of course, you are still a prisoner, but for the present it will perhaps be best to avoid any formal proceedings. I understand that both Lord Lammersfield and Mr. Casement consider it advisable to keep the whole matter as quiet as possible, at all events until the return of the Prime Minister. After that we must decide what steps it will be best to take."

"I am very much obliged to you," I said. "There is one question I should like to ask if I may."

He took off his spectacles and polished them with his pocket-handkerchief. "Well?" he observed encouragingly.

"I should like to know whether Savaroff's daughter is in custody—the girl who gave the police their information about me."

"Ah!" he said, with some satisfaction, "that is a point on which you all appear to have been misled. I have just enlightened Mr. Casement in the matter. The information on which the police acted was not supplied by a girl." He paused. "It was given them by your cousin and late partner, Mr. George Marwood."

"What!" I almost shouted; and I heard Tommy indulge in a half-smothered exclamation which was not at all suited to our distinguished company.

Sir George, who was evidently pleased with our surprise, nodded his head.

"Mr. Marwood rang up Scotland Yard at half-past ten last night. He told them he had received an anonymous letter giving two addresses, at one of which you would probably be found. He also gave a full description of the alterations in your appearance."

I turned to Latimer. "I suppose it was Sonia," I said. "I never dreamed of her going to him, though."

"It was very natural," he replied in that unconcerned drawl of his. "She knew that your cousin would do everything possible to get you under lock and key again, and at the same time she imagined she would avoid the risk of being arrested herself."

"Quite so, quite so," said Sir George, nodding his head sagely. "From all I can gather she seems to be a most dangerous young woman. I shall make a particular point of seeing that she is arrested."

His words came home to me with a sudden swift stab of pity and remorse. It was horrible to think of Sonia in jail—Sonia eating out her wild passionate heart in the hideous slavery I knew so well. The thought of all that she had risked and suffered for my sake crowded back into my mind with overwhelming force. I took a step forward.

"Sir George," I said, "a moment ago you were good enough to say that the Government would try and make me some return for the injustice I have suffered."

He looked at me in obvious surprise. "Certainly," he said—"certainly. I am convinced that they will take the most generous view of the circumstances."

"There is only one thing I ask," I said. "Except for this girl, Sonia Savaroff, the Germans would now be in possession of my invention. If the Government feel that they owe me anything, they can cancel the debt altogether by allowing her to go free."

Sir George raised his eyeglass. "You ask this after she did her best to send you back to penal servitude?"

I nodded. "I am not sure," I said, "that I didn't thoroughly deserve it."

For a moment Sir George stared at me in a puzzled sort of fashion. "Very well," he said; "I think it might be arranged. As you say, she was of considerable assistance to us, even if it was unintentionally. That is a point in her favour—a distinct point."

"How about our friend Mr. Marwood?" put in Lammersfield pleasantly. "Between perjury and selling Government secrets I suppose we have enough evidence to justify his arrest?"

"I think so," said Sir George, nodding his head solemnly. "Anyhow I have given instructions for it. In a case like this it is best to be on the safe side."

My heart sank at his words. Charming as it was to think of George in the affectionate clutch of a policeman, I could almost have wept at the idea of being robbed of my own little interview with him, to which I had been looking forward for so long. It was Lammersfield who broke in on my disappointment. "I should imagine," he said considerately, "that you two, as well as Latimer, must be half starving. I suppose you have had nothing to eat since breakfast."

Tommy rose to his feet with an alacrity that answered the question so far as he was concerned, and I acknowledged that a brief interval for refreshment would be by no means unwelcome.

"Well, I'm afraid I can't spare Latimer just yet," he said, "but you two go off and have a good lunch. Come back here again as soon as you've done. I will ring up the War Office and the Admiralty while you are away, and we will arrange for a couple of their men to meet us here, and then you can explain about your new explosive. I fancy you will find them quite an appreciative audience."

He pressed a bell by his side, and getting up from the table, accompanied us to the door, where I stopped for a moment to try and express my thanks both to him and Sir George.

"My dear Mr. Lyndon," he interrupted courteously, "you have been in prison for three years for a crime that you didn't commit, and in return for that you have done England a service that it is almost impossible to overrate. Under the circumstances even a Cabinet Minister may be excused a little common civility."

As he spoke there came a knock at the door, and in answer to his summons the impassive butler person appeared on the threshold.

"Show these gentlemen out, Simpson," he said, "and let me know directly they return." Then, shaking my hand in a friendly fashion, he added with a quizzical smile, "If you should happen to come across any mutual acquaintance of ours, perhaps you will be kind enough to convey my unofficial congratulations. I hope before long to have the privilege of offering them personally."

I promised to deliver his message, and, following our guide downstairs, we passed out into the street.

"I like that chap," said Tommy. "He's got no silly side about him. Joyce always said he was a good sort."

He stopped on the pavement, and with his usual serene disregard for the respectabilities proceeded to fill and light a huge briar pipe.

"What's the programme now?" he inquired. "I'm just dying for some grub."

"We'll get a taxi and run down to the flat and pick up Joyce," I said. "Then we'll come back to the Café Royal and have the best lunch that's ever been eaten in London."

Tommy indulged in one of his deep chuckles.

"If anyone's expecting me in Downing Street before six o'clock," he observed, "I rather think he's backed a loser."

It was not until we were in a taxi, and speeding rapidly past the House of Commons, that I broached the painful subject of George.

"I don't know what to do," I said. "If he's at his house, he has been arrested by now, and if he isn't the police will probably find him before I shall. It will break my heart if I don't get hold of him for five minutes."

Tommy grunted sympathetically. "It's just on the cards," he said, "that Joyce might know where he is."

Faint as the chance seemed, it was sufficient to cheer me up a little, and for the rest of the drive we discussed the important question of what we should have for lunch. After a week of sardines and tinned tongue I found it a most inspiring topic.

As we reached the Chelsea Embankment a happy idea presented itself to me. "I tell you what, Tommy," I said. "We won't go and knock at Joyce's flat. Let's slip round at the back, as we did before, and take her by surprise."

"Right you are," he said. "She's probably left the studio door open. She generally does on a hot afternoon like this."

The taxi drew up at Florence Court, and telling the driver to wait for us, we walked down the passage and turned into Tommy's flat. There were several letters for him lying on the floor inside, and while he stopped to pick them up, I passed on through the studio and out into the little glass-covered corridor at the back.

It was quite a short way along to Joyce's studio, and from where I was I could see that her door was slightly ajar. I stepped quietly, so as not to make any noise, and I had covered perhaps half the distance, when suddenly I pulled up in my tracks as if I had been turned into stone. For a moment I stood there without moving or even breathing. A couple of yards away on the other side of the door I could hear two people talking. One of them was Joyce; the other—the other—well, if I had been lying half-unconscious on my death-bed I think I should have recognized that voice!

There was a sound behind me, and whipping noiselessly round I was just in time to signal to Tommy that he must keep absolutely quiet. Then with my heart beating like a drum I crept stealthily forward until I was within a few inches of the open door. I was shaking all over with a delight that I could hardly control.

"... you quite understand." (I could hear every word George was saying as plainly as if I were in the room.) "I only have to ring up the police, and in half an hour he'll be back again in prison—back for the rest of his life. He won't escape a second time—you can be sure of that."

"Well?"

The single word came clear and distinct, but it would be difficult to describe the scorn which Joyce managed to pack into it. It had some effect on George.

"You have just got to do what I want—that's all," he exclaimed angrily. "I leave England tonight, and unless you come with me I shall go straight from here and ring up Scotland Yard. You can make your choice now. You either come down to Southampton with me this evening, or Lyndon goes back to Dartmoor tomorrow."

"Then you were lying when you said you were anxious to help him?"

With a mighty effort George apparently regained some control over his tongue.

"No, I wasn't, Joyce," he said. "God knows I'm sorry for the poor devil—I always have been; but there's nothing in the world that matters to me now except you. I—I lost my temper when you said you wouldn't come. You didn't mean it, did you? Lyndon can never be anything to you; he is dead to all of us. At the best he can only be a skulking convict hiding from the police in South America or somewhere. You come with me; you shall never be sorry for it. I've plenty of money, Joyce; and I'll give you the best time a woman ever had."

"And if I refuse?" asked Joyce quietly.

It was evident from the sound that George had taken a step towards her.

"Then Lyndon will go back to Dartmoor and stop there till he rots and dies."

There was a short pause, and then very clearly and deliberately Joyce gave her answer.

"I think you are the foulest man in the world," she said. "It makes me sick to be in the same room with you."

The gasp of fury and astonishment that broke from George's lips fell on my ears like music. He was so choking with rage that for a moment he could hardly speak.

"Damn you!" he stuttered at last. "So that's your real opinion, is it! That's what you've been thinking all along! Trying to use me to help that precious convict lover of yours—eh?"

I heard him come another step nearer.

"I'll make you pay for this, anyhow," he snarled. "Sick at being in the same room with me, are you? Then by God I'll give you some reason—"

With a swift jerk I flung open the door and stepped in over the threshold.

"Not this time, George dear," I said.

If the devil himself had shot up through the floor in a crackle of blue flame, I don't think it could have had a more striking effect on my late partner. With his mouth open and his face the colour of freshly mixed putty, he stood perfectly still in the centre of the room, gazing at me like a man in a trance. For a second—a whole beautiful rich second—he remained in this engaging attitude; then, as if struck by an electric shock, he suddenly spun round with the obvious intention of making a dart for the door.

The idea was distinctly a sound one, but it was too late to be of any practical value. Directly he moved I stepped in, and catching him a smashing box on the ear with my right hand sent him sprawling full length on the carpet. Joyce laughed gaily, while lounging across the room Tommy set his back against the door and beamed cheerfully on the three of us.

"Quite a little family party," he observed.

Joyce was in my arms, and we were kissing each other in the most shameless and unabashed way.

"Oh, my dear," she said, "I hope you haven't hurt your hand."

"It stung a bit," I admitted, "but I've got another one—and two feet." I put her gently aside. "Get up, George," I said.

He lay where he was, pretending to be unconscious.

"If you don't get up at once, George," I said softly, "I shall kick you—hard."

He scrambled to his feet, and then crouched back against the wall eyeing me like a trapped weasel.

I indulged myself in a good heart-filling look at him.

"So you've been sorry for me, George?" I said. "All these three long weary years that I've been rotting in Dartmoor, you've been really and truly sorry for me?"

He licked his lips and nodded.

I laughed. "Well, I'm sorry for *you* now, George," I said—"damned sorry."

If anything, the putty-like pallor of his face became still more ghastly.

"Don't do anything violent, Neil," he whispered. "You'll only regret it. I swear to you—"

"I shouldn't swear," I said. "You don't want to die with a lie on your lips."

The sweat broke out on his forehead, and he glanced desperately round the room, as though seeking for some possible method of escape. The only comfort he got was a shake of the head from Tommy.

"You—you don't mean to murder me?" he gasped.

I gave a fiendish laugh. "Don't I!" I cried. "What's one murder more or less? I know you've put the police on to me, and I'd sooner be hanged than go back to Dartmoor any day."

Tommy rubbed his hands together ghoulishly. "What are we going to do with him?" he asked. "Cut his throat?"

"No," I said. "It would make a mess, and we don't want to spoil Joyce's carpet."

"Oh, it doesn't matter about the carpet," said Joyce unselfishly.

"I've got it," said Tommy. "Why not throw him in the river? The tide's up; I noticed it as we came along."

Whether he intended the suggestion seriously or not I don't know, but I rose to it like a trout to a fly. There are seldom more than two feet of water at high tide at that particular part of the Embankment, and the thought of dropping George into its turbid embrace filled me with the utmost enthusiasm.

"By Jove, Tommy!" I exclaimed. "That's a brilliant idea. The Thames water's about the only thing he wouldn't defile."

I stepped forward, and before George knew what was happening I had swung him round and clutched him by the collar and breeches.

"Open the door," I said, "and just see there's no one in the passage."

With a deep chuckle Tommy turned to obey, while Joyce laughed with a viciousness that I should never have given her credit for. As for George— well, I suppose in his blind terror he really thought he was going to be drowned, for he kicked and struggled and raved till it was as much as I could do to hold him.

"All clear!" sang out Tommy from the hall.

"Stand by, then," I said, and taking a deep breath, I ran George through the flat down the passage, and out into the street, in a style that would have done credit to the chucker out at the Empire.

There were not many people about, and those that were there had no time to interfere even if they had wanted to do so. I just got a glimpse of the startled face of our taxi driver as he jumped aside to let us pass, and the next moment we had crossed the road and fetched up with a bang against the low Embankment wall.

I paused for a moment, renewed my grip on George's collar, and took a quick look round. Tommy was beside me, and a few yards away, down at the bottom of some steps, I saw a number of small boys paddling in the water. There was evidently no risk of anybody being drowned.

"I'll take his feet," said Tommy, suiting the action to the word. "You get hold of his arms."

There was a brief struggle, a loud scream for help, and the next moment George was swinging merrily between us.

"One! Two! Three!" I cried.

At the word "three" we let go simultaneously. He flew up into the air like a great wriggling crab, twisted round twice, and then went down into the muddy water with a splash that echoed all over the Embankment.

"Very nice," said Tommy critically. "But we ought to have put a stone round his neck."

One glance over the wall showed me that there was no danger. Dripping, floundering, and gasping for breath, George emerged from the surface like a frock-coated Neptune rising from the waves. He seemed to be trying to speak, but the shrieks of innocent delight with which his reappearance was greeted by the paddling boys unfortunately prevented us from hearing him.

I thrust my arm through Tommy's. "Come along," I said. "We must get out of this before there's a row."

Swift as we had been about it, our little operation had already attracted a certain amount of notice. People were hurrying up from all directions, but without paying any attention to them, we walked back towards the taxi, the driver of which had apparently been too astonished to move.

"Gor blimey, Guv'nor," he ejaculated, "what sorter gime d'you call that?"

"It's all right, driver," said Tommy gravely. "We found him insulting this gentleman's sister."

The driver, who evidently had a nice sense of chivalry, at once came round to our side.

"Was 'e?—the dirty 'ound!" he observed. "Well, you done it on 'im proper. You ain't drowned 'im, 'ave ye, gents?"

"Oh no," I said. "He's addressing a few words to the crowd now." Then seeing Joyce standing in the doorway I hurried up the steps.

"Joyce dear," I said, "put on a hat and come as quick as you can. It's quite all right, but we want to get out of this before there's any bother."

She nodded, and disappeared into the flat, while I strolled back to the taxi.

It was evident from a movement among the spectators that George was making his way towards the steps. Some of them who had come running up kept turning round and casting curious glances at us, but so far no one had attempted to interfere. It was not until Joyce was just coming out of the flats, that a man detached himself from the crowd and started across the road. He was a big, fat, greasy person in a bowler hat.

"Here," he said. "You wait a bit. What d'ye mean by throwing that pore man in the river?"

I opened the door of the taxi and Joyce jumped in.

"What's it got to do with you, darling?" asked Tommy affably.

"What's it got to do with me!" he repeated indignantly. "Why, it's just the mercy o' Gawd—"

"Come on, Tommy," I said.

Tommy took a step forward, but the man clutched him by the arm.

"No yer don't," he said, "not till ... Ow!"

With a sudden vigorous shove Tommy sent him staggering back across the pavement, and the next moment we had both jumped into the taxi and banged the door.

"Right away," I called out.

I think there was some momentary doubt amongst the other spectators whether they oughtn't to interfere, but before they could make up their minds our sympathetic driver had thrust in his clutch, and we were spinning away down the Embankment.

Joyce, who was sitting next to me, slipped her hand into mine.

"I love to see you both laughing," she said, "but I *should* like to know what's happened! At present I feel as if I was acting in a cinematograph play."

We told her—told her in quick, eager sentences of how the danger and mystery that had hung over us so for long had at last been scattered and destroyed. It was a broken, inadequate sort of narrative, jerked out as we bumped over crossings and pulled by behind buses, but I fancy from the light in her eyes and the pressure of her hand that Joyce was quite contented.

"It's—it's like waking up after some horrible dream," she said, "and suddenly finding that everything's all right. Oh, I knew it would be in the end—I knew it the whole time—but I never dreamed it would happen all at once like this."

"Neither did George," chuckled Tommy. "How long had he been with you, Joyce?"

"About twenty minutes," she said. "He came straight to me from Harrod's, where he's spent most of the day buying stores for his yacht. He had quite made up his mind I was coming with him. I don't believe he's got the faintest idea about what's happened this morning."

"He will have soon," I said. "That's why I threw him in the river. He's bound to go back to the house for a change of clothes, and he'll find the police waiting for him there."

"That'll be just right," observed Tommy complacently. "There's nothing so good as a little excitement to stop one from catching cold."

"Except lunch," I added, as the taxi rounded the corner of Piccadilly and drew up outside the Café Royal.

What the manager of that renowned restaurant must have thought of us, I find it rather difficult to guess. It is not often, I should imagine, that two untidy mud-stained men and a beautiful girl turn up at four o'clock in the afternoon and demand the best meal that London can provide.

Fortunately, however, he proved to be a gentleman of philosophy and resource. He accepted our request with perfect composure, and by the time we had succeeded in making ourselves passably respectable he presented us with a menu that deserved to be set to music.

Heavens, what a lunch that was! We ate it all by ourselves in the big empty restaurant, with half a dozen fascinated waiters eyeing us from the end of the room. They were probably speculating as to whether we were eccentric millionaires, or whether we had just escaped from some private lunatic asylum, but we were all far too cheerful to care what they thought. We ate, we drank, we laughed, we talked, with a reckless jubilant happiness that would have survived the scrutiny of all the waiters in London.

"I know what we'll do, Joyce," I said, when at last the dessert was cleared away and we were sitting in a delicate haze of cigar smoke. "As soon as things are fixed up I'll buy a good second-hand thirty-ton boat, and you and I and Tommy will go off for a six months' cruise. We'll take Mr. Gow as skipper, and your little page-boy as steward, and we'll run down to the Mediterranean and stop there till people are tired of gassing about us."

"That will be beautiful," said Joyce simply.

"I'll come," exclaimed Tommy, "unless the Secret Service refuse to give me up." Then he stopped and looked mischievously across at Joyce and me. "It's a pity we can't ask Sonia too," he added.

"Poor Sonia," said Joyce. "I am so glad you got her off."

"Are you really?" asked Tommy. "That shows I know nothing about women. I always thought that if two girls loved the same man they hated each other like poison."

Joyce nodded. "So they do as a rule."

"Well, Sonia loved Neil all right; you can take my word for it."

Joyce laughed softly. "Yes, Tommy dear," she said, "but then, you see, Neil didn't love *her*—and that just makes all the difference."